INSIDE CHINA'S GRAND STRATEGY

Asia in the New Millennium

Series Editor: Shiping Hua, Center for Asian Democracy,
University of Louisville

This series aims to publish creative works on Asia with new materials and/or with new interpretations. We welcome manuscripts that look at the challenges and opportunities of Asia in the millennium from the perspective of politics, economics, and cultural-historical traditions. Projects that study the impact of Asian developments on the world are also welcome. Priority will be given to those manuscripts that examine the history and prospect of the democratization process of Asia. Also of our interest are those theoretically, empirically, and policy oriented works that can be used as teaching materials at undergraduate and graduate levels. Innovative manuscript proposals at any stage are welcome.

Advisory Board

William Callahan, University of Manchester, Southeast Asia, Thailand
Lowell Dittmer, University of California at Berkeley, East Asia and South Asia
Robert Hathaway, Woodrow Wilson International Center for Scholars,
   South Asia, India, Pakistan
Mike Mochizuki, George Washington University, East Asia, Japan and Korea
Peter Moody, University of Notre Dame, China and Japan
Brantly Womack, University of Virginia, China and Vietnam
Charles Ziegler, University of Louisville, Central Asia and Russia Far East

Books in the Series

The Future of China-Russia Relations
Edited by James Bellacqua

The Mind of Empire: China's History and Modern Foreign Relations
Christopher A. Ford

Challenges to Chinese Foreign Policy: Diplomacy, Globalization, and the Next World Power
Edited by Yufan Hao, C. X. George Wei, and Lowell Dittmer

INSIDE CHINA'S GRAND STRATEGY

The Perspective
from the
People's Republic

YE ZICHENG

Edited and Translated by
STEVEN I. LEVINE AND GUOLI LIU

THE UNIVERSITY PRESS OF KENTUCKY

Scholarly publisher for the Commonwealth,
serving Bellarmine University, Berea College, Centre College of Kentucky,
Eastern Kentucky University, The Filson Historical Society, Georgetown
College, Kentucky Historical Society, Kentucky State University, Morehead
State University, Murray State University, Northern Kentucky University,
Transylvania University, University of Kentucky, University of Louisville,
and Western Kentucky University.
All rights reserved.

Editorial and Sales Offices: The University Press of Kentucky
663 South Limestone Street, Lexington, Kentucky 40508-4008
www.kentuckypress.com

15 14 13 12 11   5 4 3 2 1

Map by Dick Gilbreath

Library of Congress Cataloging-in-Publication Data

Ye, Zicheng.
   [Zhongguo da zhanlüe. English]
   Inside China's grand strategy : the perspective from the People's Republic / Ye
Zicheng ; edited and translated by Steven I. Levine and Guoli Liu.
      p. cm. — (Asia in the new millennium)
   Includes bibliographical references and index.
   ISBN 978-0-8131-2645-6 (harcover : alk. paper)
   ISBN 978-0-8131-2646-3 (ebook)
   1. China—Politics and government—1976-2002. 2. China—Economic
policy—2000- 3. China—Foreign relations—1976- 4. China—Strategic
aspects. 5. Geopolitics—Asia. I. Levine, Steven I. II. Liu, Guoli, 1961-
III. Title.
   DS779.26.Y45513 2011
   355'.033551—dc22   2010044410

This book is printed on acid-free recycled paper meeting the requirements of the
American National Standard for Permanence in Paper for Printed Library Materials.

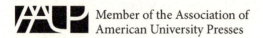

Manufactured in the United States of America.

  Member of the Association of
American University Presses

Contents

Preface to the
English Edition

Late at night on September 20, 2008, my old schoolmate and friend Professor Guoli Liu called me from the United States with some good news. The translation of my book *Inside China's Grand Strategy* was now complete and would soon be published by the University Press of Kentucky.

After the phone call, I was very excited and could not fall asleep for a long time. I was happy as well as a bit anxious. I was happy because this edition of my book would enable more English-speaking readers to acquire a better understanding of China's grand strategy of peaceful development. But I was anxious because the Chinese original had been completed in 2002 and published in 2003 (with a Korean edition appearing in 2005), by now a number of years had passed, and both China and the international community had undergone some significant changes. For example, when I wrote my book, the Iraq War had not yet occurred, and, by September 2008, it had been going on for more than five years. Also, when I wrote my book, China was making numerous preparations for the Olympics, and by now the Olympics had been successfully concluded. The whole world had witnessed how the new Beijing staged a magnificent ceremony. Have the contents of my book passed the test of time? Is the point of view expressed in it already passé? Might the book mislead readers?

I have reviewed the main contents of my book several times. Happily, I am convinced that it is neither one of those works that is out-of-date before it is published nor one of those absolutely worthless and philistine works that should be immediately consigned to the remainder bins. Of course, some of the statistics cited in the book have changed a lot by now. For example, over the period 2000–2007, the U.S. GDP rose from $9.83 to $13.8 trillion, and U.S. military spending rose from $400 to $700 billion, and, over the period 2002–2007, China's GDP increased from $1.02 to $3.2 trillion, its per capita GDP increased from $900 to more than $2,000, and its foreign exchange reserves rose from $286.4 billion to $1.5 trillion. But the main features of China's grand strategy set forth in the book have not changed very much, and English-speaking readers wishing to understand China's situation should still find it worth reading.

The preface provides a rough sketch of the history and culture of China's grand strategy. In Sun Zi's *Art of War*, in the contention between the states of Wu and Yue, in the unification of the six kingdoms by the state of Qin, as well as in other works and the course of history itself, one can discern the wisdom of China's grand strategy. The strategic goal of reviving the Chinese nation that was set by Mao Zedong and Deng Xiaoping has been affirmed and developed by China's current leaders and the Chinese people. In particular, Deng's goals of peaceful development, reform and opening, and a focus on economic development and his policies of one country two systems, establishing the rule of law, and developing the market economy remain today the core objectives of China's grand strategy. Now we may add to these the goals of sustainable development, the building of a harmonious society and a harmonious world, peaceful relations with its neighbors, and entering into the world community. China possesses the historical, cultural, political, and economic conditions to achieve the great project of national renascence. These conditions continue to exist. My book criticized those theories that predicted the decline or collapse of China. Such viewpoints have already been discredited and will continue to be in the future.

The economic priorities that my book identifies are still the strategic choices in contemporary China, and even the rapid growth in China's military budget has not changed this reality. China must become a great democracy, but certainly not along the lines of Western democracy. My book clearly spells out the concept of Chinese-style democracy, a concept that more and more people accept. Those readers who think that China will take the path of Western-style democracy may be quite disappointed, but time will tell whether China will continue along the path of Chinese-style democracy.

Maintaining normal relations with the United States is key to China achieving its strategic objectives. And, since this book was completed, Sino-U.S. relations have undergone great changes, becoming more mature and more stable and, in the process, validating the viewpoint that I presented. There may be conflicts between China and the United States, but there is nothing inevitable about a large-scale war between the two countries. China is neither an ally nor an adversary of the United States. Sino-

U.S. cooperation has increased over the years. The viewpoint—which I criticized—that there will inevitably be a war between China and the United States is obviously wrong and outmoded. The common interests that bind the two countries exceed the contradictions between them.

At the same time, how China manages its relations with other great powers is also an important factor in determining whether it can implement its grand strategy. My book takes the long view with respect to these relations with other powers. Sino-Russian relations have continued to develop in a stable fashion, and the Sino-Russian strategic partnership has withstood the test of time. Some new contradictions have developed in relations between China and the European Union; the main ones are differences in ideology and values that have produced conflicts in the areas of politics and economic relations. China's relations with India have generally improved even though India periodically plays the "China threat" card. What I am particularly pleased with in looking back six years is the viewpoint I expressed with respect to Sino-Japanese relations, namely, that "there can be two tigers on the mountaintop." Although this contravened the conventional wisdom, it seems that it has actually come to pass. After going through a rough patch, Sino-Japanese relations are again on track and developing normally.

China's relations with its other neighbors have also seen great changes, yet the main trend is that which my book emphasized, namely, the development of common interests. In the four subregions of Northeast, Southeast, South, and Central Asia, China, adhering to the common good, has upheld regional security and stability, actively participated in the peaceful resolution of the North Korean nuclear issue, promoted the process of establishing a free trade agreement with the countries of Southeast Asia, and cooperated with the countries of Central Asia in combating terrorism and promoting economic development. It has also participated in the process of South Asian cooperation.

My book views China's domestic situation as the key factor in achieving its grand strategy. It addresses critical issues that have been, are now, and will for a long time remain the most important issues for China. These are unemployment and underemployment, bribery and corruption, establishing the rule of law, the economic differential among various regions, the wide gap between rich and poor, developing human talent, economic development, population, resources, the environment, and public spirit. In 2008, China witnessed the March 14 Lhasa Incident, the

May 12 Wenchuan Earthquake, the collapse of the Shanxi dam, the incident of poisoned milk powder, and other important and urgent domestic events that demanded solutions. The greatest threat to China—its greatest enemy—is its own domestic problems.

When I was writing this book, cross-strait relations were very tense. They posed a great challenge to the strategic question raised in this book of how to win over Taiwanese public opinion. What should be done if Chen Shui-bian declared independence? What should be done if the United States got involved in this process? At that time, quite a few people in China held the pessimistic view that a cross-strait war was inevitable. My view was that the mainland should focus on economic development, promote unity, and demonstrate patience and greater concern for the Taiwanese people. It should have confidence in a long-term solution to the Taiwan question and demonstrate strategic thinking by adopting a more flexible interpretation of the "one China" principle. Time has provided its answer to these questions.

The publication of the English edition of this book owes much to the great efforts of a number of people. My students He Lin, Huang Mei, and Cao Hua initially produced a draft English translation. My old schoolmate and friend Professor Guoli Liu of the College of Charleston recommended that my book be published in the United States. He also did a lot of work on the draft translation. I would like to express particular thanks to Professors Steven I. Levine and Ronald N. Montaperto, who worked tirelessly on translating and editing this book to ensure its ultimate publication in English. Finally, I want to thank Professor Hua Shiping of the University of Louisville and the editors of the University Press of Kentucky, who have guided this book through the publication process.

An English version of my book is being issued in the United States, not because the book is particularly well written, but because of the rising interest in China among U.S. academics. Its publication reflects the rise of China in recent years and the desire on the part of the international community to understand it. The views expressed in this book are those of neither Chinese officialdom nor of the Chinese scholarly community. They are simply the views of an individual Chinese scholar who wishes China to be great and hopes that a great China will contribute more to world peace and stability. I alone am responsible for all the problems and shortcomings herein. If this book makes even a small contribution to those readers wishing to understand China, I will feel greatly honored.

Further Thoughts on the Life Expectancy of U.S. Hegemony

In 2008, many important economic events occurred in rapid succession in the United States. There was a subprime mortgage crisis. Fannie Mae and Freddie Mac, the country's two largest mortgage companies, were faced with serious financial difficulties. The government had no choice but to take control of them. On September 15, the country's fourth-largest investment bank, Lehman Brothers, with capital holdings of more than $640 billion, declared bankruptcy. Another investment bank, Merrill Lynch, was taken over by Bank of America. AIG, the country's largest insurance company, faced a crisis, and the U.S. government declared that it would recapitalize it. Then Morgan Stanley and Goldman Sachs abandoned investment bank status and became bank holding companies. Wall Street confronted a serious economic crisis. In order to cope with it, on September 20, the government announced that it would invest as much as $700 billion in a rescue plan to help the U.S. economy weather the worst times since the world economic crisis of 1929. It also turned to the world community to request assistance, hoping that other economically powerful members of the G7 would take measures to save the market.

In sum, this crisis is much more serious than the incidents several years ago involving Enron, Anderson, WorldCom, Xerox, and Merck. Just as those cases raised the anguished question of whether U.S.-style capitalism could survive, the subprime and the Lehman crises raise the question of the future of the United States as a great power and the changing structure of the international community.

In China, there are also many points of view regarding how to look at the United States. One viewpoint is that the 2008 economic crisis points to the end of U.S. hegemony. A second holds that five hundred years of Western dominance is now in doubt. A third contends that unipolarism is over and that the age of multilateralism and multipolarity has arrived. A fourth is that China has already entered onto the world stage and has become one of the world's leading powers, along with the United States and Europe.

It is, however, too soon to tell which, if any, of these viewpoints is correct because it is not yet clear how the situation will develop. I think we must first acknowledge that there are numerous problems with the domestic economy of the United States and that these problems have definitely weakened the position and influence of the United States with respect to international economic, political, and military affairs. If these problems are not managed well, and if the measures taken to address them fail, then the crisis will get worse and will eventually end the reign of the United States as the world's only superpower. There can be absolutely no doubt on this score.

This does not mean, however, that the only possible future for the United States is bleak. It is also possible that its future will be a good one, and it may also be that, after traversing a difficult period of crisis, it will get back on the right economic track. This is because the factors that I discuss in this book that led to long-term economic growth in the United States are still present. These include a stable political system, a highly developed legal system, a developed education system, abundant human talent, rich resources, a favorable geopolitical environment, top-notch science and technology, and continued military superiority.

The United States may recover its developmental vitality and gain more respect internationally providing it does the following things. It must correct the errors it made in unleashing the Iraq War, show more respect internationally for the opinions of other great powers, increase its consultation and cooperation with other countries, cease pursuing arbitrary international policies of force and unilateralism, stop forcing its ideology and values on developing countries, use military force with restraint, and strengthen its self-control. Domestically, it must correct excessive consumption, strengthen financial controls, and deal effectively with economic crime.

In sum, U.S. hegemony may already be on the decline. The days of glory when the United States could do whatever it liked are gone never to return. But, if it reflects deeply on the current crisis and chooses the correct path out, its international influence may still be very strong and long lasting.

Introduction

Understanding
a View from Beijing

Guoli Liu and Steven I. Levine

China's rapid rise as a global economic power has resulted in its growing
political influence and military capability. Scholars in the United States,
Europe, and Japan have engaged in serious debates about China's grand
strategy and its implications.[1] Apart from some China scholars and international relations experts, however, the outside world has not paid close
attention to the academic analysis and policy debate about China's emerging grand strategy inside China itself. There is little systematic scholarly
analysis by Chinese scholars available in English.[2] In order to answer the
question "What does China think?"[3] we need to pay close attention to
what Chinese scholars have been arguing about China's grand strategy. It
is time to introduce to the English-speaking world important writings by
Chinese scholars about China's grand strategy.

It is in this connection that we strongly recommend serious consideration of the key arguments in *Inside China's Grand Strategy*. This is the
first original, systematic, book-length analysis of China's grand strategy
by a leading Chinese scholar of international relations. The author, Ye
Zicheng, is a professor of international politics in the School of International Studies of Peking University. He has written numerous influential
books, including *Opening to the Outside World and China's Modernization* (1997), *Geopolitics and Chinese Diplomacy* (1998), *New China's Diplomatic Thought* (2001), *China's Diplomatic Thought during the Spring*,

Autumn, and Warring States Periods (2003), and *The Development of Land Rights and the Rise and Fall of Great Powers* (2007).[4] He is among the first Chinese scholars to advocate that China assume growing responsibility as an emerging great power.[5]

Among Chinese scholars, Ye Zicheng stands out as an original thinker and a rational analyst. He is among the first group of Chinese international relations scholars to emerge during the era of reform and opening. He entered the Department of International Politics at Peking University in 1978. At that time, Peking University was one of only three universities in China with a department of international relations.[6] After completing his undergraduate and graduate studies, Ye joined the faculty of Peking University in 1985. When the Department of International Politics became the School of International Studies in 1996, he became the founding chair of the Department of Diplomacy. He is a leading scholar on international politics with an emphasis on Chinese foreign relations and diplomatic thought.

This English edition of *Inside China's Grand Strategy* is the result of long-term cooperation among several Chinese and U.S. scholars. In 2005, He Lin, Huang Mei, and Cao Hua completed the first-draft translation at Peking University. Guoli Liu did the preliminary editing of the manuscript. Then Steven I. Levine and Ronald N. Montaperto, U.S. scholars of Chinese foreign policy and international politics, assumed responsibility for editing the entire manuscript, including retranslating certain portions of the book to achieve greater clarity. The translation and editing process took five years. As coeditors, we were determined to be faithful to the original. We did not add anything to the manuscript. Keeping the interest of our readers in mind, and with Professor Ye's consent, we deleted some less important or redundant parts of the Chinese version. It is our sincere hope that our editing will enhance the book's readability without changing any key argument of the original. Our purpose is not to present our own views on China's grand strategy or to take issue with any of Professor Ye's arguments, facts, and analyses. This is his book and his voice. Our job as editors and translators has been to transmit that voice to English readers as faithfully as possible, no more and no less.

We hope that readers will discover many thoughtful and interesting ideas in this important book. We would like to highlight a few of these ideas that we as editors found particularly interesting. In contrast to the popular notion in the West that China is an emerging superpower,[7] Ye argues that, while China has the potential to become a world power, it is not yet such a power. In his view, China suffers from the following short-comings. First, it has not achieved complete national reunification. The issue of Taiwan is still a big drag on China's international influence. Second, China's population is too great and its per capita GDP relatively low. Compared with advanced countries, the levels of education and health care in China are very low. Third, the level of scientific and technological creativity in China is relatively low. Fourth, China's international influence is rising but has not reached a level commensurate with its comprehensive national strength. Nevertheless, in Ye's opinion, China possesses the preconditions for becoming a world power. Its economy is in the take-off stage with regard to modernization. Rapid economic development is the most important prerequisite for China's growth as a world power. At the same time, Ye recognizes the importance of political reform. He argues that democracy is both a value and a political goal. Developing democracy is currently a major global trend. China should become a democratic great power, a great power with human rights and the rule of law, and a country respected by international society. However, it should resist pressure to become a Western-style democracy. It should actively learn, absorb, and reconstruct the experience of democracy in the context of Chinese realities.

Ye's view of China's relations with the United States deserves special attention. After the Cold War, the United States became the world's sole superpower. Therefore, the Sino-U.S. relationship became the most important one in China's foreign relations and, arguably, the most important bilateral relationship in the world. China does not interfere in U.S. domestic affairs, and it hopes that the United States will not interfere in its domestic affairs. It believes that it does not present a challenge to the United States. Rather, it is the United States via its arms sales to Taiwan and its military alliances and military cooperation with China's neighbors that constitutes a challenge to China, threatening its containment. The Sino-U.S. relationship encompasses both cooperative efforts and challenges.[8]

In examining the strategic choices involved in China's policies toward the United States, Ye critically reviewed the following scenarios. The worst case is a confrontation with the United States. If war is thought to be inevitable, China should prepare effectively and maximize its interests. However, this is a bad plan, one that should be adopted only in the case of absolute necessity. That is, China should act only if, despite its best efforts, the United States defines it as an enemy and behaves accordingly or if the United States supports a declaration of independence by Taiwan. But this will harm both Chinese and U.S. interests and should be avoided. In contrast, the best case is Sino-U.S. cooperation leading to a new alliance. Both sides should recognize that their common interests are best served by acting together, just as during World War II and the 1970s–1980s, when both formed a de facto alliance to resist the Soviet threat. The advantage for China would be that such an alliance would support global peace and stability and provide some restriction on U.S. unilateralism. It could also get more of the capital, market access, technology, and military equipment necessary for its modernization as well as an easing of U.S. pressure on the Taiwan issue. This is the best choice for China, Ye asserts, but it is also unrealistic. Put simply, the two countries lack the basis, in terms of both ideology and national interests, and the will to form an alliance. Any alliance with the United States would require China to subordinate its interests, which, in turn, would degrade its independent status as a world power. It is unacceptable for China to become a U.S. ally at the cost of losing its national self-identity. A new alliance would be possible only if its unilateralism caused a major loss of international support for the United States and the United States was to realize the utility of acting on the basis of its common interests with China.

Ye sees the third possibility of neither alliance nor confrontation as more realistic. There will be conflicts and cooperation between China and the United States. "Consequently," as he notes in chapter 3, "the only strategic choice for China is to try its best to improve ties, enlarge areas of common interest, and accept that the relationship will reflect both cooperation and confrontation. It should use reasonable and restrained means to resist U.S. actions that threaten its interests and try gradually to steer the relationship onto a normal track. This is neither the best nor the worst choice, but it has the best chance of success and should, therefore, be adopted." This strategic choice synthesizes many possibilities and will be useful in different situations. For example, when conflict seems imminent, China can try to manage the situation to prevent escalation to violence. Also, even if the two nations cannot establish a true alliance, they can cooperate in such key areas as trade, education, the fight against terrorism, and the protection of the environment. They should emphasize achieving balance in their relations. When troubles arise, they should manage them and always leave room for improvement. And, when relations are smooth, they should anticipate potential conflicts and adopt preventive measures. China should not confront the United States on its own initiative. If the United States tries to force confrontation, China should not be afraid and should be prepared. Even when the United States is entirely responsible for a downturn in relations, China should exercise restraint and always seek opportunities to change the U.S. position. The United States cannot force its will on China as it does with small countries, nor can it try to solve conflicts between the two as in Afghanistan or Iraq.

In Ye's view, the greatest threat to China is not from the United States but from the accumulation of its own growing internal problems. China has experienced rapid growth and development for three decades, but the development is unbalanced, fragile, and unstable. If such problems as corruption, unemployment, the widening gap between rich and poor, social security, and social protection are not dealt with properly, they may cause turbulence and slow the historical process of China's rejuvenation and rise.

In terms of China's relations with other great powers, Ye thinks that China's relationship with Russia is the best of all. Strategically, that relationship is essential to China's quest for great power status. In addition to its role as a source of energy, Russia's military and dual use technologies are essential to enhancing China's comprehensive national power. It is important to China's security that the long common border, particularly in the northwest, be stable. Since the Beijing-Moscow strategic partnership is not aimed at any third country, both nations are free to develop relations with the United States, Japan, and Europe without undermining their bilateral ties. In fact, the interests of the two countries require them to carry out strategic cooperation. Taken together, the threat posed to Russia by NATO's eastward expansion, the broadening of the Japanese-U.S. security alliance, and the Chechen and Taiwan issues mean that China and Russia have some anti-U.S. strategic interests in common. Nevertheless, the overriding national interests of both China and Russia require them to give priority to their relations with the United States and seek to improve them. Ye argues that China should support Russia's efforts to regain its status as a world power.

Ye also suggests that it is of crucial importance for China to manage its relations with Japan well. Beijing should not regard competition with Japan for world power status as a zero-sum game. China's becoming a world power is not an obstacle to Japan's becoming one, and vice versa. Ye believes that China and Japan can develop cooperative and complementary relations. Neither can do without the other if they want to develop a cohesive East Asia. It is worth noting that Ye made this argument for improving Sino-Japanese relations in 2003 when those relations were deeply troubled owing to rising nationalism in China and the unrepentant attitudes of certain Japanese leaders toward aggression by Japan against its neighbors during World War II. Ye argues that it is important for Japan and China to find new ways to raise relations to a new level. The two countries have conflicting views on a variety of issues, including sovereignty over the Diaoyu Islands, future priorities for the security treaty with the United States, the status of Taiwan, and memories of the Japanese invasion as a factor affecting bilateral ties. As both nations claim the Diaoyu Islands, the two sides should exercise restraint, maintain the status quo, take no actions to occupy the territory, and try to find ways of joint development and utilization. Recent improvement in Sino-Japanese relations demonstrates the acuity of Ye's analysis of this critical bilateral relationship.

On the critical issue of Taiwan, Ye argues that development takes priority over unification. Clearly, unification is more likely than permanent separation. However, the key variable is the course of China's development program. If China's economy and political life remain stable, independence will not be an option for Taiwan. On the other hand, if the mainland falters, the proindependence forces might be encouraged to take a desperate risk. Thus, China should build its own long-term unification strategy on the knowledge that the final resolution of the Taiwan problem depends on its own political and economic development. Such strategic thinking provides insights for understanding the relation between unification and China's rise to global prominence.

In contrast to the hypernationalist view that favors unification preceding development, Ye argues that the processes of China's integration and growth are actually the same process. That is, China's rapidly increasing power will also strongly accelerate the unification process. Development and unification both are core interests of China, and the Taiwan problem is a difficult and central issue. But it cannot now be said that, without unification, there will be no development. Development should promote unification, but, because development is the determinative factor, modernization should continue as the first strategic priority. As long as the Taiwan problem does not deteriorate to the point of conflict, development should be China's primary goal. Development will lead to unification and will also strengthen China's unity when it is eventually achieved. The more developed mainland China is, the better the chances for peaceful unification. Unification and development are not two discrete processes. Rather, they intersect in time, in space, and even in content.

Ye argues that China can develop an effective strategy for Taiwan on the basis of historical experience and the requirements of modernization and development. He outlines the core content of the strategy as follows. It is essential to understand that independence for Taiwan is impossible as long as the mainland sticks to the principle of peaceful unification, maintains political and economic stability, and continues to grow economically. While some military pressure against the Taiwanese separatist forces is necessary, the priority should be winning the hearts of the people of Taiwan. China's leaders must not forget that time is on the side of those seeking unification. The goal will be achieved more rapidly if Chinese leaders understand and respect the concerns of the people of Taiwan. If Taiwan declares independence, the mainland will respond forcefully. But, as long as there is the possibility of peaceful unification, force will not be used. Finally, the mainland must be flexible in applying the one China principle. Any action that promotes the cross-strait relationship should be taken. For example, a possible solution is a quasi federation with the substance but not the structure of a federal system. Taiwan would renounce independence, in return for which the mainland would renounce the use of force, and the two sides could make it clear that, while Taiwan might not have the freedom of an independent country, it would have considerably more latitude than the Hong Kong and Macau special administrative regions.

Cross-strait relations are greatly influenced by the United States. In Ye's view, the United States uses Taiwan to contain China and to benefit the U.S. arms industry. It preserves the status quo in order to be able to trade with both sides. It uses the Taiwan issue as a way of encouraging peaceful evolution in China. If China develops smoothly, the common interests between the United States and China will increase, while those between Taiwan and the United States will decrease. Unification is China's core interest, but protecting Taiwan is not even an important interest for the United States. Taiwan will gradually be marginalized in the U.S.

hierarchy of interests. The more developed and stronger China is, the less likely the United States will have a full-scale confrontation with China over Taiwan.[9] Therefore, there is every reason for the mainland to be confident about the future. It is clear that China is a great power in international society and has enough power and determination to prevent Taiwanese independence. Taiwan cannot be independent in Ye's view. Its future depends on the mainland.

Cross-strait relations since 2000 have experienced up and downs. With the transition of power in Taiwan from Chen Shui-bian to Ma Ying-jeou in May 2008, a new opportunity for cross-strait peace and cooperation has emerged. The danger of war in the Taiwan Strait has been significantly reduced. Accordingly, Beijing's policy has further shifted from preparing for the worst-case scenario to building mutual trust and enhancing cooperation. It seems that Ye is correct in his analysis of the dynamic yet complex cross-strait relations. The strategy of focusing on development rather than increasing immediate pressure for unification has led to a more stable relationship across the Taiwan Strait.

Ye emphasizes that domestic sources are driving China's emerging grand strategy of peaceful development. China's dynamic growth and peaceful relations with the outside world have indicated that the strategic choice made by Deng Xiaoping and his supporters is correct. China's peaceful development requires deep reform that will provide both institutional and technological innovations. In nearly three decades, China has made enormous progress and built a firm foundation for future development as a great power. At the same time, it has accumulated a large number of domestic problems while going through a series of profound changes. If the critical problems cannot be solved or alleviated effectively, they may cause a crisis and lead to a calamitous impact on political and social stability. In recent times, Chinese citizens often put corruption, bureaucratism, the increase in unemployment and laid-off workers, and the widening gap between the rich and the poor as the main factors affecting social stability in China.[10]

According to Ye, the tough problems that China is confronting today can be resolved only through the deepening of reform. Widespread corruption has, in fact, weakened the Chinese government's managerial ability, but the Chinese political system still retains a certain mobilization power. China may prevent a major social crisis if it properly manages politics, implements system innovation, overcomes corruption and polarization, and distributes the fruits of the economic growth more rationally among all members of society. If the reformers improve the oversight system effectively via democratic construction at the basic level, pursue an inner-Party power checks-and-balances mechanism, China will move in the direction of democratization with Chinese characteristics. Over the long run, democracy might be the only way for the regime to sustain legitimacy. It is important to examine the transition from a revolutionary party to a governing party and democracy under the new leadership. Renewed debate in China about democracy and numerous local democratic elections might lead to new efforts at building a new political order.[11]

How would Chinese-style democracy develop in Ye's view? Fundamental political change could start with grassroots efforts and intra-Party democracy and expand incrementally to more open and free elections at higher levels of the government and still allow the Chinese government to maintain the stability necessary for economic development.[12] There will be no real checks and balances without democracy. Without checks and balances, there will be no real solution to corruption, and there will be no real peace and stability in China in the long term. Suppression works only temporarily, the cost is too high, and it undermines the credibility and legitimacy of the government. That is why deep reform is necessary. Such deep reform is not simply propaganda promoting such notions as "rectification of Party discipline," "mass line," and "people oriented," but real political reform, which is not simply administrative but political in nature—transforming the relationship between the Party and the government, between Party leaders and the rank and file, and between the government and the citizens. Such fundamental political reform will continue to affect the international environment of China.[13]

As an ideal grand strategy, peaceful development represents the dream of the Chinese people to achieve prosperity and power in a peaceful environment. This is a dream of growing prosperity, a healthy environment, social harmony, a diverse culture, dynamic interaction with the outside world, and friendly and peaceful relations with all countries. This dream is consistent with the common aspiration of the majority of the people in the world. People who believe in peaceful development will reject Samuel Huntington's vision of "the clash of civilizations" or John Mearsheimer's "tragedy of great power politics."[14] In reality, China's development has not been and will not be smooth. China today confronts multiple challenges, including resource constraints, environmental degradation, a shortage of skilled labor, weak social security, a weak health safety net, deficits in social trust, and diminishing returns on investment. Nevertheless, it continues to move ahead rapidly in spite of daunting challenges. Many times alarmists have proclaimed the "coming collapse of China."[15] Such crisis calls have repeatedly turned out to be overstated. It seems reasonable to argue that the Chinese reality is somewhere between the model of economic miracle[16] and the warning of crisis or collapse. The drive to achieve peaceful development and the fear of growing crisis are both powerful forces motivating China's reformers to carry out deep reform. Motivations can change, and history shows how the motivational change of a rising great power can wreak havoc in world politics. Ultimately, much of the international confidence in China's intentions depends on its firm embrace of international responsibility and domestic reforms. The fundamental goal of the deep reform is to restructure the Chinese political and economic systems in order to adapt to a changing international environment. Whether China can succeed in its deep reform and maintain its grand strategy of peaceful development will affect not only the welfare of all the Chinese people but also the future of the world. Because the deep reform requires the hard work of many generations of Chinese people, the grand strategy of peaceful development is likely to last a very long time if there are no major catastrophic incidents to interrupt the implementation of this grand strategy.

The 2008 global financial crisis clearly indicates that the world economy is entering turbulent and uncharted territory. As its economy is more intertwined with the global economy than ever before, China is finding that sustainable development is coming under enormous pressures. It has already established itself as the world's largest manufacturer of a wide range of goods, adding new product areas such as personal computers and many categories of consumer electronics to its long-standing dominance in clothing, toys, footwear, and sporting goods. It absorbed more than $700 billion in foreign direct investment between 1979 and 2007. Its swelling foreign exchange reserves exceeded $2.3 trillion by 2010.[17] Any significant downturn in the global economy will inevitably affect China's economy. Much of China's grand strategy of peaceful development has been based on a relatively stable and peaceful international environment and open trading system. With global financial turmoil, such assumptions can no longer be taken for granted. What role will China play in managing the global financial and trading system? What impact will the international financial crisis have on China? Will it be able to maintain its policy of reform and opening? Such questions demand careful consideration. Now is the time for more active and meaningful dialogue between China and the outside world. We hope that this English edition of *Inside China's Grand Strategy* will not only contribute to the Western understanding of China's emerging grand strategy but also further advance the ongoing academic debate among scholars and policymakers about China's growing yet uncertain role in a changing world.

1

China's Development as a World Power

Objective Conditions, Strategic Opportunity, and Strategic Choices

Following the revival of China, four kinds of objections have been raised to the idea of its becoming a world power.

The elephant mentality. According to this viewpoint, it is unrealistic to believe that China can achieve its objective of becoming a world power. "It is impossible for China to catch up with the West, not to mention surpassing it, in the twenty-first century. There is no way to tell whether it will even be able to do so in the twenty-second century. Thus, we ought to jettison the unrealistic objective of overtaking the West." Internationally, China should not pick fights with the world, and it should not try to become a superpower on a par with the United States. There is no need for it to seek to become a "tiger" like the United States; indeed, since it lacks the capability, this is impossible. Nor should it join the company of the "wolves," namely, Russia, Japan, and India. Of course, China cannot act like a sheep that others devour. It should be like a gentle elephant that stands apart from the tigers, wolves, and sheep, having no conflict with them, and not contending with them for food.[1]

The theory of natural growth. This view is that it does not matter whether China *wants* to develop into a world power. The crucial point is that it *needs* to develop; its status as a world power will follow naturally. It should not struggle to achieve the status of a world power. When it develops to the level of a world power, sooner or later it will achieve world power status.[2]

The theory that conditions are lacking. The core argument from this perspective is that China has so many domestic problems and is backward in so many aspects that it presently lacks, and will continue to lack, the qualifications to be a world power. Therefore, there is no point in it even trying. Though it has made great achievements in economic reform since the late 1970s, further reflection indicates that, in spite of its rising status, China lacks three decisive elements necessary to becoming a world power: a favorable security environment, hard military and economic power, and the soft power of politics, society, and ideology.

The theory that China will collapse. In his book *The China Dream,* Joe Studwell, the editor-in-chief of the U.S. journal *The Chinese Economy,* stated that the Chinese economy is a mansion constructed on sand.[3] Probably the best example of this doom-and-gloom genre is *The Coming Collapse of China,* by Gordon Chang, who believes that China's entry into the WTO in 2001 was the starting point of its impending collapse.

None of these viewpoints stands up to scrutiny. Rather, China possesses both the objective conditions and the historical prerequisites necessary to become a world power.

The Objective Conditions and Historical Prerequisites Necessary for China to Become a World Power

China Possesses the Objective Conditions to Become a World Power

We may consider the attributes of a great power with respect to natural geography and economic potential under the following headings:

China is the third largest country in area. Some scholars think that being a world power requires a special sort of territorial foundation; that is, countries aspiring to world power status must be continent-sized powers like Russia, the United States, and China. France, on the fringe of a continent, and island nations like the United Kingdom and Japan do not meet this criterion. This viewpoint is somewhat overstated since history has witnessed a number of world powers—including the earliest world power, the Roman Empire, and the Spanish and Ottoman empires—that were not, in fact, continent-sized land powers. Nevertheless, it remains true that an extensive territory is an important prerequisite to becoming a world power.[4]

Countries with territories of more than 1 million square kilometers

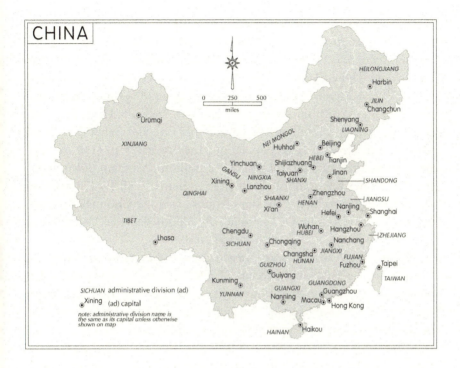

are the largest in the world. There are twenty-eight such countries whose total land mass of 99,680,000 square kilometers represents 74 percent of the world's total 133,480,000 square kilometers. Among them there are twelve would-be great powers, including Russia (17,070,000), Canada (9,970,000), China (9,600,000), the United States (9,360,000), Brazil (8,510,000), Australia (7,710,000), India (3,280,000), Mexico (1,950,000), Indonesia (1,930,000), Iran (1,640,000), South Africa (1,220,000), and Egypt (1,000,000). Other countries with large territories include Argentina (2,760,000), Kazakhstan (2,710,000), Saudi Arabia (2,150,000), Sudan (2,500,000), Algeria (2,380,000), Libya (1,750,000), Mongolia (1,560,000), Peru (1,280,000), Chad (1,280,000), Niger (1,260,000), Angola (1,240,000), Mali (1,240,000), Columbia (1,130,000), Bolivia (1,090,000), Ethiopia (1,090,000), and Mauritania (1,020,000). The territorial expanses of some large economic powers are as follows: Turkey (770,000), Japan (370,000), Germany (350,000), the United Kingdom (240,000), France (550,000), Italy (300,000), and South Korea (99,000).

China is the most populous country in the world. Countries with populations exceeding 50 million as of 1995 may be counted among those with the largest populations in the world. There are twenty-three such countries, accounting for 4.168 billion, or 74 percent, of the total global population of 5.673 billion. Among them are China (1.3 billion), India (1 billion), the United States (263 million), Indonesia (200 million), Brazil (159 million), Russia (148 million), Japan (125 million), Mexico (92 million), Germany (82 million), Iran (64 million), the United Kingdom (58.5 million), France (58 million), Egypt (58 million), and Italy (57 million). Other countries with large populations include Pakistan (130 million), Bangladesh (120 million), Nigeria (112 million), Vietnam (74 million), the Philippines (69 million), Turkey (61 million), Thailand (58 million), and Ethiopia (56 million). The populations of some economically powerful countries are as follows: Australia (18 million), Canada (29.6 million), Spain (39 million), and South Korea (45 million).

China is the world's sixth largest economy in terms of GDP. Any country with a GDP that exceeds US$200 billion has the potential to become a world economic power. There were twenty-two such countries in 1997, accounting for US$25.8 trillion of the world's total GDP of US$29.9 trillion, or 86 percent. These countries are the United States (US$7.69 trillion), Japan (US$4.77 trillion), Germany (US$2.32 trillion), France (US$1.53 trillion), the United Kingdom (US$1.22 trillion), Italy (US$1.16), China (US$1.06), Brazil (US$773 billion), Canada (US$583.9 billion), Spain (US$570.1 billion), South Korea (US$485.3 billion), Russia (US$403.5 billion), the Netherlands (US$402.7 billion), Australia (US$380 billion), India (US$373.9 billion), Mexico (US$348.6 billion), Switzerland (US$313.5 billion), Argentina (US$305.7 billion), Belgium (US$268.4 billion), Sweden (US$232 billion), Austria (US$225.9 billion), and Indonesia (US$221.9 billion).

According to World Bank data published on April 2, 2002, the first twenty-one countries in terms of GDP in the year 2000 are as follows: the United States (US$9.84 trillion), Japan (US$4.84 trillion), Germany (US$1.87 trillion), the United Kingdom (US$1.41 trillion), France (US$1.294 trillion), China (US$1.08 trillion), Italy (US$1.074 trillion), Canada (US$687.8 trillion), Brazil (US$595.4 billion), Mexico (US$574.5 billion), Spain (US$558.5 billion), South Korea (US$457.2 billion), India (US$456.9 billion), Australia (US$390.1 billion), the Netherlands (US$364.8 billion), Argentina (US$284.9 billion), Russia (US$251.1 billion), Switzerland (US$239.7 billion), Sweden (US$227.3 billion), Belgium (US$226.6 billion), and Turkey (US$200 billion). (Austria and Indonesia, which made the list in 1997, had GDPs of US$189 billion and US$153.2 billion, respectively, in 2000.) These twenty-one countries generated US$26.93 trillion of the global GDP of US$31.49, or some 85 percent.[5]

China is a country with significant political and military power. China is one of five countries to hold permanent seats on the UN Security Council. The other four countries are the United States, the United Kingdom, France, and Russia. These are also the five big nuclear powers. What is more, China has become the third country capable of sending manned craft into outer space.

China Has Sufficient Comprehensive National Strength to Develop into a World Power

The concept of a world power is based on comprehensive national power, not just one or two indicators. Deng Xiaoping pointed out that comprehensive national strength should be viewed in an all-around way. According to research by Chinese and foreign scholars, comprehensive national strength is composed of the following elements. It is the power of a sovereign country, including both hard power, such as economic and military power, and soft power, such as spiritual culture, national historical tradition, and national cohesiveness. National power also includes both present power and potential power.

The German scholar William Fuchs of Berlin University, a professor of theoretical physics, is perhaps the earliest Western scholar to study international relations from the perspective of comprehensive national strength. His *National Power Equation* (1965) incorporated the results of extensive research and computation with various complicated formulas.[6]

Other scholars before and after him also advanced similar concepts. The U.S. scholar Ray S. Cline is one of the better-known figures in this field. He served as deputy director of the CIA, the head of the Bureau of Intelligence and Research in the State Department, and the director of the Center for Strategic and International Studies at Georgetown University for a long time. He published two books: *World Power Assessment* in 1975 and *World Power Trends and U.S. Foreign Policy for the 1980s* in 1980.[7] Cline divides national strength into physical and spiritual elements. The physical element is composed of population, territory, GDP, energy, minerals, industrial production, food supplies, trade, and military power. The spiritual element includes strategic intentions and national willpower.

According to a report issued by the Japan Comprehensive Planning Bureau commissioned by the Economic Planning Department, national strength is composed of three capacities: international capacity, survival capacity, and coercive capacity. International capacity includes the economy, monetary power, science and technology, fiscal power, and mobility. Survival capacity includes area, population, resources, national defense, national will, and relations with allies. Coercive capacity includes military power, strategic resources and technology, economic power, and diplomatic power.

The U.S. scholar Nicholas John Spykman listed ten elements of comprehensive national strength: territory, border characteristics, population, raw material, economy and technology, financial power, national homogeneity, social homogeneity, political stability, and public morale. Another prominent international relations specialist, Hans J. Morgenthau, pointed out nine elements of comprehensive national strength: geography, natural resources, industrial capacity, military preparedness, population, national character, national morale, diplomatic skill, and quality of government. Yet other U.S. scholars, Robert Cox and Robert H. Jackson, emphasize five elements: GDP, per capita GDP, population, nuclear capacity, and international prestige.[8]

Joseph Nye, a former U.S. deputy undersecretary of state and dean of the Kennedy School of Government at Harvard University, argues that national power is composed of both hard power and soft power. Hard power is the power to control others; it includes basic resources and military, economic, and scientific and technological power. Soft power includes national cohesion, culture, international legitimacy, and participation in the international system.[9]

Chinese scholars have also expressed their views on this fundamental question. They believe that comprehensive national power means the organic total of all the strength of a sovereign country, including population and natural resources and soft power and hard power. There are several variants of this view.

In the first variant, there are seven elements, namely, natural power, manpower, economic power, scientific and technological power, educational power, national defense power, and political power. In the second variant, there are four elements: basic power (population, resources, national cohesion), economic power (industry, agriculture, science and technology, finances, and business capacity), defense power (strategic resources, technology, military, and nuclear power), and diplomatic power (foreign policy, approaches to dealing with international affairs, fundamental positions, and foreign exchanges and aid). In a third variant, there are eight elements: basic national indicators (territory, geographic location, natural resources, climate, terrain, strategic territory), population, economy, science and technology, defense power, political power, spiritual power, and foreign relations. In a fourth variant, there are seven elements: politics, economy, science and technology, national defense, culture and education, diplomacy, and resources. In a fifth variant, there are ten elements, distributed between hard power and soft power. Hard power here comprises economic power (the foundation), military power (the means of enforcement), and scientific-technological power (the leading force). Soft power is composed of open, stable, enduring, and adaptive domestic political, social, and economic systems; strong cultural, political, moral, and cohesive power; theoretical guidance; strategic insight and diplomatic skill; effective domestic and international management, including effective mobilization of domestic and international resources; well-educated and culturally advanced citizens; and high living standards.[10]

As may be seen, there are many common elements within these varying definitions of what constitutes comprehensive national strength. Table 1 presents a guide to the views of a number of the aforementioned authors.

My own view is that it is more productive to understand so-called comprehensive national strength as comprising a country's survival ability, development capacity, and international influence.

Different countries have different requirements for comprehensive national power. If a small country adopts the strategy of allying with a big power, it may be inclined to think that it is not necessary to possess its own military forces because, if something happens, it may not be able to defend itself by relying on its own forces. If it does try to build up its own military to defend itself, it is likely to discover that it lacks the wherewithal to do so. Moreover, if it is attacked by a larger neighbor, it may still be unable to defend itself. For these reasons, I do not propose to discuss the comprehensive national power of middle and small countries.

Furthermore, comprehensive national power has, of necessity, different requirements in different times. Formerly, natural resources, such as land, and the basic necessities of life, including food and minerals, were

Table 1. The Assessment of Comprehensive National Power of Great Powers

	(a)	(b)	(c)	(d)	(e)	(f)	(g)
United States	304 (2)	100 (1)	100 (1)	68 (1)	4572 (1)	79 (1)	551 (1)
Soviet Union/Russia	458 (1)	73 (2)	71 (2)	41 (2)	3286 (2)	43 (5)	252 (4)
Japan	108 (5)	41 (3)	57 (3)	35 (3)	2869 (4)	52 (2)	365 (2)
Germany	116 (4)	23 (4)	19 (5)	27 (4)	2775 (5)	50 (3)	354 (3)
United Kingdom	68 (9)	23 (4)	10 (6)	23 (5)	2454 (8)	42 (6)	210 (6)
France	74 (8)		6 (7)	23 (6)	2680 (6)	43 (4)	221 (5)
Canada	61 (10)			21 (8)	3137 (3)	38 (7)	155 (8)
India	36 (12)			13 (10)	1335 (11)	21 (11)	100 (11)
Australia	88 (6)			13 (9)	2566 (7)	30 (9)	124 (9)
Indonesia	55 (11)				1107 (12)	15 (12)	
Brazil	137 (3)				1607 (10)	23 (10)	102 (10)
China	83 (7)	17 (5)	35 (4)	22 (7)	2157 (9)	32 (8)	196 (7)

Note: Values given are mean score and, in parentheses, rank. Sources (by column) are as follows: (a) Ray S. Cline, *World Power Trends and U.S. Foreign Policy for the 1980s* (Boulder, CO: Westview, 1980). (b) Data from a 1978 study by the Japanese Research Institute. (c) Data from a 1987 study by the Japanese Research Institute. (d) Yu Hongyi, "Estimating and Appraising Comprehensive National Strength," *Technology Progress and Countermeasures* 5, no. 5 (1989): 52. (e) Wang Songfen, *Main Countries' Comprehensive National Strength* (Changsha: Hunan Press, 1996). (f) Data from a revised version of Wang's *Main Countries' Comprehensive National Strength*. (g) Huang Shuofeng, *New Theory of Overall National Strength* (Beijing: China Social Sciences Press, 1999), 119.

the basic conditions of comprehensive national power. Nowadays, human resources, that is, women and men with a higher education, have become the decisive element in a country's total power. For example, combat effectiveness used to be measured by the number of troops and the level of morale. Now, the most important element is the quantity of high-tech weapons and equipment.

Whether a country has the will to achieve global influence is also important in assessing the likelihood of its achieving that influence. If a country lacks the will, it may not regard the possession of such influence as important to it. In the 1920s and 1930s, few Americans put much stock in membership in the League of Nations. In the 1960s, Mao Zedong stated that it did not matter whether China was a member of the United Nations since China itself was like a United Nations of many nationalities. At the time, China was disinclined to take part in or play an active role in international activities. In some cases, the conditions for its participation were lacking; in others, it lacked the will to participate.

Therefore, in this discussion, greater emphasis is placed on what sort of comprehensive national power a would-be or potential great power must possess.

The three dimensions that constitute the comprehensive national strength of any given country can be elaborated as follows.

Survival capacity. The necessities for national survival include territory, geographic location, natural resources, climate, topography, strategic territory, population, national cohesion, nationality structure, economic power, military power, etc. Theorists of the realist school assert that all countries must give top priority to national security. Therefore, each country must possess the necessary survival capacity, including territory, population, natural resources, and requisite economic strength (a certain level of GDP and per capita GDP). The survival capacity requirements of a would-be world power with global influence are much greater than they are for ordinary countries. For example, a country with only 3 or 4 million people and a territory of only several thousand square kilometers cannot become a world power no matter how hard it may try. We can summarize the prerequisites for becoming a world power as follows: a population greater than 50 million, total territory (including territorial waters) of no less than 1 million square kilometers, a GDP ranking within the top thirty, total foreign trade among the top thirty, per capita GDP based on purchasing power of over US$3,000, the capacity to sustain the normal life of its people and its social order on the basis of its own economic resources, and the capacity to defend its national security, safeguard its national unity and territorial integrity, and protect the security of the lives and property of its people by relying on its own military forces. To qualify as a potential world power a country must possess at least two or three of these prerequisites.

Developmental capacity. Developmental capacity includes a mature, well-functioning, and stable system, including political, economic, and legal institutions; a stable and mature middle class playing a balancing and stabilizing role in society; a relatively developed national education system; a high percentage of citizens with a quality education that includes advanced science and technology; human resources developed to the midlevel on a world scale; per capita GDP per annum, figured according to purchasing power, at or above US$6,000; world levels in the basic fields of, and leadership or parity in at least certain fields of, science and technology; the capacity to halt environmental degradation, promote ecological equilibrium, and commence sustainable development; the capacity to resolve a shortage of natural resources by increasing production, devising substitutes, and importing or producing synthetic materials; the military capability to protect national development; the capability to maintain and support foreign trade, transportation, and strategic resources; and the ability to maintain a relatively fast and healthy rate of growth. Another important factor is the national development trend, that is, whether the country has entered a phase of relatively rapid growth.

International influence. These capabilities include influence deriving from the expansion of the population, the economic system, the territory, and resources; national cohesion and willpower; participation in international organizations and meetings in the fields of politics, the economy, culture, education and sanitation, sports, military, security, and the environment; occupying a fairly important position in and playing an active role in international organizations; exercising a constructive influence in the process of solving international problems; playing an important part in setting the rules of the world system and constructing new international political and economic orders; playing an important role in regional affairs and cooperating with other major regional powers in resolving regional issues; accepting the main rules and values of world civilization and contributing to a developmental path that reflects the characteristics of one's own country while studying and borrowing from the experience of other leading countries; making creative contributions to world civilization and development and sharing new experiences and models to address various political, economic, social, and culture issues; possessing the necessary military, economic, and political power to safeguard peace and stability in the region and the world; providing ethical inspiration and influence on the basis of one's own country's stable social system, continuous creativity in science and technology, strong market and productivity, and advanced culture with national characteristics.

These three dimensions are likewise the main criteria in judging whether a given country possesses the qualifications to be considered a great power. It is evident that the concept of comprehensive national power is complicated and that it cannot be measured using only one or two indicators. Therefore, while we must consider per capita GDP, we cannot limit ourselves entirely to this one indicator. Factors can play different roles in calculating comprehensive national power depending on the country in question.

For instance, military power is an important element in a country's comprehensive power. It is not only a survival factor but also a developmental one and an even more important element with regard to international influence. But the salience of military power is very different with respect to survival capacity, development, and international influence. For example, from the angle of survival capacity, China, a large country with both land and sea borders, should possess the military capacity to defend both its territorial seas and its land against attack and aggression from the sea. From the angle of development, China should possess the military capacity to protect its overseas transportation and foreign trade and at a minimum the capability to conduct military activities in its coastal waters. As a world power with world influence, China should possess the military capacity to conduct warfare on the high seas and in concert with other major powers to safeguard world peace and stability. International influence, however, is not merely a matter of military strength; it also depends on a certain degree of cultural influence and the possession of an advanced social system. Sometimes moral influence plays a more important role than military power. Why did fascist Germany lose the Second World War? Of course, the military capacity of the Allies ultimately exceeded that of Germany, but there is another important reason for its failure. The Germans claimed to be a superior race, advocating the elimination of inferior nationalities and, thus, purifying Europe, and promoting the theory that superior races should rule the world. This type of thinking contradicted the main trend of world civilization and evoked almost unanimous opposition on the part of the major countries in the world.

The Soviet Union used to possess superior military power on a par with that of the United States, but this military power did not translate into equivalent international influence, let alone manage to guarantee the survival of the Soviet Union itself. The Soviet military could only stand by and observe first the disintegration and then the extinction of the Soviet Union. Its huge nuclear arsenal was useless. After the Soviet Union disintegrated, Russia inherited most of the Soviet military power, but, even though it remains strong in military terms, it has not been able to play the role of a world power since 1992 and is unlikely to be able to exert global influence for some time to come.

There is no doubt that survival capacity, developmental capacity, and international influence are integrally related to each other.

Survival capacity and developmental capacity are the foundation of comprehensive national power. International influence is based on survival and development. Without survival capacity and developmental capacity, there can be no international influence. When a country can survive and develop, it may then exert a certain degree of international influence, but such international influence does not arise automatically. Only if it strives to secure and then utilize its capacity will a country be able to enjoy a commensurate degree of international influence. Sometimes, even though a given country's survival capacity and developmental capacity have exceeded those of many other countries, its international influence remained minimal—for example, if it adopted a closed policy, isolationism, and a purely regional outlook and was unwilling to participate in international affairs or if most members of the international community did not welcome its participation. For example, during the U.S. isolationist period—which began in 1823 when President James Monroe announced the Monroe Doctrine, whereby the United States abjured interference in European affairs and proscribed European interference in the Americas—the Congress and the president did not concern themselves with or participate in the affairs of Europe or the other regions of the world. Consequently, although the United States already possessed considerable strength—becoming by the end of the nineteenth century the strongest country in the world, its power far exceeding that of Great Britain, which had the greatest influence in world affairs—it did not have much international influence. Even its participation in World War I did not render it a world power. That is because the majority in Congress adopted a policy of isolationism and was unwilling to participate in the League of Nations, the main international organization, which President Wilson himself had energetically promoted. Only after World War II did the United States finally became one of two world superpowers and, after the Cold War, the lone superpower.

By the 1980s and 1990s, Japan had already become a powerful country with a GDP second only to that of the United States, a position it retains to this day. Yet it is not a world power because it lacks the international influence of a great power. In military affairs, it is controlled by the United States and takes its diplomatic cues from Washington. It has long been unwilling to engage in sincere, conscientious, and deep introspection on its invasion of neighboring countries and has lacked the courage to take responsibility for its own past. Therefore, its aspiration to become a great power is stifled by the United States, while its perspective on the wars of aggression that it waged inevitably evokes suspicion on the part of its East Asian neighbors, including the Chinese people. Hence, Japan has the attributes of, but does not enjoy the influence of, a great power.

In a very short time, Singapore, a small country that has been independent for only forty years, has become a well-educated, prosperous, and socially stable country despite its lack of natural resources and any other special advantages. This is because it pioneered its own development model, achieved an impressive record of accomplishments, and was blessed with outstanding leaders. Because of the sagacity of these leaders, it enjoys greater international influence than other small countries. In 1997, the GDP of Singapore reached US$101.8 billion, ranking thirty-fourth in the world in absolute terms. Its per capita GDP was US$32,940, ranking fourth in the world. (If calculated according to purchasing power parity [PPP], its per capita GDP ranked first in the world.) Even after experiencing the financial crisis of 1997, by 2000 Singapore— with a population of 3.74 million people—had a GNP of US$92.5 billion, ranking thirty-ninth in the world according to absolute value, but its per capita GNP reached US$24,666, placing it in the top twenty countries. But Singapore is too small and its power, relative to that of other countries, too weak for it to become a country with great international influence. So, even though its international influence exceeds its national power, because of limits on its power, Singapore cannot become a world power.

The influence of individual countries with petroleum resources is relatively small, but the collective influence of OPEC is rather large. Countries like Kuwait, Saudi Arabia, Iran, and Iraq exert influence disproportionate to their size and population because of their huge petroleum reserves. Their combined influence on the world economy is considerable. Individually, however, they are unlikely to become world powers.

In terms of comprehensive national strength, China probably ranks fifth or sixth in the world, but it suffers from the following serious shortcomings. First, it has not achieved complete national reunification. The issue of Taiwan is still a big drag on its international influence. Second, its population is too big and its per capita GDP relatively low. Compared with many other countries, its levels of education and health care are very low. Third, scientific and technological creativity is relatively low. China is at the stage of copying the advanced technology of the West, and there is a large gap between it and developed countries with respect to advanced and new types of technology. Fourth, its international influence is rising but has not reached a level commensurate with its comprehensive national strength. With respect to many important international issues, its influence is still relatively less than that of other countries. In sum, China has the potential to become, but is not yet, a world power.

China Has the Historical Prerequisites to Become a World Power

What is a world power? What countries can be considered world powers? In world history, what countries can be regarded as great powers? The culture of some ancient civilizations exerted a very great impact on world civilization, so those ancient civilizations can, perhaps, be regarded as great powers. Ancient Egypt, which arose around 2000 B.C., is one such example. It stretched from North Africa to West Asia and later included the Assyrian Empire. But it was not, I think, a great power. It produced the earliest world civilization, and, at its apex (1567–1085 B.C.), its influence expanded to the two-river basin, namely, the third falls of the Nile within what is now the territory of Sudan. The influence of ancient Babylon exceeded even that of Egypt. Babylon gave birth to the earliest cities, the first social reforms, the first law code, and the earliest writing system. It is recognized as the cradle of Western civilization, and it played an enormous role in the development of human civilization. At its peak, during the era of Hammurabi (1792–1750 B.C.), the Babylonian Empire unified the two-river basins. At its apex (680–669 B.C.), the kingdom of Assyria, located in another part of Babylon, included Iraq, part of Iran, parts of Turkey and Syria, and northern Egypt.

Ancient Greece also exerted great influence on world civilization. The spirit of freedom and democracy represented by Pericles and Socrates, the pursuit of science and reason represented by Aristotle, and the unprecedented large-scale empire created by Alexander the Great made enormous contributions to the development of modern Western civilization. Jewish civilization contributed numerous world-famous people, including Karl Marx, Albert Einstein, Sigmund Freud, and dozens of Nobel laureates in the sciences. Jewish spiritual philosophy originated in ancient times and reached its peak in the Hebrew kingdom of the eleventh to the ninth centuries B.C.[11] Some scholars consider the Persian Empire, which spanned the continents of Europe, Asia, and Africa, to be the first great empire. Not only did it possess its own material and spiritual civilization, but it also maintained a huge empire and managed a huge institutionalized civilization. Therefore, its cultural content was more mature, richer, and deeper than that of Egypt or Assyria. The Persian Empire embraced three major centers of ancient civilization, the two-river basin, Egypt, and the Indus River. It also abutted a fourth, Greece.[12] But none of these ancient civilizations can be regarded as world powers. Their influence was mainly spiritual and cultural, and their political, economic, and military influence was confined to relatively small areas.

During the course of world history, a number of countries have been considered world powers. Between 30 B.C. and A.D. 283, the Roman Empire was at its zenith and a veritable superpower. Other great powers included the Byzantine Empire, beginning in the third century A.D., the Arabian Empire of the seventh and eighth centuries A.D., and the Ottoman Turkish Empire that was founded in the fifteenth century.

The Ottoman Empire was one of the most powerful countries in the fifteenth century. The Turkish conquest in 1453 of Constantinople, the capital of Byzantium, signaled its rise. By the end of the fifteenth century, its territory stretched from Central Asia through West Asia to North Africa, the Balkan Peninsula in Southeast Europe, and the southern part of Western Europe. In 1529, the Ottoman armies approached Vienna and Italy. The population of the Ottoman Empire, some 14 million people, was more than twice that of Spain, a European power with a population of 5 million, and more than five times that of England, with a population of 2.5 million. The influence of the Ottoman Empire on Europe, North Africa, West Asia, and Central Asia persisted until the nineteenth century.

The consensus of Western historians is that, over a period of nearly one thousand years, from the initial landing of the Moors in Spain to the second Turkish siege of Vienna, Europe was under constant threat from Islam.[13] Only the Islamic civilization threatened the existence of Western civilization, and it did so on two occasions, the Ottomans besieging Vienna first in 1529 and then again in 1683. After that, the Ottoman threat receded, and the empire assumed the strategic defensive. It totally disintegrated during the First World War.

In fact, prior to A.D. 1500, only the Roman and the Byzantine empires were regarded as world powers in the West. The Arabian kingdom and the Ottoman Empire appeared in the Middle East and West Asia. If we include China, we may say that, prior to A.D. 1500, in global terms the East prevailed over the West. The East was on the offensive and the West on the defensive. Western armies never invaded the East, but large Eastern armies menaced the West on numerous occasions.

During the 500 years from A.D. 1500 to the twentieth century, a fundamental change occurred in the trend of history. With the exception of late-nineteenth- and early-twentieth-century Japan, all the world powers were Western countries. These included Spain in the sixteenth century, Great Britain in the seventeenth and eighteenth centuries, the Russian Empire between the eighteenth century and the twentieth, the Austro-Hungarian Empire between the seventeenth century and the nineteenth, the United States from the nineteenth century to the present, Germany from the late nineteenth century to the early twentieth, France from the late nineteenth century through the early twentieth, and the Soviet Union before and after World War II. Among these countries were not merely great powers in a generic sense but actually superpowers or global superpowers. Great Britain in the nineteenth century, the United States after World War II, and the Soviet Union from the 1950s to the 1980s graduated from the ranks of great powers to become superpowers. Since the 1990s, the United States has become a global superpower.

Obviously, from A.D. 1500 to the present, there have been enormous changes in the global distribution of power, and the balance of power has shifted from the East to the West. Among the fifteen great powers that appeared over the past five hundred years, only China, first under the Ming dynasty and then under the Qing, and modern Japan belonged to the East; the twelve others were Euro-American, as were the three superpowers (Great Britain, the United States, and the Soviet Union) and the lone world superpower (the United States). A major shift has occurred in the historical position of the East and the West. Since 1500, the Western great powers have become more dominant and the Eastern countries enslaved and exploited. The birth and development of the great powers have changed world history, and, without these great powers, one might even say that there would be no world history.

Of course, there are significant differences among the great powers. By the late nineteenth century, the United States was already a great power, but its position was entirely different from its position at the end of the twentieth century. By the late nineteenth century, it was already the world's leading economic power, but it was not a member of the great power system and, therefore, had little influence. It was satisfied with the isolationist status of master of the Western Hemisphere. Its influence at the end of the twentieth century was so much vaster that it can hardly be compared to its influence in the late nineteenth century. Consequently, we can divide the great powers into three types.

The first type is the global superpower. It has enormous influence on a global scale. Up to the present, the United States is the only such country in world history. It developed from a superpower into a global superpower. Its influence reaches everywhere, and its power is unrivaled. Not only does it enjoy influence over ordinary countries, but it also influences Europe and Russia (through NATO) and China and Japan (through the U.S.-Japan Security Treaty and arms sales to Taiwan). It stations military forces throughout the world and has unmatched military, political, economic, and cultural influence. In certain respects, its power exceeds the sum total of the comprehensive strength of several other great powers combined.

At one time, the British Empire enjoyed similar influence. In the first half of the nineteenth century, Great Britain was the strongest power, enjoying the greatest influence in world affairs. Yet it cannot be spoken of in the same breath with the contemporary United States. For example, even at the height of its power, it had little influence with Russia, Japan, and Latin America.

The second type is the superpower. Usually such states exert a significant degree of influence in two, three, or even more regions of the world. There have been only three superpowers in world history, the nineteenth-century British Empire, the post–World War II United States, and the post–World War II Soviet Union.

There have been times when two great powers coexisted, for example, the Roman Empire and the Han dynasty, but they had very little contact

Table 2. Estimated Strategic Nuclear Warheads

	ICBM-Borne Warheads	SLBM-Borne Warheads	Aircraft-Borne Warheads	Total
Soviet Union	6,420	2,787+	680	9,887
United States	2,118	5,536	2,520	10,174

Source: Paul Kennedy, *The Rise and Fall of the Great Powers: Economic Change and Military Conflict from 1500 to 2000* (New York: Random House, 1987), 503.

with each other. The Roman Empire dominated Europe, North Africa, and West Asia; the Western Han dynasty was the strongest power in East Asia. The two were comparable in the scale and range of their power. The British Empire can also be regarded as a world superpower; its influence was greater than that of other contemporaneous world powers, and the scope of its power was also greater.

Between the 1940s and the 1980s, the bloc of East European countries headed by the Soviet Union and the bloc of Western countries headed by the United States also belonged to this superpower category. They were independent of each other and confronted each other. Neither side could control the other. They constituted different systems—indeed, different worlds. Each possessed nuclear forces far in excess of what was required for strategic deterrence and capable of destroying the world many times over (see table 2).

The third type is the world power. Often these countries are the great powers in a multipolar world. None of them compares to the United States or the Soviet Union, but they exert considerable influence in a particular region or with respect to particular issues even though none of them has sufficient power to influence the entire range of world issues. During the nineteenth century, when the British Empire was the dominant power, it was still unable to control and influence the other great powers with which it shared the stage of history, even though its power far exceeded theirs. It and these other states were independent of each other for a very long time, and, more recently, their relations became overlapping and competitive, the pattern that characterized relations among European countries in the seventeenth and eighteenth centuries and the European powers and Japan in the nineteenth century.

China was once a world power and a superpower. China is a unique country in the history of world civilization. Nearly all the more than twenty great civilizations in world history have vanished. Persian civilization was long the most influential civilization in North Africa and West Asia, yet it was extinguished by Alexander the Great of Macedonia. Thereafter, a number of Hellenized states appeared in what had been Persian territory. Greek civilization exerted tremendous influence for a time and then was extinguished by Macedonia and Rome. Roman civilization, the most influential of Western civilizations, was destroyed by Germanic tribes from the north of Europe and by the Turks. Unlike all these other civilizations, China is the only country that has continuously maintained its historical civilization for some five thousand years, including its spoken and written language and its scholarly cultural traditions, which are enduring symbols of the nation. This unique continuity expresses its creativity and its capacity for self-renewal.[14] As some foreigners recognize, throughout most of its long history, China was among the richest and strongest countries in the world. This is what guaranteed China's status as a superpower in history.

Comparing the Roman Empire with the Qin and Han dynasties. Everybody acknowledges that the Roman Empire was the greatest world power in ancient times. Rome ruled all or parts of contemporary Italy, France, England, Spain, Portugal, Switzerland, Austria, Greece, Serbia, Bulgaria, Romania, Turkey, Iraq, Syria, Egypt, Libya, and Tunisia. It was the first real world power in the West and the greatest among ancient Western civilizations. At its zenith, the Roman Empire had a population of more than 50 million and a territory in excess of 6.5 million square kilometers. Excluding desert and areas that could not be controlled at that time, Rome actually controlled between 3 and 4 million square kilometers. Many scholars believe that the Roman Empire represents the true beginning of Western history and that Europe subsequently developed on the foundation of ancient Roman civilization.[15] Yet few people consider the Han dynasty, which was established before the Roman Empire, as a world power. Chinese historians point out that 202 B.C., the date of the founding of the Han dynasty, was almost the same time as the rise of the Roman Empire (200–197 B.C.). The decline of the Roman Empire occurred almost simultaneously with that of the Han dynasty. The Yellow Turban Rebellion of A.D. 184 signaled the beginning of the decline and fall of the Eastern Han. The Roman Empire began its decline in the second century A.D. and split in two in the fourth century, and the Western Roman Empire was attacked and conquered by Germanic peoples. During their heydays, the Han dynasty and the Roman Empire were the

two greatest powers of their time, boasting huge territories, large populations, and highly developed economies and culture with which those of
no other empires could compare.[16] In some respects, the Han dynasty was
even stronger and more advanced than the Roman Empire.

The largest empire in the ancient Western world was ruled from
Rome. At its maximum extent in A.D. 211, it controlled both sides of the
Mediterranean Sea, most of the territory around the Black Sea, and England as well. It encompassed some 60 million people speaking many different tongues and had a standing army of 350,000. In addition, thirty
divisions of 10,000 soldiers each were garrisoned abroad in the border
provinces and on the frontier. In the East, however, an even larger empire
endured for over four hundred years. In 220 B.C., the Han dynasty ruled
no fewer than 60 million people. In scale and organizational capacity,
it surpassed the Roman Empire. Its writ extended from Korea to West
Asia and Asia Minor and included most of the territory of contemporary China, with the exception of Hainan and Tibet. The army of the Han
dynasty exceeded 1 million men, and the road system, built during the
Qin dynasty, totaled 6,800 kilometers, while the Roman Empire's road
system, stretching from Scotland to Rome and from Rome to Jerusalem,
was only about 5,984 kilometers.[17] The Han dynasty further expanded the
road system it inherited from the Qin. The Chinese Empire also developed far more sophisticated and larger-scale monetary, economic, and
security systems than those of Rome. In those years, the people of Rome
were proud of being Roman citizens; yet, in China, for a number of reasons, the process of assimilation was even deeper. Pride in the superiority of China's culture was not simply the prerogative of the elite but the
aspiration of the many non-Chinese peoples who lived under the sway
of the Han dynasty. The superiority of the Chinese way of life, which
included advanced agriculture, an elegant and refined language, and
highly advanced arts, powerfully attracted the subject peoples within the
empire, who respected their conquerors and desired to be assimilated.
The superiority of this culture combined an emphasis on harmony with
the imperial examinations, the refined ethical system of Confucian philosophy, and Legalist statecraft. Unlike in the Roman Empire, where only
the higher strata of conquered societies were assimilated, in China the
assimilated peoples as a whole quickly identified themselves as Chinese,
adopted Chinese language, dress, and methods of agricultural cultivation.
Unlike the Roman Empire, where conquered native elites merely paid lip

service to their new masters, China achieved a unity that was supported by the masses, who believed firmly in national unification.

A comparison of the Tang dynasty with the Eastern Roman Empire leaves no doubt that China was the most advanced country of its era. Surveying world history of that era, Chinese scholars believe that China was the leading state. It was the first of the leading states to enter the age of feudal society, a full seven hundred years before Europe, and it reached its apogee during the Tang dynasty. The Tang boasted the most developed urban economy in the world; its capital, Changan (the contemporary Xian), was the largest political, economic, and cultural center in the world. With a population of close to 1 million, Changan was an important world trading center, attracting both Chinese and foreign merchants. At this time, the level of European productivity was quite low, and the natural economy was dominant. Not until the eleventh century did cities begin to develop in Europe. Constantinople, the capital of the Eastern Roman Empire and the only city with which one can compare Changan, was the richest and most populous city in Europe at that time. It had a population of just 800,000. Another international city was Baghdad in the Arabian Empire. Changan was the most advanced and largest in population and size of these three large cities. Many engineering projects completed during the Sui and Tang periods were the most advanced in the world at that time. The Zhaozhou bridge was the earliest large-scale stone-arch bridge in the world. Not until the mid-nineteenth century were such comparatively large arched bridges built in Europe. The Grand Canal, built during the Sui dynasty, was the longest canal at that time. The Tang dynasty also constructed advanced irrigation works. In that same era, China's textile industry, mining, metallurgy, navigation, papermaking, printing, pottery, sugar industry, etc. were the most advanced in the world. The earliest European paper mills did not come into existence until the twelfth century in Spain and the thirteenth century in Italy. The Tang imperial examinations were an integral part of the most advanced bureaucratic system in the world and subsequently served as a major source for the civil service system in the West. Tang China was the most advanced country in the world. Japan and other countries sent many students to study in China, and they contributed to the reform process in Japan. They made a thorough study of the Tang dynasty political and economic system and established the Japanese writing system on the basis of Chinese characters. Japan also sent students to Korea, which had

begun learning from China even earlier. The advanced economy and cul-
ture of the Tang dynasty also attracted many people from the West. Tang
China became the center of economic and cultural exchanges between
East and West.[18]

The large-scale, advanced, and prosperous capital cities of China
long served as magnets attracting people from afar. According to historical research, of the ten largest and best-known cities in the ancient
world, the seven largest were the capitals of successive Chinese dynasties.
Changan, the capital of the Sui and Tang dynasties, had an area of eighty-
four square kilometers and a population of 1 million. (During the Han
dynasty, Changan was thirty-five square kilometers.) Luoyang, the capital of the Northern Wei dynasty, covered an area of seventy-three square
kilometers. The Yuan capital of Dadu, which, as Beijing, served as the
capital during the Ming and Qing dynasties, covered fifty to sixty square
kilometers. Their areas and populations were all larger than that of contemporaneous foreign cities. Rome had only fourteen square kilometers,
Baghdad thirty-one square kilometers, and Byzantium (Constantinople)
only twelve square kilometers. These Chinese capital cities were not only
large in area; they were built quickly, and their layout and construction
were advanced and rational. They represented the most advanced level of
urban construction in the world at that time.

The Song dynasty was not nearly as strong as the Han and Tang
dynasties, but Song China was still among the most advanced countries
of its era. Jacob d'Ancona, an Italian Jew who traveled to Song China,
called it the strongest maritime shipping power of his day. Contemporary
Europeans called Citong (contemporary Quanzhou), the Song dynasty
capital and the most flourishing city in the empire, the City of Light. As
a trading port, Citong surpassed the most flourishing European ports of
its day. Song China's population exceeded 100 million. Hangzhou had a
population of more than 1 million, and it was considered the largest and
richest city in the world. Fourteenth-century Venice only had 100,000
people, Florence 50,000–60,000, and Paris 250,000.[19]

Quanzhou was the world's greatest city. It attracted large numbers of
foreigners; more than thirty nationalities and races lived and traded in
the city, including Franks, Saracens, Indians, Jews, Venetians, Alexandri-
ans, Belgians from Flanders, Englishmen, and African merchants.

A comparison between China during the Ming dynasty and contemporary Europe indicates that China was the strongest country of that

era as well. The noted historian Paul Kennedy has pointed out that Ming China was one of the strongest countries in the world.[20] In A.D. 1500, Europe was in no way superior to Asia. In fact, Europe's weaknesses outweighed its strengths. Its four greatest weaknesses were the following: (1) Europe had a paucity of natural resources. It was neither the most fertile nor the most populous region of the world. Both India and China could boast of their superiority in these respects. (2) From a geopolitical perspective, Europe's topography was unfavorable. To the north and west, it was surrounded by ice and water. On the east, it was frequently invaded by many strong forces. The Turkish Empire posed the greatest threat at this time. The memory of the fall of Constantinople in A.D. 1453 was still fresh. (3) Europe was fragmented politically and had never really been unified. It was a mélange of petty principalities, small city-states, and small kingdoms. The larger states, like France, England, and Spain, were constantly at war with each other. (4) Europe also lagged behind Asia in science, technology, culture, and military power. In every dimension, the cultural and scientific inheritance of Europe during this era was borrowed from Asia, or, at the least, one might say that the core centers of world civilization were all at the same level. In terms of comprehensive national power, fifteenth-century Europe, like Europe now, was just one of the most important centers of power. No one could have predicted that it would soon dominate the world.

The turning point came in the great era of navigation. The voyages of Columbus and Magellan in search of the New World were a great impetus for European development. After this, Europe entered the age of the Renaissance, the Protestant Reformation, and the Industrial Revolution, resulting in the European miracle. Seizing this opportunity over the course of the next two to three hundred years, Europeans changed the course of history. For the first time ever, Europe forged ahead of the East. In reality, the history of Zheng He's seven voyages westward demonstrated that China's navigational capacity surpassed that of Europe. The seven oceangoing voyages led by Admiral Zheng He of the Ming dynasty between 1423 and 1432 were the greatest voyages in the world at that time. They preceded those of the Europeans. Zheng traveled longer distances, had more advanced instruments, and commanded larger ships and crews. In this East-West competition, China initially enjoyed a competitive advantage, but it proved unable to transform its potential strength into real power. The main difference was that the great Western voyages of exploration were driven by economic gain. The West continually seized great quantities of gold, silver, and treasure from the New World, such spoils supplying a powerful motive for continuing these voyages. By contrast, the Chinese voyages were aimed at displaying to the world the authority and wealth of the emperor. Riches were bestowed on local peoples in exchange for their submission to the emperor's authority. No one realized that this was a perfect opportunity to develop China. China skipped its date with Lady Luck and soon paid a heavy price for this folly as Europe took full advantage of this strategic opportunity.

Next let us compare Great Britain and China under the Qing dynasty. Prior to 1840, the latter was the greatest trading country in the world. Then the Industrial Revolution created a brand-new mode of production. The productivity of labor advanced by leaps and bounds, making Britain unquestionably the most advanced country in the world. The output of pig iron in Britain was just 70,000 tons in 1788 but had increased to 320,000 tons by 1811, a more than fourfold increase in twenty-three years. Starting its textile industry virtually from scratch, Britain quickly became the biggest exporter of cotton yarn in the world. Because of material abundance and rising living standards, its population increased from 9 million in 1700, to 16 million in 1800, and to 41.8 million in 1900. Between 1800 and 1900, its GDP increased fourteenfold. Over that hundred-year period, the annual average increase in GDP was from 2 to 2.35 percent.

Nevertheless, over a very long period of time, the Qing dynasty occupied a superior position compared to Britain. According to Paul Kennedy, Britain's industrial production in 1750 accounted for only 1.9 percent of the world total, while China's in that same year accounted for 32 percent. In 1800, Britain accounted for 4.3 percent of world industrial output, China for 33 percent. Right up to 1860, Britain accounted for a little more than 19.9 percent, while China's share had slipped to 19.7 percent. That was the year that Britain outproduced China for the first time. At this time, Britain's energy consumption was five times that of the United States and of Germany and six times that of France. Its population was just 2 percent of the world's total, but it accounted for 45 percent of world industrial manufacturing capacity, one-fifth of world trade, and two-fifths of trade in industrial goods. Meanwhile, it was building up its infrastructure, including its transportation, postal, and telecommunications systems. In 1880, it accounted for 23 percent of world trade, China only 12.5 percent. In 1900, Britain accounted for 18 percent, China only 6 percent. Britain left China far behind.[21] A similar situation existed regarding China and the United States. In 1800, the United States accounted for only 0.8 percent of world industrial output, China for 33.3 percent. At this time, U.S. industrial output was only one-fortieth of China's. By 1830, the United States accounted for 2.4 percent, China for 29.8 percent. By then, the U.S. total was one-twelfth of China's. In 1860, the United States accounted for 7.2 percent, China 19.7 percent. In 1880, the United States surpassed China, accounting for 14.7 percent, China only 12.5 percent. Huntington says that, in 1750, all the Western countries together accounted for only 18.2 percent of world manufacturing, a figure that rose to 23.3 percent in 1800 and 31.1 percent in 1830. From 1800 to 1860, China's share of world manufacturing declined from 32.8 to 19.7 percent.[22]

According to another economist, Angus Maddison, China's GDP in 1820 calculated in 1990 terms was US$199.2 billion, the largest in the world. Britain's was US$34.8 billion, fourth in the world. India's was US$110.9 billion, France's US$37.3 billion. China accounted for 28.7 percent of world GDP, more than the 26.5 percent of India, France, and Britain combined. Britain's per capita GDP was US$1,756 in 1820, first in the world. China's per capita GDP was US$525, or 29.9 percent of Britain's and 89 percent of the average per capita world GDP at the time. Only in the latter half of the nineteenth century did China's leading position gradually erode. By 1890 its share of global GDP fell to 13.2 percent, by 1919 to 9.1 percent, and by 1952 to 5.2 percent. Its per capita GDP fell to 50 percent of the world average in 1890, 36.7 percent in 1919, and 23.7 percent in 1952.[23]

History cannot fully explain the present, nor does history repeat itself. But what differentiates the history of China from those of other countries is its continuous and unbroken character. That China was able to become a great power many times over the course of more than two thousand years was due to its strong points and the superiority that it enjoyed. This also confers on contemporary China some cultural and historical resources that can be made use of today to expedite growth. Contemporary China must draw on the experience and lessons of its past. The essence of several thousand years of China's glorious history can then shine forth with renewed glory under the new conditions of our age.

Factors Influencing China's Development as a World Power

Political Conditions Influencing China's Development as a World Power

In addition to its potential advantages and resources, the strategic determination and leadership capability of a national government and its elites are very important factors in determining whether a given country develops into a world power. As noted in the preface, three generations of Chinese leaders share the common understanding that, through the efforts of the Chinese people generation after generation, China can become a middle-level developed country by the hundredth anniversary of the founding of the People's Republic of China and approach the level of a developed country through great efforts. Although Chinese leaders made some big mistakes in the past, since the beginning of the era of reform and opening up China has revised its development goal and policy direction and reaffirmed the path of modernization and development. It has strived to safeguard world peace and stability, focused on the central task of economic construction, and made great efforts to develop productivity, increase comprehensive national strength, and raise people's living standards. The goal is to achieve political democracy, economic development, and spiritual civilization and restore China to the ranks of the world's great powers. This will remain China's strategic objective for the next half century. This strategic objective is also a strong motivator that serves to unite the Chinese people inasmuch as it is an ideal they all share. It is a powerful spiritual force that stimulates the wisdom, activism, and sense of responsibility of the Chinese people.

Possessing a clear strategic objective and the firm resolution to realize it are essential if China is to take advantage of the objective conditions and its own great potential to become in reality a world power. Meanwhile, the political and economic system of socialism with Chinese characteristics provides unique advantages for achieving this strategic objective.

China's socialist system was long influenced by the Soviet model. This model contained dual contradictions with respect to how to develop the advantages and potential of the country. On the one hand, the Soviet system of socialism was itself an important factor in the disintegration of the Soviet Union. The Soviet Union, at one time a superpower on a par with the United States, collapsed just five years into its era of reform. The lessons and influence of this experience are far-reaching. Many people have tried to solve the puzzle of the Soviet Union's disintegration, but there are many factors involved and many possible explanations. Granted, many external factors were involved, including the Cold War and military competition with the United States, but these were not the decisive factors that brought about the collapse of the Soviet Union. I firmly believe that the fundamental reasons for this collapse lay within Soviet society itself. It was not the result of some sort of Jewish conspiracy or the victory of some sort of U.S. or Western strategy of peaceful evolution. Within Russia itself, there are various opinions on the causes of the Soviet collapse. The one I find most persuasive is that the traditional Soviet socialist model was unable to renew itself in a timely manner. Even if this was not the most important or the most decisive factor, it certainly was one among them. Nevertheless, the Soviet model was a very positive historical contribution. It provided an alternate model of industrialization to the Western model pioneered in England. Unlike the British model, Soviet-style modernization began with heavy, not light, industry. This model was the expression of a political and economic system in which state power was highly centralized. Such extreme centralization of state power planted the seeds of subsequent Soviet failure, but there was a glorious period marked by great successes that led to the dramatic rise of Soviet power. By the late 1930s, in a process that took just over a decade, the Soviet Union transformed itself from a backward agriculture country into an industrialized and powerful one, second only to the United States. Victory in World War II made it a world power, and, in the 1950s and 1960s, it attained the status of a superpower.

China's prereform socialist system had much in common with the Soviet model. More than two decades of reform have brought about qualitative changes that led to the building of socialism with Chinese characteristics. Under the old, hermetically sealed system, the Party and the government were joined at the hip, power was concentrated in the hands of a few leaders, and the planned economy was based on unitary ownership and egalitarianism. As a result of reform, a new political and economic system has developed in China. The functions of the CCP have been separated from those of the state, and China is moving toward political democracy and a state based on the rule of law under the principle of CCP leadership. China is likewise moving toward a market economy with multiple forms of ownership and distribution. In this way, socialism with Chinese characteristics can avoid many of the defects of developing countries that have adopted Western-style electoral competition and are subject to the evils of ethnic and religious strife. Moreover, it can also avoid the basic defects of Soviet-style socialism while enjoying the advantages that derive from socialism's ability to focus natural resources and social forces on the task of achieving the nation's main strategic objectives.

The capacity of the CCP leadership for improvement and innovation is the key to whether China can make the most of its system of socialism with Chinese characteristics. The quality of a country's political system has nothing to do with the number of political parties. The key lies in whether the government can embody and achieve the will of the majority of people. Just as Deng Xiaoping said: "Three factors are important in appraising a political system, political structure, and government policy. The first is whether the political situation is stable; the second is whether it promotes national unity and improves the people's livelihood; the third is whether productivity is steadily improving."[24] During the reform era, there have been major changes in the leadership system of the CCP, and the quality of leadership has been greatly enhanced. This is the main reason why China has been able to maintain rapid economic growth and political stability for more than twenty years. Although the CCP leadership faces a severe test in the face of such problems as serious corruption, the abuse of power for personal gain, and the lack of effective supervision, the system of socialism with Chinese characteristics will keep China on track to becoming a world power and is the key to promoting and accelerating this process. The CCP has advanced the goal of building a socialist democratic system based on the rule of law that will facilitate the process of renewal within the Party. The CCP's goal of building a comparatively well-to-do society by focusing on economic development accords with the national will of the overwhelming majority of the Chinese people for the long term and is a strong factor in promoting China's growth.

Rapid Economic Growth: The Most Important Prerequisite for China's Development as a World Power

In the more than quarter century since China adopted its reform policy in 1978, it has achieved the rapid economic growth that has been the most exciting development of the late twentieth century and the early twenty-first. The questions of how to assess China's achievements over this period and its prospects for future development have generated intense debates both at home and abroad. The following are two typical views.

Some people hold a pessimistic view of China's achievements and prospects. They believe that growth has reached its limit and that China is in danger of repeating South America's cycle of boom and bust. Some Western scholars argue that, even though China has made great strides, overall it still lags a century behind the United States and Western Europe, that there has still been no fundamental change in the agricultural character of its economy. They say that analysts who believe that it will soon become a world power are excessively optimistic. In the first place, it cannot sustain such rapid economic development over a long period of time. Even according to the figures of its own State Statistical Bureau, there exists a large gap between China and the West with regard to quality of education, scientific research, and social system. Moreover, the foundation of development is still extensive rather than intensive, requiring ever greater investment of funds and resources, a situation that cannot continue for long. Second, even though GDP is an important indicator, it does not suffice to give an accurate reflection of a country's economic development. Third, China's labor productivity is still very low, only a small fraction of that of the West. China also lags behind other countries in software development. Some scholars argue that its present situation is similar to that of South America and that it may well repeat that region's cycle of boom and bust.[25]

Another viewpoint holds that the systematic overestimation of China's achievement is part of a Western conspiracy. In asserting that it is a powerful enemy by exaggerating its economic achievements, forces hostile to China are able to fabricate their China threat theory. The United States, an extremely nationalistic country, exaggerates the power and potential of one or another country in order to suggest the possibility that sometime in the remote future that country may catch up with it. It designates such a hypothetical enemy in order to mobilize its resources against it. During the Cold War, U.S. elites constantly exaggerated the strength of the Soviet Union and trotted out various myths such as the United States having fewer missiles than the Soviet Union and Soviet GDP having reached 70 percent of U.S. GDP. Later on, these elites did the same vis-à-vis Japan. For example, Ezra F. Vogel's *Japan as Number One* was a best seller in the United States.[26] Now the United States uses the same formula with respect to China. A lot of the China threat theories come from the United States or elsewhere in the West. Examples are the perceived threats posed by China as number one in the future (a kind of China threat theory in a disguised form), the "mega trends of Asia," the "advantage of Confucian culture," and Chinese PPP. Unfortunately, these sensational myths are regarded as the most valuable treasures when introduced to China. Some Chinese intentionally accepted such overestimates. Some Chinese themselves like to overstate the achievement of China in order to overcome the Chinese sense of inferiority due to over one hundred years of bullying by the West: "They haven't discovered that the repetition of these so-called miracles has been regarded as evidence of China's wild ambition by the United States and Japan. China thus becomes the new 'very respected enemy' of the United States. The predicament faced by China is, not that the United States does not pay attention to it today, but pays too much attention to it."[27]

Even after discounting for statistical errors, however, China's achievements are very impressive. Yet the gaps among different regions in China and between urban and rural areas are huge. There is room for continued growth. It is quite likely that China will maintain a high rate of growth. This is not a matter of blind optimism.

Naturally, the Chinese must overcome the inferiority complex deriving from the past century of humiliation, and we should not try to conceal our historical failures by intentionally exaggerating our achievements. There can be no doubt on this score. At the same time, we must distinguish between the conspiracy of those who deliberately exaggerate China's achievements and those who arrive at that same conclusion by applying various analytic methods. There may well be people who are hostile to China and deliberately exaggerate its achievements in order to propagate the theory of a China threat. But they should not be confused with those scholars who have conducted serious analysis of China's development prospects. Moreover, the former Soviet threat to the United States was not simply a figment of propaganda. Although its power was exaggerated, generally speaking the Soviet Union did possess significant power, especially military power equivalent to that of the United States. Similarly, Japan's power was also exaggerated, but its impressive growth in the 1960s–1980s was not a phantasm. Its subsequent stagnation is no reason to deny its past success. There can be no doubt that there is a conspiracy to deliberately exaggerate China's achievement and play up the theory of a China threat. The CIA is suspected of participating in such a conspiracy by overestimating its projections of China's future economic performance. According to a 1995 report summarized by CIA Information Committee vice chairman Fuller, calculated in terms of PPP, China's economy will exceed US$20 trillion in 2020. By comparison, the U.S. economy is expected to be US$13 trillion that year and the Japanese just US$5 trillion. Thus, like Germany in the past, China already poses a threat to the United States, which therefore should, the argument goes, contain China. A 2002 CIA report asserts that China's GDP in 2001, based on PPP, was US$5.56 trillion. This figure is more than US$2 trillion higher than the US$3.45 trillion of Japan's GDP.[28] This is a deliberately exaggerated figure.

It is one thing to exaggerate China's achievements and quite another to accurately estimate its past and future economic growth. Two kinds of methods are used to assess the size of an economy. One is the traditional foreign exchange rate computing method, namely, comparing China's GDP with those of other countries after conversion into U.S. dollars according to the official yuan–U.S. dollar exchange rate. The other method, the one used by the World Bank, is based on so-called PPP. It compares the real purchasing power of a country's currency with that of other countries' purchasing power. There are different ways of converting to PPP; consequently, there are different standards for PPP calculation. Meanwhile, there are varying forecasts of China's future growth, ranging from high (more than 9–10 percent annually) to medium (7–8 percent annually) and to low (4–6 percent annually). The conclusions reached vary considerably depending on which method is used and what the predicted rate of growth is.

As far back as 1986, in *The Rise and Fall of the Great Powers,* Paul Kennedy noted the comparatively large discrepancies among forecasts dealing with the Chinese economy. An article in the *Economist* noted that a number of economists asserted that, if China could maintain its 8 percent annual growth rate, its GDP would exceed the combined GDP of the United Kingdom and Italy by 2000 and far exceed that of any major European country by 2020. These same specialists forecast that, by 2020, China's GDP would reach US$5.06 trillion, compared with France's at US$2.1 trillion, India's at US$2 trillion, Italy's at US$1 trillion, and the United Kingdom's at US$900 billion.[29] We can see now that these predictions were too optimistic. China's GDP reached US$1.069 trillion in 2000, still ranking behind those of Germany (whose unification was naturally not anticipated), the United Kingdom, France, and Italy. If measured by PPP, however, the forecast was pretty close to the mark. The IMF and the World Bank, which have generally been quite upbeat as regards the Chinese economy, began publishing reports on China in 1993. According to the IMF, when calculated according to PPP, China's GDP in 1993 was not US$440 billion but rather US$1.7 trillion. If that is, indeed, correct, China was the third largest economy in the world after the United States and Japan. By the same token, China's per capita GDP was US$1,450, not US$370. World Bank estimates were even higher, namely, US$2.35 trillion in 1992 calculated according to PPP, or just a shade below Japan's US$2.37 trillion GDP. According to the 1994 edition of the British publication *Information Digest,* China's GDP (measured in PPP) was US$3.08 trillion in 1994 and would reach US$10.45 trillion by 2004. This would make it US$2 trillion higher than the projected U.S. GDP in 2004. These projections were obviously too high and far removed from reality.[30]

Since then there have been many optimistic forecasts regarding China's future development:

1. In a 1997 article, Professor Dwight Perkins, a political economist at Harvard University, noted that, between 1978 and 1995, China's growth rate was equivalent to the growth rates of South Korea and Taiwan in the 1960s–1970s. South Korea took thirty years to industrialize and modernize. Since China's situation in 1978 was worse than South Korea's in 1960 and China was so much larger, it stood to reason that it would take China longer to industrialize and modernize than it had South Korea, yet, in reality, it had taken just a little over ten years. According to Perkins's calculation, China's per capita GDP in 1995 was three times what it was in 1978. Calculated in terms of PPP, China's GDP in 1978 was US$500 billion, and its per capita GDP was US$500; its per capita GDP rose to US$1,200 in 1991 and US$1,700 in 1995, and its GDP reached US$2 trillion in 1995. South Korea's per capita GDP in 1960 was US$850, and Taiwan's per capita GDP was US$1,400. By 1990, South Korea's per capita GDP had risen to US$10,000 and Taiwan's per capita GDP to US$14,000. In other words, in just thirty years, South Korea and Taiwan achieved the per capita GDP that it took Europe 150 years—from 1820 to 1970—to attain. If China maintains a 7 percent growth rate every year until 2010, it can reach Europe's 1970 level. If the rate is just 5 percent, it will take over forty years (i.e., until 2020) to reach that goal.[31]

2. Another forecast of long-term economic trends in China, cover-

ing the years 1994–2015, was issued by the Rand Corporation in 1996. According to that study, Chinese per capita purchasing power in 1994 was US$4,200, or 16.3 percent of the U.S. figure. The Rand analysts estimated that China's best-case average annual GDP growth would be 4.9 percent. Thus, its per capita GDP would reach 18.8 percent of the U.S. level by 2000, 25.6 percent by 2010, and up to 28.9 percent by 2015. Its GDP would overtake that of the United States by 2006, rising to 110 percent by 2010 and 127 percent by 2015.[32]

3. According to the 1997 World Bank report *China 2020*, China's 1995 per capita GDP was US$290. If its domestic savings rate declined from 40 to 35 percent over the next ten years, this would depress the annual growth rate by 1.5 percent. But its annual growth rate between 1995 and 2000 was actually 8.4 percent. If its growth rate declined by 1.5 percent over the period 2000–2020, by the latter year its GDP would far exceed that of the United States, and its per capita GDP would be half the current U.S. per capita GDP, or about the level of Portugal today. In 1997, the World Bank also issued a second report on the Chinese economy, one calculated according to per capita PPP and stating that China's 1997 per capita GDP was US$3,570, compared to the U.S. figure of US$28,740, which was eight times that of China. That same year, China's GDP reached US$4.38 trillion, compared to the U.S. figure of US$7.69 trillion, that is, 1.75 times that of China.[33]

4. In 1997, the Asian Development Bank published a report titled *Emerging Asia*. According to this report, there are three possible scenarios for China's economy in the period 1995–2025. The optimistic plan envisions China continuing along the path of economic reform, with productivity maintaining a relatively rate of high growth and per capita GDP increasing annually by 6.6 percent. The pessimistic scenario projects a per capita GDP increase of 4.4 percent annually. According to the third, median projection, per capita income will increase by 6.05 percent annually, resulting in a Chinese per capita GDP equal to 10.8 percent that of the United States in 1995 and 38.2 percent by 2025.[34]

5. In 1998, Angus Maddison, an economic historian with the OECD, made a forecast concerning China's economic prospects. His more pessimistic estimate projected a 7.5 percent annual average GDP growth rate from 1978 to 1995, followed by a 5.5 percent growth rate from 1995 to 2010. Per capita annual growth would, he predicted, decline from 6 to 4.5 percent during the same period. By 2015, China's GDP would exceed that

of the United States, accounting for 17 percent of world GDP. The Chinese per capita GDP would equal one-fifth of the U.S. figure.[35]

6. According to the U.S. scholar Julia Chang Bloch, the size of China's economy doubled between 1985 and 1993. On the basis of 1993 World Bank PPP figures, China was the world's third largest economy, after the United States and Japan. Even if only a relatively low rate of economic growth occurred, China's would become the second largest economy around 2006.[36]

7. A 1999 report by the Sustainable Development Group of the Chinese Academy of Sciences forecast China's annual GDP growth rate at 7 percent between 2000 and 2010 and 6.5 percent between 2010 and 2020. It predicted that China's per capita GDP would reach US$3,000 by 2030 and US$6,000 by 2050.[37]

8. In 1995, the China Study Group of the Chinese Academy of Sciences predicted that China's average annual GDP growth rate would fall between 9.3 and 10.2 percent between 1995 and 2000, between 8 and 8.7 percent between 2000 and 2010, and between 7 and 7.8 percent between 2010 and 2020. If this forecast is accurate, China's per capita GDP, which was US$2,100 in 1994, will have grown 7.6 percent on average between 1994 and 2015. By 2015, its GDP will have exceed that of the United States, although on a per capita basis it will still be only one-quarter of the U.S. level.[38]

9. In 2002, the China Institute of Contemporary International Relations reported that China's GDP was 9.58 trillion yuan in 2001, that is, US$1.16 trillion calculated in terms of the then prevailing exchange rate. It predicted that China's GDP would reach US$2 trillion by 2010 and US$4 trillion by 2020.[39]

Comparing these estimates with the reality of China, we can see that the basic tendency is to overstate the country's economic development and underestimate its problems. For example, the World Bank estimated China's per capita GDP (calculated according to PPP) at US$3,500 in 1997, and the Rand Corporation estimated it at US$4,200 in 1994. Obviously, both these estimates are gross overstatements.

In my opinion, China possesses all the preconditions for becoming a world power. Its economic miracle is in the takeoff stage (a part of the modernization process) and can be the starting point of and foundation for its development into a world power. Of course, we must pay serious attention to critiques of the Chinese economy, but these should not alter our fundamental assessment of China's economic development prospects. Whatever methods are used to assess the country's likely development over the next twenty to thirty years, it is an objective fact that China has made enormous strides forward in the more than a quarter century since the policy of reform and opening up to the world was introduced.

From 1989 to 2001, China's GDP shot up from 1.69 to 9.59 trillion yuan. The average annual growth rate was 9.3 percent, far exceeding the 3.2 percent world average (figured from 2.7 percent for developed countries and 5.2 percent for developing countries). China enjoyed the highest growth rate in the world. Its per capita GDP, calculated according to the foreign exchange rate method, was US$190 in 1978, rising to US$780 in 1999, US$840 in 2000, and US$899 in 2001, an average annual increase of 8.2 percent. Its per capita income ranking improved from 194th in 1978 to 141st in 2000 among 209 countries and regions in the world. It reached US$3,291 in terms of per capita PPP. It moved up from the ranks of the lower-income countries to the ranks of the lower-middle-income countries according to World Bank criteria. (The global average was US$7,410.)

The total value of China's imports and exports rose from US$20.6 billion in 1978 to US$509.7 billion in 2001, a twenty-five-fold increase. The volume of its foreign trade increased from 1.5 percent of total world trade in 1978 to 4 percent by 2001. Its global trade ranking increased from twenty-fifth in 1978, to fourteenth in 1989, to sixth in 2001. Foreign direct investment (FDI) in China increased to US$46.9 billion in 2001. That amount was fourteen times the figure for 1989. China has long attracted the largest amount of FDI among all developing countries.

The Chinese people's standard of living has improved in step with the country's rapid economic growth. The average annual salary of urban employees grew from around 2,000 yuan in 1990 to 10,870 yuan in 2001, a more than fivefold increase. The proportion of personal income spent on food (Engel coefficient) dropped from 60 to 37.9 percent in urban areas and from 70 to 47.7 percent in the countryside from 1978 to 2002. Rural per capita income rose from 601 yuan in 1989 to 2,366 yuan in 2001, an increase of 62 percent, discounting for inflation. Urban per capita income rose from 1,376 to 6,860 yuan, a twofold increase, discounting for inflation. Savings deposits increased from 500 billion yuan in 1989 to 8 trillion yuan in 2002. From 1990 to 2002, the average life expectancy increased from 68.5 to 71.4 years; rural per capita living space grew from 17.8 to 25 square meters; urban per capita living space increased from 6.7 to 10 square meters. From comparatively few, the number of land-line telephones grew to more than 200 million, while the number of cell phones increased from none to more than 180 million. The number of people traveling abroad increased from 3 million in 1990 to 12.1 million in 2001. Private ownership of an automobile increased from 15 percent of all vehicles in 1990 to 40 percent in 1999 and has increased even more rapidly in recent years. Many indicators show that Chinese living standards have basically reached comparatively well-off levels.

The national economy of China continued to grow at a fairly rapid pace in 2002. GDP leaped to 10.24 trillion yuan. Calculated in constant prices, GDP increased by 8 percent in 2002 over the previous year. The foreign trade surplus was US$30.4 billion. China actually utilized US$52.7 billion of FDI, an increase of 12.5 percent over the previous year. Foreign exchange reserves reached US$286.4 billion at the end of 2002, an increase of US$74.2 billion over the previous year. Foreign trade surged forward. The annual total volume of imports and exports reached US$620.8 billion in 2002, a 21.8 percent increase over the previous year. Total exports were US$325.6 billion, a 22.3 percent increase; total import value was US$295.2 billion, a 21.2 percent increase.[40] Calculated according to foreign exchange rate, China's GDP was US$1.02 trillion in 2002, earning it the ranking of sixth in the world. Calculated according to PPP, it was US$4.11 trillion, or 49 percent that of the United States. Urban and rural savings increased from 21 billion to 7.5 trillion yuan. China is already first in the world in the annual production of more than eighty agricultural and industrial products. Among the most important of these are grain, meat, fish, and fish products, cotton, poultry and eggs, fruit, vegetable oils, vegetables, yarn, cotton cloth, silk fabrics, knit goods, clothing exports, woolen textiles, televisions, refrigerators, washing machines, electric fans, electric irons, electric rice cookers, microwave ovens, tractors, motorcycles, miniature cars, telephones, bicycles, ceramic wares, leather goods, coal, steel, cement, chemical fertilizer, and cell phones.[41] Even though its role in the world economy is still not great enough, China is playing an increasingly important role in East Asia. For example, its exports to Japan have reached US$61.7 billion, surpassing the US$57.5 billion in U.S. exports to that country. China has become the largest importer of Japanese goods.

More importantly, China is already on the fast track of economic growth and already has the momentum for continuous development. It is widely recognized as the most important of the ten major emerging markets in the world, accounting for 40 percent of the emerging market. By GDP, it is the second largest market in the world, accounting for 10 percent of the world market. This is China's greatest developmental advantage. It is also the basis for its ongoing prosperity and long-term development.[42]

In 2003, Stephen Roach, the chief economist for the U.S. investment firm Morgan Stanley, commenting on those who doubt the reality of China's economic achievements, said:

Many people have consistently doubted the reality of China's economic miracle, especially in the past five years, but the powerful trend of China's economic growth will continue for a long time and there should be no doubt whatsoever regarding the vigorous growth of the Chinese economy. Though the economic scale of China is rather small, it is increasing rapidly and exerting great influence on the global economy. At present, China's economy accounts for just 4 percent of the world economy's total of $32 trillion, but in a weakening global economy, China's economic growth accounted for 17.5 percent of world GDP growth in 2002, second only to the U.S. and greater than the contribution of Germany, Japan, and Britain. China accounted for 65 percent of world import growth in 2002, making China first in the world. China may be able to sustain an average annual growth rate of 7.3 percent for the next 10 years.[43]

Even some hard-liners in the United States acknowledge China's economic achievements and are optimistic about future prospects. On June 2, 2002, then U.S. deputy secretary of defense Paul Wolfowitz said that China has steadily developed in recent years and that there was no reason for the United States to doubt that it could reach U.S. and Japanese levels of GDP.[44]

To be sure, the Chinese economy is facing a number of difficulties and problems. For example, China is overly dependent on foreign capital, technology, and markets. Domestic demand accounts for only 26 percent of its economic growth. Therefore, it should rely more on domestic demand. China also faces the problem of how to deal with deflationary pressures and growing economic disparity at home. It can solve these problems only through further economic reforms. If it does introduce such reforms, not only can it continue to develop, but it can also lead the international economy within ten years. Its labor market is greater than that of all OECD countries taken together. Therefore, within a short space of time, its rapid growth will stimulate dramatic changes in the relative cost of factors of production, depress the cost of labor over the long term, and have a profound influence on the global distribution of income.[45]

As China's economy has grown, there has been a corresponding significant increase in its overall national strength. In the three-hundred-plus-page *2003 Report on China's Sustainable Development Strategy*, the Chinese Academy of Sciences assessed China's sustainable development and overall national strength for the first time. Unlike past reports, this one treated ecological and environmental factors as important indicators. The seven indicators employed in the report are economic power, scientific and technological power, military power, level of social development, ecological power, government regulatory and control power, and diplomatic capacity. In comparison with twelve other countries—the United States, Great Britain, Russia, Japan, Italy, India, Germany, France, Canada, Brazil, Australia, and South Africa—China was ranked seventh in terms of sustainable overall national power in 2000. Overall, its score was half that of the United States. Several individual rankings are as follows: In economic power, China ranked third behind the United States and Japan; in military strength, it ranked fourth behind the United States, Japan, and Great Britain. In addition, its diplomatic capacity, ecological power, and government regulatory and control power ranked fifth, sixth, and thirteenth, respectively. Its level of social development and scientific and technological power ranked eleventh. Total sustainable development power is made up of five major support systems: survival, developmental, environmental, social, and intellectual.[46]

According to the *Global Competitiveness Report: 2002–2003*, published by the World Economic Forum, in terms of international competitiveness China ranked thirty-ninth in 2001 and rose to twenty-ninth in 2002. Among the areas in which it excelled were domestic economic power and state managerial capacity, in which it stood in the front ranks; its competitiveness in science and technology was comparable to the fairly high ranking of the newly industrialized countries; it ranked in the middle with regard to national quality competitiveness, business administration competitiveness, and internationalization. It was rated relatively deficient in financial system competitiveness and infrastructure.[47] The most important economic development indicator of world power status, namely, the growth and trajectory of GDP, suggests that China will become one of the top two or three countries in the world by the 2020s–2030s and, basically, possess the economic strength to become a world power. Chinese officials say that, although China has maintained a 9 percent annual growth rate over the past twenty years and accomplished an economic miracle, its future growth rate will, in accordance with Japan's experience of diminished growth over the past twenty years, decline from that 9 percent figure. China, however, is quite different from Japan and has enormous potential for growth. Regional differences and the urban-rural gap are both quite large. These differences present important problems for the economy, but they also offer great scope for further development. China can maintain an average annual growth rate of 7 percent. Its total output ranked sixth in the world in 2002, accounting for 3.7 percent of world total output. It may surpass France by 2005 and become the third largest economic entity in the world by 2020, when its GDP will reach 35 trillion yuan, or more than US$4 trillion (according to the present exchange rate), equal to Japan's current level. This will put it ahead of France, the United Kingdom, and Germany. Per capita GDP will rise from US$800 per annum to US$3,000. In terms of comprehensive national strength, by 2020 the U.S. advantage over China will be reduced from three times to two. The Chinese people's living standards will rise from the current lower-middle-income level to the middle-income level. China's human development index will improve from its current upper-middle level of 0.7 to 0.8.[48]

It is entirely likely that China can realize the goal of modernization because of three major advantages that it possesses: (1) an enormous, competent, and relatively low-cost workforce; (2) the enormous and as yet not fully realized market potential of its 1.3 billion people; (3) a relatively developed and comprehensive industrial system. It can jump-start its economic development by using innovations in information technology.[49]

Specialists assert that, in view of China's workforce, market potential, and basic infrastructure, there is no reason to underestimate its future development potential. For example, the total length of its expressways, which was just six thousand kilometers at the end of 1998, increased to ten thousand kilometers in 1999, sixteen thousand kilometers in 2000, and nineteen thousand kilometers in 2001. This is an unprecedented rate of development compared to other countries. Another example is cellphone use. Ten years ago, there were almost no cell phones in China, but the number in use by 2002 had reached 150 million, greater than the population of Japan, and first in the world. The number was expected to rise to 300 million by 2005. Another significant indicator is the rapid growth in automobile production. In 2002, automobile sales shot up to 3.2 million, a 40 percent increase over the previous year. China has surpassed Great Britain, France, and Italy to become the world's fourth largest market after the United States, Japan, and Germany.[50] It will soon have more than 10 million automobiles, and it is only a matter of time until it surpasses Japan, becoming the number two market in the world. General economic growth is also linked to urban development. China's urban development has entered a period of unprecedented growth. In 1992, the country had a total of twenty cities with populations of more than 1 million people; by 2002, that number was 166. The process of dynamic urbanization in China is a powerful force driving economic growth.[51]

Expectations are that China's total foreign trade will reach US$2 trillion by 2020[52] and that the average annual growth rate of its foreign trade will be at or above 7.2 percent over the next twenty years.[53] "As long as globalization is not reversed, the free flow of capital into China and the free flow of labor power out of China will be two major irresistible tides of the twenty-first century. . . . History may well judge that the dramatic rise of China was one of the most important catalysts in the laboratory of globalization."[54] Therefore, even though globalization is a large trap for many developing countries, for China it is a great international strategic opportunity.

If China can avoid great internal turmoil and major economic failures at home, it will be able to approach or overtake the GDP of the United States by 2050. That will enable it to become a world power and bring about a great rejuvenation of the Chinese nation. "China will be certain to achieve the transformation that Liang Qichao spoke of; namely, from the ashes of 'the old Middle Kingdom,' the golden phoenix of a new contemporary world power will arise."[55]

INTERNATIONAL STRATEGIC OPPORTUNITIES FOR CHINA TO
GROW INTO A WORLD POWER: CONTROVERSIES
AND ASSESSMENTS

The Controversy over Peace and Development and a Basic Assessment
of the International Environment for China's Growth

In recent years, Chinese scholars have debated the question of how to
assess the international environment of China's development. One school
of thought argues that peace and development are no longer the main contemporary themes. The present era, it is said, is one of struggle between
the South and the North, an imperialist era under hegemonic conditions.

According to this perspective, the historic opportunity for peace
and development that history presented to China beginning in the 1980s
ended with NATO's war against Yugoslavia. In fact, history has not yet
even entered the era of true peace and development. Unfortunately, the
present peaceful intermission is probably very limited. The historical
opportunity for peace and development that China successfully grasped
in the 1980s was fading by the end of the twentieth century. The realities
of the Taiwan issue have already punctured the illusions of Chinese paci-
fists. Peace and development are merely castles in the sand. After NATO's
expansion eastward and the revision of the U.S.-Japan Security Treaty,
time no longer favored China. Moreover, it became clear that the capitalist center would not allow peripheral capitalist countries to develop.
Because exploitation and oppression of the underdeveloped countries by
the developed countries are the foundation of safeguarding the developed
countries, the developed countries will not allow the developing countries
to develop. So the hallmark of the current era is the struggle between the
South, which is safeguarding its right to develop, and the North, which
seeks to limit and exploit the South's right to develop. Thus, it is impossible for China, a developing country, to develop within a world system
centered on the West. This perspective is a reprise of dependency theory
and its thesis about center-periphery relations, which flourished in the
1960s but fell out of favor in the 1980s.[56]

In the modern world, economic crises deriving from the struggle
for overseas market, goods, and raw materials are not the only cause of
war among the capitalist countries. Even without economic crisis, economic and trade competition among nations persists and can lead to war.
History demonstrates that territorial disputes, the struggle for political

hegemony, and religious conflicts all have been causes of war. Economic development can promote economic exchanges and interdependence, but, since it can also increase contradictions and friction, it cannot always be treated as a factor promoting peace. Neorealism contends that nation-states remain the main actors in the existing international system. Conflicts are inevitable because countries pursue their own power and security. Although the actions of nation-states are restricted by the structure of the international system, the likelihood of war has increased because of the unequal distribution of power and interests.

Whether peace and development are the hallmark of the present is a suitable subject for discussion. Additional research is needed on many contemporary issues, including the question of whether changes in the international environment are really favorable to China's development. Those who argue that peace and development are not the main themes of the present deserve an audience. They say that we should not discuss peace and cooperation alone, without also considering war and security threats. We should not focus on the economy and development alone, without also stressing politics and security. We should not talk about globalization and interdependence alone, without also discussing national interests and state sovereignty. In sum, we must view things in their totality and not restrict ourselves to a one-sided view of reality. We should take note of U.S. hegemonic behavior and the contradictions between the United States and various other countries, but we should also take note of the possibility of cooperation among the United States, Russia, China, and other countries. On this issue, the views of some authors are one-sided. They overemphasize the hegemonic behavior of the United States and the contradictions among great powers like the United States, Russia, and China after the Cold War. They underestimate the existence of strategic cooperation between Russia and the United States and between China and the United States. Some authors argue that, as Zhang Ruizhuang puts it, "the end of the Cold War has not eliminated but increased the danger of nuclear war." The imbalance of power between Russia and the United States "has increased rather than reduced the possibility of a nuclear war." They believe that the United States may force Russia into a corner and, thus, make it "more dependent on nuclear deterrence."[57] It is clear that such views underestimate the degree of compromise and cooperation between Russia and the United States. Russia's behavior after 9/11 and the development of relations between Russia and the United States over the past several years have already demonstrated that the possibility of nuclear war between the two countries has been greatly reduced rather than increased.

I agree with the fundamental proposition that peace and development are the main contemporary trends. This is an indisputable fact that favors China's becoming a world power. Although wars and disturbances are constants in the post–Cold War international environment, in general a prolonged period of world peace has prevailed. Since the beginning of human society, there has been no end to war, nor will there ever be absolute world peace. World peace is only a kind of relative peace and mainly judged by great power relations. The world wars of the twentieth century broke out when the world powers were divided into different hostile military blocs. World wars were, in fact, wars among the world powers. As long as there is no war between the great powers, there will be an era of relative peace in the world.

Although there are some problems among the six great powers—the United States, Europe, Russia, Japan, India, and China—there is no likelihood of a major war. The prospects for cooperation among them are greater than the prospects for struggle and conflict. This is the greatest change in the wake of 9/11 and also represents China's international strategic opportunity.

The changes in great power relations are the result of profound transformations in the structure of post–Cold War international politics. In the key great power relations, including those between Europe and Japan, Europe and India, Europe and the United States, Japan and the United States, and India and Japan, there are no major contradictions. They are stable and cooperative. The decisive factor in great power cooperation is the relations among China, Russia, and the United States as well as their relations with other great powers. The relationship between Russia and the European countries has been a consistent focal point of Russia's foreign policy, and both sides enjoy what are basically normal relations. Relations between Russia and China are steadily developing, and Russia has somewhat improved its relations with Japan.

China enjoys friendly, good neighborly relations with Russia and has established an overall partnership with Europe. There has been significant improvement in its relations with India. Although Sino-Japanese relations have been stagnant, there has been no serious setback. Sino-U.S. differences over the Taiwan issue are the likeliest potential cause of

war between the two countries, but 9/11 has offered new common interests and greatly reduced the possibility of war. Even more important is
that Chinese and U.S. leaders are building more normal relations, relations based on common national interests. Although there is no reason
for euphoria yet, neither is there cause for alarm.

The decisive factor in relations among the great powers today is the
nature and evolution of their relations with the United States, the sole
superpower. In 2002, the U.S. government clearly stated that good relations could be established among the great powers and groupings of great
powers. President George W. Bush said: "We will establish good relations
in order to safeguard the peace among the great powers."[58] The National
Security Strategy of the United States of America, issued in September
2002, also expressed this idea.[59]

In support of this U.S. view, the most important foundation of great
power cooperation is common efforts to oppose international terrorism
and safeguard world peace. This point was clearly reflected in the 2002
national security strategy.

Another possible foundation of cooperation is Western values as
represented by the United States and its allies. Americans view Europe,
Japan, and India as democracies that are allies and partners of the United
States. Although they consider the foundations of freedom and democracy in Russia still shaky, at least Russia has begun the process of establishing a democratic system. In their eyes, China is a cipher because it is
still a socialist state under the leadership of the CCP, and Americans are
not sure whether such a country will cooperate with the United States.
The U.S. national security strategy acknowledges that China has begun
to move toward political opening, allowing individual freedom in many
respects, and conducting elections in villages and townships, but it still
criticizes China's system of CCP leadership. Unlike the first Bush administration, which viewed China as a strategic competitor, current U.S.
leaders tend to think that, like Russia, China is becoming a cooperative
partner of the United States.

The key to whether the world is entering a period of cooperation is
whether the newly rising great powers will cooperate with the United
States. The United States pays particularly close attention to Russia,
China, and India. Americans take note of their differences with Russia,
India, and China, but these differences do not prevent the United States
from building cooperative relations with them.

The United States is dissatisfied with the Russian elite's suspicion of it and is itself skeptical about Russia's efforts to prevent the proliferation of nuclear, chemical, and biological weapons. The Americans blame the slow progress in Russo-U.S. relations on Russia's own weakness. Nevertheless, the relationship has already changed from one of confrontation to one of cooperation, with notable results for bilateral relations.

The main divergence between the United States and India is that Washington harbors doubts about India's intention to develop nuclear weapons and missiles. It also worries about the slow pace of economic reform in India. Yet, with respect to great power relations, the greatest change in U.S. policy is vis-à-vis India. The United States used to view India as an unimportant country, but now U.S. national security strategy is looking at India anew and sees it as a world power with which the United States shares ever-growing strategic interests.

The United States criticizes China for not making "the basic choice about the nature of the state" (i.e., China not choosing the Western model), for adopting an out-of-date policy direction, and pursuing advanced military capabilities that could threaten its Asian-Pacific neighbors. China and the United States disagree on the issues of human rights, nonproliferation, and Taiwan, but the U.S. national security strategy does not regard China as the main rival. The United States looks forward to transition in China, but, meanwhile, it tries hard to establish a constructive relation with a changing China. The two countries have cooperated well in many areas of common interest.

For quite some time to come, there will be no great powers that can compete against the United States for global leadership. U.S. leadership is the prerequisite for the current period of great power cooperation. China certainly has a different perspective regarding two of the U.S. points regarding the period of great power cooperation. First is with respect to so-called U.S. leadership. China does not object to the United States, as the world's most powerful country, shouldering a heavier burden in safeguarding world peace and stability, but it can never recognize its right to lead the world. Second, China hopes that the great powers will establish cooperation on the basis of world multipolarity and diversity. It objects to any U.S. effort at imposing Western values on it. It will not become a country that follows Western-style democracy, as the United States expects. These differences, however, should not hinder China, the United States, and other great powers from cooperating on international affairs. With regard to these two issues, contradictions and friction may develop between China and the United States, and great power struggle may occur within the context of great power cooperation. During such cooperation, China must remain highly vigilant regarding U.S. interference in its internal affairs and attempts to apply pressure on it and scrutinize U.S. proposals carefully. The U.S. national security strategy indicates that the United States hopes for great power cooperation, but, reading between the lines, one can easily detect the persistence of unilateralism.

Generally speaking, the initiation of the period of great power cooperation coincides with China's concept of peace and development as the main contemporary theme. There is no chance of a new world war breaking out. China can secure a long-term peaceful international environment. This basic judgment is an important part of its international strategic opportunity. For China, the opportunities afforded by great power cooperation are greater than the challenges presented. The current international environment offers extremely favorable conditions for it to grow into a world power.

From the viewpoint of China, largely similar conclusions can be drawn. Over the twenty- to thirty-year period that it will need to develop into a world power, there will be a favorable environment as well as some unfavorable external factors. The general trend, however, is favorable for its growth. From 2001 to 2030, the international situation will be tense in some regions, small-scale wars and conflicts will not cease, but there will be no large-scale regional war. There will be no great power war that could affect international peace and development.

In terms of the history of China's growth as a world power, the international environment over the next thirty years will be more favorable than the two periods 1949–1978 and 1979–2000. The positive aspect of the first period, during which China followed the strategy of leaning to the side of the Soviet Union in the 1950s, was achievements in economic construction. Through several five-year plans, it built a national economic system from scratch, obtained the atomic and hydrogen bombs, and developed an earth satellite. On the negative side, it experienced a period of confrontation first with the United States, then with the Soviet Union, and with both simultaneously as well as bad relations with neighboring countries. It fought a war in Korea, confronted the United States in the Taiwan Strait crises, tangled with India in a border conflict, was involved in the Vietnam War, and engaged in border conflict and military clashes and confrontation with the Soviet Union. In this period, it was unable to secure a peaceful international environment. External factors included the U.S. military blockade and economic sanctions as well as ideological conflict between China and the former Soviet Union. Internal factors included Mao Zedong's misjudgment about the likelihood of world war and the negative impact on Chinese foreign policy of leftist errors. Even in such an unfavorable international environment, China's economy still increased by a large margin, though growth was of low quality. Nevertheless, this period led to a significant increase in China's comprehensive national power.

In the second period (1979–2000), China secured a more peaceful international environment than during the first. It established diplomatic relations with the United States, relations between China and Western countries improved steadily, and Sino-U.S. relations experienced their best period in history. Under the banner of its independent foreign policy, China improved relations with the Soviet Union, and, after the Soviet Union disintegrated, it developed a strategic partnership with Russia. It resumed and improved relations with its neighbors and settled a number of territorial disputes. It focused on the central task of economic construction, promoting economic reforms and foreign trade. In addition, it also benefited from U.S. and European economic growth during the 1990s. Its comprehensive national power and international status both improved significantly. Negative factors included twists and turns in Sino-U.S. relations, especially U.S. sanctions against China in 1990, U.S. sales of large quantities of advanced fighter planes to Taiwan, Washington's interference in China's internal affairs under the pretense of human rights, and the dispatch of U.S. warships to the Taiwan Strait in 1996. The U.S. bombing of China's embassy in Belgrade, Yugoslavia, in May 1999 and the April 2001 collision of a U.S. reconnaissance plane with a Chinese fighter brought relations to a low point. U.S. debates on China policy pitted those who favored engagement against advocates of containment. Consequently, U.S. policy toward China often vacillated.

China made a number of changes in its international environment since the beginning of the twenty-first century. It made a good start in the new century by joining the WTO in 2001. This offered a better opportunity to integrate its economy with the world economy. It obtained the right to host the Olympics in 2008, and the Chinese soccer team entered the World Cup competition for the first time, a pleasant surprise for the

Chinese. China and ASEAN decided to begin the process of developing a free trade zone, which was good news for the development of the regional economy. The establishment of the Shanghai Co-Operation Organization brought relations between China and Central Asia to a new stage.

Of course, even though changes in great power relations have enhanced the prospects for world peace, this does not mean that there are no contradictions among the great powers or that China should not be attentive to the anti-China force in the world. A wave of China threat theory has appeared in the world as some people perceive China's growth as a threat and advocate collective containment. Invoking various excuses, some hard-liners in the United States call for the containment of China. After 9/11, unilateralism raised its head in the United States, while multilateralism took a beating. There are also powerful right-wing forces in Japan that favor the containment of China. Therefore, China must remain on guard.

The Debate on Economic Globalization and the Impact of Globalization on China's Economic Development

Opponents of globalization assert that it is a trap that developed countries set for developing countries and that it disadvantages developing countries. They say that it is a new way for the North to exploit the South. The tide of globalization polarizes developing countries. The developed countries enjoy numerous advantages relating to advanced technology, language, culture, the rules of the international system, and so forth. The trend of globalization generally favors the developed countries. Some scholars have pointed out that, although the countries of the North account for only 20 percent of world population, they produce 82.7 percent of world GDP, 82 percent of world trade, 80 percent of bank deposits, 94 percent of funding for research and development, 94 percent of commercial loans, and 80 percent of domestic investment. Meanwhile, the condition of many developing countries has deteriorated. Between 1965 and 1980, there were 200 million people in developing countries who lived in poverty. Over the thirteen years from 1980 to 1993, this number quintupled to 1 billion. In the 1980s, 10 of 98 developing countries experienced economic decline. In the 1990s, 25 of 102 developing countries suffered economic decline.[60] Moreover, the proportion of the total value of global trade of the forty-eight poorest countries dropped from 0.8 percent in 1980 to 0.5 percent in 1997. The income ratio of the richest 20 percent and the poorest 20 percent of the world's population changed from 60:1 in the early 1990s to 74:1 at the end of the 1990s. Aid to developing countries from the developed world has been greatly reduced.[61] In 2000, 926 million people in high-income countries representing 15 percent of world population accounted for 79.5 percent of world GDP; 2 billion people in low-income countries representing 35 percent of world population enjoyed only 2.4 percent of world GDP. The wealth of the three richest individuals in the world exceeds the total GDP of the forty-nine least developed countries. Globalization increases the risk faced by developing countries, for example, the financial crisis in Latin America, East Asia, and Russia caused by the circulation of capital. A number of Latin American countries have experienced repeated crises. Some critics believe that globalization is a conspiracy of the Western powers to deprive developing countries of their sovereignty.

Several characteristics of globalization are harmful to developing countries. First, globalization has imposed unprecedented restrictions on the nation-state and on national sovereignty. Sovereign states and nation-states can no longer do what they wish. Their freedom of action is restricted by rules devised by the West, particularly the United States. The greatest restriction, the result of Western and world pressure, has been to deprive them of the right to develop biological, chemical, and nuclear weapons, a right previously recognized as inherent in the concept of national sovereignty. The Iraqi crisis and the Korean nuclear crisis are instances of the international community restricting the rights of sovereign states. Moreover, because of the double standard that they employ, the United States and Western countries will not even allow some developing countries to utilize nuclear energy for peaceful purposes. Every developing country that manufactures nuclear reactors is subject to pressure from the United States and Western countries, which suspect that the developing countries might conceal the production of nuclear weapons under the guise of building nuclear reactors for energy production. Second, globalization originated in the United States and Western countries. Its main feature is the imposition by core Western countries of the Western free market economy, democracy, the Western legal system, open and transparent forms of behavior, and Western values on developing countries in the context of exporting goods, technology, and capital. Third, the sovereignty of states is threatened by the concept of human rights that globalization proclaims. The most powerful countries treat human rights as a universal value that trumps sovereignty and is one of the foundations of the newly established international order. The strategy of so-called humanitarian intervention that the United States and NATO developed after the Cold War has been used to launch the war in Yugoslavia, the Afghan War, and the Second Gulf War, all without the authorization of the United Nations. This policy initiated a new stage in the West's oppression of developing countries.

My basic view is that the Scientific and Technological revolutions (especially globalization), the Information Revolution, economic liberalization, integration, and the knowledge economy have brought unprecedented challenges to the developing countries, but opportunities as well. Globalization is not at all identical with Westernization, even though globalization popularizes and implements some Western values. For example, the market economy, which originated in the West, has become a global norm now, the concept of a planned economy having fallen by the wayside. The concept of human rights has been enhanced everywhere. Democratization has become the new development model and choice of social development in many countries. More and more countries have accepted the principle of nonproliferation of nuclear, biological, and chemical weapons. The contents of universal human values have been enriched. In the process of globalization, there has emerged a trend of growing polarization. On the other hand, regional integration and cultural diversity are also developing. Polarization aside, many countries in the South have achieved significant levels of development under globalization. Life expectancy there has been increasing, living standards have improved to some extent, education and culture are developing, and the illiteracy rate is dropping. Of particular significance is that the average GDP growth rate of the developing countries is higher than that of the developed countries. Although the main benefits of international capital flow are enjoyed by the transnational capital of developed countries, the flow of capital and technology has actually promoted economic growth in the developing countries. Otherwise, why would so many developing countries have set aside their doubts and welcomed foreign capital investment? One cannot say that FDI has been forced on them by the developed countries. Because developing countries have adopted a variety of different measures to counter globalization, they have either profited from or been injured by it in various ways.

Globalization has provided a brand-new, favorable environment for China's rapid growth. The opportunities have far exceeded the challenges, and it is fair to say that China is the greatest beneficiary of the post–Cold War era of globalization. The period when China is growing into a world power is also one in which a new wave of world development is occurring. From the vantage point of history, every such wave produces winners and losers. The rise of new powers and the decline of old ones is a law of world history.

The collapse of the Soviet Union and the end of communism in Eastern Europe in 1990 ended one era and began a new one. Superficially, this new era appeared to be one of unipolar U.S. hegemony, but, in fact, it is neither that nor the so-called end of history. Rather, it is just the beginning of a new era. This is an era of information-based technology, globalization, economic integration, and a knowledge economy. The United States is far ahead of all other countries in science and technology, and this pattern of leadership will not change for a long time to come. This does not mean, however, that other countries have no chance to develop. World history indicates that the goddess of fortune does not smile only on a single country or people.

Developing countries confront just two possible fates in this new era. One is to face growing marginalization; the other is to seize this rare opportunity and exert themselves to their utmost to develop themselves and narrow the gap with developed countries.

The Information Revolution has greatly accelerated world economic development. Something that used to take one hundred years to accomplish can now be done in twenty, ten, or even fewer years. Between 1953 and 1973, world industrial output reached the total output of the century and a half between 1800 and 1953. World manufacturing output in 1980 was 30 times greater than that of 1900. The volume of world trade in 1973 was 5.2 times that of 1913.

Globalization refers to the growing trend of the global flow of technology, goods, capital, human talent, production, and markets. The rapid growth of world trade is the first trend of globalization. From 1950 to 2000, the volume of world trade grew more than fifty times, from US$120 billion to more than US$6.1 trillion. The second trend of globalization is the global circulation of capital. Worldwide foreign investment was US$650 billion in 1985 and rose to US$2.3 trillion in 1996. Total world direct investment in 2000 reached US$6 trillion. Every day, many billions of dollars circulate throughout the world. The third trend of globalization is the transnational reorganization of production. This is reflected in the rapid growth of transnational corporations (TNC). There were more than 7,000 TNCs in the 1960s with 27,300 subsidiaries. By 2000, the total number of TNCs had jumped to 35,000, with 700,000 subsidiaries. The output value of the 630 Western TNCs accounted for one-third of gross world output value, or about US$10 trillion. Trade among these TNCs accounts for more than 60 percent of total world trade. The output of the 200 largest TNCs exceeded the GDP of 182 sovereign states.[62]

The fourth trend of globalization is the growing role of international organizations in economic integration. There are now more than 160 member states in the WTO, which contributes to the economic integration of the world by promoting free trade, investment, and information exchange. At the same time, regional economic integration has been developing apace. Besides NAFTA and the European Union, there are APEC, ASEAN, and free trade agreements among ASEAN, China, and Japan.

The fifth trend of globalization is the growing mobility of people. In 1950, there were only 25.3 million international tourists. That figure rose to 500 million in 1993 and 650 million in 2000.

Globalization does not necessarily mean the impoverishment and marginalization of developing countries. In fact, it also offers opportunity for developing countries. Western capital is driven by the profit motive and will inevitably flow into places where profit is greatest. If there is an opportunity, capital, which recognizes no national boundaries, will flow there. The tide of globalization has given rise to a large number of TNCs not totally controlled and supervised by national governments. In many fields, the cost of investment in Western countries has become higher and higher; therefore, Western capital is inclined to flow into those places that offer relative political stability, low-cost labor, land, and know-how. Some developing countries have been quite successful in seizing these opportunities to attract foreign investment; others achieved early success but later declined; still others failed entirely or even regressed.

From the 1970s to the 1990s, Singapore, Hong Kong, Taiwan, South Korea, and a number of countries in Southeast Asia developed very successfully. Since achieving independence in 1965, Singapore, a small island nation, has become a leader of the emerging nations of East Asia. Hong Kong has also performed very well, as has South Korea. Their history indicates that East Asian countries can take advantage of the Technologi-cal Revolution to catch up with and overtake Western countries. Their experience is an inspiring example for China inasmuch as their history and culture are similar to China's and, in some cases, they are actually a part of China. They demonstrate China's great potential to take advantage of the Technological Revolution.

China's achievements in recent years have been related to globaliza-tion, and China has been one of the beneficiaries of globalization. From 1978 to 2002, its total trade turnover grew thirtyfold, from US$20.6 to US$620.8 billion, increasing from 1.5 to 4 percent of world trade in 2001. Its ranking shot up from twenty-fifth in 1978 to sixth in 2002. It has absorbed more than US$400 billion of foreign investment since 1978, second only to the United States. In 2002, it actually used US$52.7 billion in FDI, surpassing the United States to become the number one country in attracting FDI.[63] Calculated in terms of the foreign exchange rate, Chi-na's GDP was US$1.02 trillion in 2002, ranking sixth in the world. Cal-culated in terms of purchasing power, its GDP reached US$4.11 trillion, which equaled 49 percent of U.S. GDP. An important difference between China and many Latin America countries that suffered economic crisis because of absorbing foreign capital improperly is that most of the FDI in China is long-term and relatively little speculative. According to the data issued by the State Administration of Foreign Exchange Control, by June 2002 China's external debt balance was US$169 billion, of which medium- and long-term external debt was US$117 billion, accounting for 69.4 percent. Short-term external debt was US$51.8 billion, account-ing for 30.6 percent. By every measure, China's external debt was well within the international safety line.[64]

The Debate about China's Security Environment

One view suggests that its security environment is so dangerous that China must take precautions to avert the danger, which grows more severe every day. By itself, U.S. power far exceeds China's. If the United States draws Japan, Southeast Asia, India, and Australia into its orbit, then China is destined to fail. This is no mere strategic intention, according to the proponents of this view; the United States has already put this plan into effect. It has deployed missile defense systems in Japan, expanded the scope of its security treaty with Japan, and accelerated the eastward expansion of NATO. NATO and the five countries of Central Asia have established a partnership. On the pretext of attacking international terrorism, the United States stationed troops in Afghanistan and Central Asia, strengthened the U.S.-Australia Security Treaty, expanded its arms sales to Taiwan, and drew India into its orbit. President George W. Bush declared North Korea part of the Axis of Evil, launched the second war in Iraq on March 20, 2003, and threatened to strike North Korea in the name of stopping nuclear proliferation. All these actions are aimed at encircling and containing China. The security threat that China faces is more serious than at any time in the past. Therefore, it is argued, China must develop its military strength to prepare for the coming danger.

I agree that China's security environment is becoming more and more complicated, but, on the whole, it is somewhat improved and, most likely, will get even better in the future. Prior to the First Opium War (1840–1842), China's greatest security problem was invasion by nomadic people from the north and the northwest. Since unification during the Qin dynasty (221–206 B.C.), China constantly faced threats from the north, first from the Xiongnu, and then invasions by the Tartars. To counter these threats, the Qin and the Han began to build the Great Wall, and military forces were often deployed against the Xiongnu during the Han and Tang dynasties. Later wars were fought between the Song and the Jin and the Liao; Mongol power ascended, and the Yuan dynasty that it established expanded its borders. Finally, once-remote Russia became a powerful adversary that threatened China and eventually occupied more than 1.5 million square kilometers of its territory. All this is now in the past. China and Russia are friendly neighbors, having permanently solved the border problem left over by history. The northern border is now the most secure of China's boundaries. On the northwest, although national separatists and terrorists cause occasional disturbances, relations between China and the Central Asian states are friendly.

The disputes between China and India in the western sector of their border are under control. Prior to a final resolution, the two countries have agreed to address the problem through peaceful means and to take measures to stabilize the status quo along the border. China has never regarded India as a threat and does not think that there is any basic strategic conflict between itself and India. Chinese leaders think that India has neither the intention nor the ability to launch a large-scale attack on China. India's major problems are those of domestic development and the long-term and serious conflict over Kashmir between India and Pakistan. Even though some Indians invoke the China threat theory and claim that India should develop its national defense in response, the numerous large-scale armed conflicts between India and Pakistan show that China is not threatening India. There may be contradictions and friction between China and India, but there is no serious issue of national security between them.

China has been invaded from the sea more than a hundred times since 1842, bringing great harm to the country. Its growing power, the improvement of Sino-European relations, and the return of Chinese sovereignty over Hong Kong and Macao have caused the earlier conflicts between China and Europe to fade into the past. Relations between China and the European maritime powers have been normalized on the basis of the Five Principles of Peaceful Coexistence, and China and Europe are developing a comprehensive partnership. Neither side threatens the other's security.

Despite some contradictions relating to territorial waters and the question of sovereignty over some islands in the South China Sea, relations between China and the countries of Southeast Asia are relaxed. China and Vietnam have reached agreement over their land border. China and ASEAN have signed a protocol on the creation of a China–Southeast Asia free trade zone. China does not threaten any country in Southeast Asia; it considers these as partners in development that pose no threat to its national security.

China's biggest worries concern the United States. Yet China and the United States have no irreconcilable contradictions of national interest. China has neither the ability nor the desire to pose a threat to the United States. A comparison of the national power of the two countries demonstrates that the so-called China threat is merely idle chatter. The United States could pose a problem for China's national security, especially as a significant obstacle to China's national unification with Taiwan. From the perspective of U.S. history and the history of Sino-U.S. relations, however, the United States is not a threat to China. The U.S. Open Door policy of the nineteenth century was aimed at allowing the Americans to secure profits equal to those of other Western powers in China. At a time when these powers were eager to divide China, however, it was a policy that was relatively friendly toward China. China achieved its international position after World War II through bloody struggles against the Japanese aggressors, but the United States also played a positive role. Over British and Soviet objections, the United States insisted on making China a permanent member of the UN Security Council. As Mao Zedong pointed out more than thirty years ago at the beginning of the process of Sino-U.S. rapprochement, there is no reason to believe that the United States will launch a war against China. As one scholar aptly indicated: "The U.S. is a truly pacifist country. No world war or regional war was ever initiated by the Americans. They have not launched a war or attempted to launch a war against China. It would be totally wrong to treat the U.S. as a threat to Chinese national security or as a hypothetical enemy. Any strategic choice deriving from such a wrong assumption would be extremely harmful."[65] The United States may be a problem for China, but it is also the critical variable in its development as a world power. As long as it does not adopt a hostile policy toward the United States, the United States will not pose a threat to it.

Japan launched wars of aggression and twice brought great disasters on China. Now it is the second strongest military power in the world after the United States. Japan has avoided taking historical responsibility for its wars of aggression against China, and many right-wing Japanese politicians are extremely hostile toward China. But there is no reason to believe that Japan will launch an extensive war of aggression against China. It is not a major threat to China because the Japanese know that they could not achieve through war what they failed to achieve in the past and that they would pay a huge price if they tried.

For the first time since the Opium wars, or perhaps even as far back as the Qin and Han dynasties some 2,000 years ago, China faces no threat from the north. For the first time in over 150 years, it faces no maritime threats. For the first time since its loss to Japan in the 1894–1895 war, it has eliminated the threat from Japan in the east. The return of Hong Kong in 1997 was a significant event in the recovery of lost territory. Never again will China be subject to the loss of its territory. Even though the international situation is somewhat tense, the overall trend toward détente continues. The process of multipolarization has encountered obstacles, but it will continue to develop. Therefore, we can say with confidence that China can pursue its goal of economic construction in a mostly peaceful and stable international environment.

As long as China avoids any large strategic blunders, adheres to its policy of peace, opening, and reform, and manages various domestic challenges, it can become a world power in the present international environment. We should have full faith in this possibility.

Development Is Always China's Main Goal

It is said that man proposes and God disposes, but achievement still depends on human efforts. The creation of opportunity is more important than opportunity itself. China must seize the opportunity to develop. When there is no opportunity, it must create opportunity. Of course, it is important to debate the question of whether there is an international strategic opportunity for China, but more important than the debate itself is the question of how to understand strategic opportunity.

Those who argue that there is no international strategic opportunity for China believe that China is in a period of endless crisis and that the best that it can do is to maintain the status quo. Others, who think that it can make use of the international strategic opportunity, argue that it must seize this opportunity to develop itself. The conclusion, which warrants careful consideration, is that, if China fails to seize this rare opportunity, it will be unable to develop.

My own view is that, while it is certainly important to make use of this strategic opportunity, one should not consider it in absolute terms. In addition to such domestic factors as the possibility of large-scale domestic turmoil or schism or extreme nationalists gaining power and launching foreign wars, only two factors could interrupt China's development. (1) If bellicose anti-China forces rise to power in the United States and treat China as an enemy, they may force war on China. (2) If proindependence forces in Taiwan ignore the cardinal principles of the Chinese nation and the fundamental interests of more than 20 million Taiwanese people and commit the desperate error of declaring independence or making nuclear weapons, they will force the mainland to resort to war as the only means of reunification. Apart from these extreme situations, China certainly has the opportunity to develop.

There are many types of international strategic opportunities. In the preceding discussion, it was assumed that the era of peace and development is beneficial to China, that globalization, especially in the form of FDI, is useful to it, and that the relatively secure international environment in which it finds itself is beneficial to its development. If the opportunities are squandered or misused, this would represent an enormous loss for China. The key to whether a country can develop is, not international strategic opportunity, but the country's own policies. If a given country lacks good policies and is unable to make appropriate judgments concerning complicated international situations, it will be unable to develop even if international opportunities stare it in the face. Conversely, with appropriate policies, a country may be able to take the initiative, transform unfavorable factors into favorable ones, and reduce the risks that it faces. In this sense, international opportunity is a relative factor, as numerous examples throughout history demonstrate. Military history is full of examples of smaller and weaker countries defeating more powerful opponents. In modern history, there are examples of unfavorably situated countries achieving impressive development.

After the October Revolution, Russia confronted a hostile international environment and a world replete with constant wars. The Soviet Union was isolated without any significant external support on which it could rely. In the language of the times, it was a red island surrounded on all sides by hostile powers. Besieged by its enemies, there seemed no opportunity for it to develop. For a time, Soviet leaders believed that socialism could not be built in a single country and that the fate of the Russian Revolution depended on the prospects for world revolution. Lenin, Trotsky, Stalin, Bukharin, and others all believed in the need to promote, support, and even stimulate revolution in other European countries. When the prospects for European and world revolution collapsed, Lenin was the first to change his strategic thinking and advance the notion that Russia could coexist peacefully with the capitalist world and use its own national resources to build socialism in one country. Of course, he never abandoned the idea of world revolution; he merely adjusted the strategic center of the country in order to build socialism in Russia first while awaiting a new high tide of world revolution. Under the New Economic Policy, within a few years the Soviet Union restored an economy that war had destroyed and proceeded to achieve rapid industrialization. In this way, it discovered a path to develop despite the unfavorable international environment.

For Japan, the Korean War of 1950 had both positive and negative aspects. Most people today would see the outbreak of war in a neighboring country as an occurrence that shattered the peaceful environment and harmed prospects for development. But Japan reaped benefit from this catastrophe, taking advantage of the opportunity to advance its own economic development by providing various kinds of assistance and services to the U.S. military.

As long as a country avoids getting involved in a large-scale war, the opportunity for development exists. Even a world war that shatters the peace and harms most prospects for development is not an absolute barrier to development for all countries. The economy of the United States prospered during both world wars because it did not take place on its soil. The United States became the largest supplier of military and civilian goods and materials in the world, and it emerged from these wars, particularly World War II, as the biggest beneficiary. If a country pursues appropriate policies, it can achieve success, not just in a peaceful international environment conducive to development, but even in an environment of limited or large-scale war.

Another example is that of Israel, whose environment may be the worst of any state. Since its founding, it has never enjoyed a period of peace and development, nor has it had normal relations with its Arab neighbors. It has been involved in five wars with these neighbors, four of which were wars of aggression that Israel itself initiated. Meanwhile, it has been constantly in conflict or at war with the Palestinians. Apart from the vital factor of U.S. support, it has never enjoyed any international strategic opportunities, but this has not stopped it from developing. In fact, it has achieved rapid development despite its population of only 6 million people, its encirclement by hostile, oil-rich countries, and its own lack of significant petroleum resources. It is the only wealthy country in the Middle East whose economy does not rely on petroleum revenues. The Israelis have produced high-quality water-saving technology, medical science, agricultural technology, telecommunications, chemical industry, early warning airplanes, and high-performance guided missiles. The example of Israel shows that a country can develop even in unfavorable conditions.[66]

As long as a country adjusts to the times, it will encounter new opportunities for development. South Korea is a recent example. The 1998 financial crisis badly harmed it, and it seemed that it would have a long-term negative or even fatal impact on its development. But the South Koreans refused to accept such an outcome. They adjusted their internal and external policies in a timely fashion, quickly restored their economy, and become the first East Asian country to surmount the financial crisis. In recent years, South Korea has achieved respectable economic growth.

After its founding in 1949, even though the People's Republic of China enjoyed a favorable environment for growth, it let slip a golden opportunity because of leftist errors and mistaken policies. This experience taught China a bitter lesson, and it went through a period of developing under unfavorable circumstances. The 1960s and 1970s were a bad time for China both at home and abroad. Leftist errors peaked during this period, and the entire country was plunged into the maelstrom of the Cultural Revolution. In the international arena, China had hostile relations with both the United States and the Soviet Union, fought a border war with India, and experienced a breakdown of relations with Indonesia and tense relations with many Southeast Asian countries because of leftist diplomacy. Even in these difficult circumstances, however, it still made some progress. For example, the atomic and hydrogen bombs and China's earth satellite were mainly developed during this period. China also resumed its lawful seat in the United Nations.

China's recent achievement in development is another pertinent example. During the East Asian financial crisis of 1997–1998, the economies of almost all East Asian countries suffered severe setbacks, in some cases losing several decades worth of achievement. Even Russia was unable to escape the financial crisis. Because China adopted correct policies toward the crisis, its economy did not suffer. On the contrary, within this generally unfavorable environment, it discovered new opportunities, and it acted as the only stabilizer on the economic stage of East Asia.

In sum, it is important for China to *seize* opportunities to develop but even more important is for it to *create* opportunities for development. I agree with those scholars who say that whether a country can develop depends on international opportunity, but opportunity is not a static factor. It can be the result of effort. The Chinese people themselves are the main factor in determining China's opportunity for development. If China adapts to the international environment and follows the historical trend of development, it will be unstoppable.

WORLD POWER STATUS FULFILLS THE CHINESE PEOPLE'S DESIRE TO RESTORE THEIR PLACE IN THE WORLD

China should become a world power, as even some farsighted international leaders have recognized. Despite the fact that President Franklin D. Roosevelt signed the Yalta Agreement with the Soviet Union, harming

Chinese interests, he was one of a small number of Western leaders who paid serious attention to China's international status. Part of his policy toward China was to recognize its status as a world power. Yet, because it was backward, he believed that three generations of education and training would be required before it could actually take its place among the world powers.[67]

As two Chinese scholars have contended:

> World power status is a scarce commodity, and there are two outcomes to the competition for this status. Those who lose out will fall into an even more passive and depressed position than before. Therefore, it is absolutely essential for China to grasp the present, rare historical opportunity in order to enter the ranks of world powers early in the twenty-first century. For over one hundred years, many high-minded Chinese have been pursuing this goal. Attaining it will enhance the self-respect and confidence of the more than 1-billion-strong Chinese nation, reduce the likelihood of China being bullied, greatly diminish potential threats from other countries, and help China secure cooperation and support from other countries in the realm of international affairs. All this will effectively assist in safeguarding and pursuing China's proper international interests.[68]

In the words of another scholar: "China should gradually strengthen its determination to become a world power."[69]

If China does not strive to become a world power, it will never become one because world power status is not something that drops from heaven. It is only normal that it should develop into a world power. Some people suggest that it should be satisfied with the status of a regional power and should not indulge in extravagant hopes of becoming a world power. They think that it is not right for it to pursue world power status because this might bring it into conflict or even war with Russia, Japan, and India. This type of thinking is absurd.

Whether China desires and is able to become a world power depends largely on itself. At the same time, we must observe the situation of countries with conditions similar to those of China. Shortly after India achieved independence, Indian prime minister Jawaharlal Nehru posited the goal of its becoming a world power.[70] A Chinese scholar wrote: "In today's India, achieving great power status is not merely the ideal of a few politicians. It has risen to the status of a national objective. In New Delhi, India's political center, politicians and strategic elites from different political parties and ideological positions all believe that India is destined to become one of the greatest civilizations in the world. Regardless of which political party is in power, it will view the pursuit of world power status as a strategic objective that must be achieved."[71] India is a country that trails China in comprehensive national strength, yet it still aspires to be a world power. Why should China not have the same aspiration? A country is just like a person. Without any ambitions or ideals, how could someone accomplish great things?

The goal of modernization that Deng Xiaoping advocated was precisely to transform China from a Third World country to a world power in economic as well as political terms. In 1984, he proposed a three-step development strategy of modernization. The first step was to double China's 1980 GDP by 1990. The second step was to double it again by 2000, reaching a moderate level of wealth. The third step was to reach the median level of developed countries and, basically, achieve modernization by 2050. He stated: "Quadrupling GDP, building a moderately well-to-do society, and modernization with Chinese characteristics are our new concepts." During his southern inspection tour in 1992, he emphasized that China should build itself "into a middle-developed country" in one hundred years, then continue making great efforts to turn itself into a fully developed country.[72]

The third generation of leaders, headed by Jiang Zemin, put forward a bold strategy for the rejuvenation of the Chinese nation, a strategy in line with the thinking of Mao Zedong and Deng Xiaoping. It is also a key development in the historical process of China's march toward world power status. The concept of national rejuvenation was the key concept frequently invoked in the report to the Sixteenth Party Congress in November 2002.

There is a close connection between the rejuvenation of the Chinese nation and China's becoming a world power. If China does not become a world power, the rejuvenation of the Chinese nation will be incomplete. Only when it becomes a world power can we say that the total rejuvenation of the Chinese nation has been achieved.

Broad vision and ambition are essential to achieving the task before us. The goal of building China into a prosperous, strong, democratic, and peaceful country is a strategic one that can unite and inspire all Chinese for the next fifty years. The ideal of becoming a world power should be the Chinese people's ideology for the twenty-first century, an ideal that will motivate them to exert their utmost to achieve.

2

China's Rise

Key Strategic Choices

The Economy or the Military as a Priority

Some analysts hold that China should assign top priority to developing military capabilities and treat economic interests as secondary.[1] Others hold that, while there is nothing wrong with emphasizing economic development, Western countries and the United States will not allow China the time it needs to do so. Accordingly, it should focus on developing military industry and military technology, speed up constructing a navy and an air force, and invest heavily in space and aviation technologies. Still others advocate focusing on the military to stimulate overall economic development.

The growth of any great power is based on economic strength. The successful great power is the county that has the strongest industrial infrastructure. However, as Paul Kennedy pointed out, military potential is not the same thing as military strength. Politics or geography might cause an economic powerhouse to opt out of military development, while an economically deficient country might choose to build a world-class military establishment. In any given period, a country's total resources are limited, so resources allocated to military development are not available for other legitimate purposes.[2]

Historically, with respect to the development of great powers, there are five patterns of relationship between economic strength and military power. In the first, the two are equated, and any increase in economic strength results in an expansion of military power. Generally speaking, a world power is by definition a world military and economic power.

a nation may be economically strong but militarily weak. For ...le, the United States became a world-class nation at the end of the ...teenth century even though it was militarily not as strong as Britain, Germany, France, or Russia. Third, a nation may be weak economically but also be capable of exercising great military power. For example, the Napoleonic wars witnessed the climax of the French domination of Europe, even though at that time the level of French economic growth and industrialization was not high. In more modern times, the economic development of the Soviet Union was uneven, but expansionism persisted. Fourth, economic development need not result in external expansion. Since the Second World War, the economic development of Germany and Japan has been fast, but they have not adopted expansionist policies.[3] Finally, countries in economic crisis are more likely to expand. Before World War II, although the economic development of Germany and Japan was not very fast, both of them followed the path of military expansion.

It is obvious that there is a close relation between speedy economic development and external expansion, between economic growth and military expansion, between military strength and military expansion. However, that close relation can be manifested in a variety of different ways. The rise and fall of Russia (and the Soviet Union) indicates that, although emphasizing military strength may help a nation achieve great power status within a short time, it may not enable it to hold that place. The annual military expenditure of the Soviet Union accounted for as much as 11–13 percent of GNP, and it is true that the Soviet Union was growing from a world power to a superpower. But its military strength did not guarantee that status for long. If the rise of the Soviet Union was due to an emphasis on military power, so too was its fall. The United States also provides an example of the relation between economic and military capabilities. While U.S. hegemony is built on its military power, more important is the great support of its overall comprehensive national strength. U.S. success in the Cold War derives from the economic strength that dragged the Soviet Union down. Military power was directly involved, but economic issues were far more fundamental and decisive.[4]

According to the realist theory of international relations, all countries make national security their top priority. However, there is still the problem of defining *national security* and understanding what it means. The United States built a multitrillion-dollar defense system, but that did not protect it from terrorist attack. If it were to establish a national missile defense system, would it guarantee its absolute security?

History shows that it is impossible to achieve absolute security. Therefore, China cannot make absolute security its goal. But it can choose basic or relative security. That is, it should preserve its sovereignty, independence, territorial integrity, and ability to choose its domestic way of life. Despite problems with relative security, this is achievable. On the other hand, making absolute security its goal and relying on military superiority will reduce the likelihood of its becoming a world power. More important, it will lead Beijing to encounter the security dilemma. The more China develops, the more worried the neighboring countries will become, and the more they will see to their own military capabilities. Furthermore, it will give more excuse for the right wing in the United States in favor of containing China to adopt tough policies that will damage the relationship between China and the United States.

Accordingly, it is fitting that China pursue a national defense policy that calls for the construction of national defense to serve overall national economic development. In effect, it is accepting relative security in order to achieve the long-term and more important objective of becoming a strong, affluent nation.[5] As some scholars have indicated, development is the keystone of China's future, and the main threat to national security is not foreign invasion but whether China can support a stable, orderly, and healthy society.[6] Other scholars warn against focusing on military force at the expense of diplomacy:[7]

> Since America cannot deprive China of its right to develop, Chinese militarists are more likely to ruin the historical opportunity for China's great revival.

> It is very dangerous to link the great opportunity of China's development with military priority.[8]

SHOULD CHINA BECOME A DEMOCRATIC NATION?

The era of conquest by military force has long since passed. A great power must have well-developed scientific, technological, economic, and military capabilities. At the same time, political, economic, and diplomatic systems have become the core content of a country's soft power. Although the Soviet Union possessed a powerful military, it lost its global status owing to its low level of soft power, The world no longer regarded it as a system that worked. China should avoid treading the Soviet path. While China speeds up the development of its economy, military, and science and technology, it also should carry though the innovation of its institutions. The most important tasks involve political, economic, and cultural innovation.

With the experience of three decades of economic reforms, and having entered the WTO, China has for some time now been moving toward a market-oriented economy. Although the course of transforming the central planned economy to a market-oriented one has not yet been completed, the toughest tasks are largely complete. Rapid economic development has led to some international identification with the Chinese economic system, and China's successful experience has increased its influence in international society. China has become a model for economic reform for some developing countries to imitate.

At the same time, China has, as one scholar points out, achieved much in the area of political reform. Its stable political environment is a key factor in attracting foreign investment. There are, however, some problems, including political corruption and an absence of consistent law enforcement. These hurt China's international image, reduce its international influence, and hamper the growth of its comprehensive national strength. In terms of soft power, China's international influence has been at rock bottom for most of the twentieth century.[9]

Should China Follow the Western or the East Asian Model?

A minority in China believe that China can and should follow the democratic development path of the West. They argue that, since democracy is a universal value, the Western model has significant relevance. For example, China should learn the Western system in order to solve its severe corruption problem. The problem is, however, that, if it were to adopt such a course, it would probably go the way of the former Soviet Union and collapse.

A second viewpoint holds that China can follow the East Asian model. In essence, this position is that East Asian countries have their own values, values that differ from those of Western democratic countries, and, thus, that they should not and cannot copy Western models. Rather, they should adopt what is useful and reject the rest. For East Asian countries, the right to survival, labor, and development are much more important than freedom of speech. A soft authoritarian political system is more likely to promote a harmonious, peaceful political and social order. Virtually all East Asian countries except Japan have gone through a period of soft authoritarian management.

Democracy is both a value and a political goal. Developing democracy is currently a major global trend. China should become a democratic great power, a great power with human rights and the rule of law, and a country respected by international organizations and international society. However, China should resist pressure to become a country with Western-style democracy.

There are five reasons for this. First, Western democracy is based on Western history and culture, including Christianity, which is different from China's history and culture. Blindly following this path will create new problems instead of solving the ones that already exist. Second, Western democratic development has its own background and economic base. However, China's has yet to establish such levels. Third, as in Russia, in China the costs of implementation would likely be excessive. Fourth, many countries have practiced Western democracy, but few have really succeeded. Fifth, Western democratic practice has many problems of its own. In sum, China should not reject democratic values, but it should actively learn, absorb, and reconstruct the experiences of democracy in the context of Chinese realities. Since the spirit of democratic reform transcends national borders, no one can openly reject it.[10] Although most developing countries have not done better simply by adopting democracy, most developed countries are in the democratic West.

When exploring the democratic road with Chinese characteristics, three factors merit attention. First, it is necessary to develop further the essential democracy that China has been practicing all along. Marx, Engels, and Lenin distinguished between class democracy and essential democracy. In the past, China overemphasized class democracy to the neglect of essential democracy. In the latter, democracy is the ultimate social objective. It grows out of the requirements of human nature and is the means of actualizing the fundamental interests of people. It is not just a government of the people but a government that expresses the will of the people.

Since the beginning of reform and opening up, the CCP has focused on improving people's lives, enhancing comprehensive national strength, and increasing social productivity, all of which tally with the will and wish of most people. China enjoys a stable political situation; its people back the government, and productivity develops consistently. We should not put aside the traditional essential democracy of socialism. Instead, we should increase our effort to do it well.

Second, we should introduce Western democratic systems (formal democracy and procedural democracy) and combine essential democracy and systemic democracy. In the past, we saw essential democracy as the opposite to formal democracy and procedural democracy. The Chinese also believed that systemic democracy belonged to the bourgeoisie. But now this point of view appears biased. Democracy with Chinese characteristics must find a mechanism that can combine essential democracy, formal democracy, and procedural democracy. Even decent essential democracy cannot replace formal democracy and procedural democracy. To some degree, the disintegration of the Soviet Union and the East European bloc occurred mainly because of the crucial defects of formal and procedural democracy.

Third, China should unite the merits of essential democracy, systemic democracy, and the politics of wisdom. Most people regard the politics of wisdom as a product of feudalism and the blindness of the mass. Others consider it to be incompatible with law and responsibility. The politics of wisdom manifests values that transcend time and social classes. For instance, if there had been no outstanding statesmen such as Washington, Franklin, Lincoln, and Roosevelt, U.S. history would have been written differently. More important, the politics of wisdom plays a very significant role in Chinese politics. China could not be considered to be China without the wisdom of Confucius, Mencius, Laozi, Xunzi, and Han Feizi or without such wise statesmen as the Kangxi Emperor. Sun Yat-sen made China the first democratic republic in Asia. Mao Zedong unified China. Deng Xiaoping played a critical role in moving China onto the path of prosperity and power.

Chinese democracy will include the experiences of Western democracy but surpass it with the infusion of uniquely Chinese characteristics. This new formulation will symbolize the force of China's presence in the world. "Chinese democracy may become the base of an international political order within which China will be a major force."[11] Zbigniew Brzezinski pointed out that, if China can democratize, it will significantly affect the future of the world. In sum, in the next twenty years, the direction of world development will be determined by the United States, Europe, and China. It would be ideal if Europe worked closely with the United States to eliminate social and political instability. If China becomes a more democratic country, it too will play an increasingly constructive role in the world system.[12] Democratization is essential to China's emergence as a global power.

Transparency Is Necessary

Some scholars believe that China should downplay, if not deny, its intention to become a world power. People with this view believe that announcing the intention to achieve great power status combined with rapid development will arouse regional and international suspicion.[13] However, this is a mistaken view. China should confidently take the path of rising to great power status. In 1990, Deng Xiaoping advocated masking Chinese intentions. At the time, this was appropriate. Eastern Europe was in upheaval, and the Soviet Union was disintegrating. It was difficult to discern the direction of various trends. Deng counseled calm and diligent attention to achieving a variety of important policy objectives while avoiding involvement in the major controversies of the time. But, appropriate though they were at the time, his guidelines did not provide appropriate guidance over the longer term. They are not suitable today.

Although China continues to face many problems and pressures, external and internal conditions are very different. Contemporary China has weathered the storm of Soviet disintegration, successfully resisted Western pressure for peaceful evolution, implemented the policies of reform and opening up, and achieved sustained economic development coupled with political and social stability. Having achieved significant success thus far, it should stick to its traditional style of being modest and prudent, but there is no need to hide its intentions. WTO membership demonstrates its determination to participate responsibly in international affairs. It should also increase transparency and be willing to promulgate its image worldwide. While there are still some countries that want to overthrow Chinese sovereignty, on the whole, most members of international society, including most Western countries, are in broad agreement with socialist China. Therefore, China should actively and confidently participate in international society and develop close contacts with other countries. Anyway, hiding future development objectives easily leads to misunderstanding. It is far better to be open.

This is not to say that China should take the lead in international affairs, but it does mean that, since it is already a regional power, it should participate responsibly in international and Eastern Asian affairs and let the world hear its voice. Under certain conditions, it should take initiatives, especially when it comes to East Asian affairs, and it should cooperate and share leadership with other countries.

As it progresses, Beijing should pay special attention to three issues. First, Deng Xiaoping's injunction to maintain focus on the main task of building comprehensive national strength despite all external pressures remains valid. The key point is setting economic construction as the number one priority. "To see the situation as a whole, no matter what is changing, we should maintain commitment to the ten-year economic construction plan. Within ten years, the economy can double and redouble in size and productivity."[14] Second, recognizing that it is a major power and constitutes an important pole in a multipolar world, China should continue to develop its international role. It founded the Shanghai Cooperation Organization in 2001, successfully hosted a meeting of APEC, entered the WTO, and was selected to host the 2008 Olympics. Third, China should promote the building of a new international political and economic order. It insists on the principle of peaceful coexistence in international affairs and especially on noninterference in the internal politics of other countries. It is also on record as opposing hegemony and supporting equality among all nations, whether strong or weak, and the democratization of international affairs.

With respect to development strategy, playing catch-up is futile. The history of the past two decades shows that the industries introduced to developing countries by the West are resource consuming, labor intensive, and technologically backward. The catch-up strategy fosters technological dependence and actually contributes to the technological advancement of the developed countries as they farm out their low-level industries and then proceed to move to new levels of activity. This virtually guarantees that the developing nations will never reach the most advanced competitive levels.[15]

Therefore, China must innovate in order to become a world-class nation; however, innovation must transcend technology and technique and reach the level of civilization itself. China today exhibits most of the conditions required to create a new and different model of civilization, one that will meet human needs in ways that the Western model cannot.

No less a historian than Arnold Toynbee has argued that, in order to survive and flourish, human society should combine the Chinese high esteem for stability and unity with the Western habit of liveliness. In his *Study of History,* he argues that Western liveliness produces change and development, but only at the price of instability. Further, he cites Chinese rigidity, which forestalls development but does provide stability. For Toynbee, the challenge is to combine the energy of the West with the stability of China to produce a lifestyle that can sustain human progress, peace, and happiness.[16]

Contemporary Chinese civilization comprises four important elements. It contains the best of Marxism, which is embodied in the values and concepts of Chinese socialism. It also reflects the achievements of capitalism, as seen in the record of its market economy. It is the repository of traditional Chinese values emphasizing family, morality, ethics, and values. Finally, it also incorporates the achievements of other countries.

If China is the carrier of a new civilization that compensates for the weaknesses of Western civilization, its comprehensive national strength and its influence are bound to grow. Two factors support this view. First, even though Chinese values are in some sense unique, at the core they are related to universal values like peace and stability. Thus, China's approach is not likely to seem strange or out of place. Second, the new civilization would recognize and correct the already acknowledged defects of Western civilization. It would lead to the restoration of human relationships, the protection of the environment, an accounting for social as well as monetary value, and the production of public goods. Thus, conditions for the development of a new civilization are favorable. The key point, however, is that, if China hopes to contribute to a new civilization through its development, it must advance science and technology in ways that actually change human civilization. That is, rather than simply copying the technologies of Western countries, it must innovate. It needs to make discoveries and develop technologies that can change the direction of development and spark a revolution in productivity.

Some analysts argue that, after twenty years of reform and opening, China should shift away from its export-oriented strategy and focus more on internal development. In this view, continued reliance on comparative advantage is unsustainable and will eventually result in the degradation of

China's social and physical environments and could very well lead to the undermining of Chinese sovereignty. Far better in this view is for China to go it alone. More specifically, it is argued that, if China joins the existing world system, it risks being swallowed up by Western society. Second, these analysts feel that China has more to gain by maintaining its present ambiguous ties with the West, which enable it to avoid domination and maintain the socialist system it needs. Finally, they believe that the United States will deliberately set a very high threshold for Chinese integration, one that involves too high a cost for China to pay. This view is incorrect.

Historically, China's relations with the external world have evolved through various forms, most notably, from China placing itself at the center of the world, to it withdrawing, to openness, to cosmopolitan periods during which Chinese civilization was changed by and changed other civilizations. This is where China is today. Opening and reform brought it out of the isolationism of the Maoist era and also brought to bear the better aspects of all the other preceding stages. China found that it could not develop and be separate from the larger world. Isolation caused its development to lag in many crucial areas. It is only since it began to blend itself into the world community that it has been able to learn the things it needs to learn in order to become a great power. Openness relates directly to its traditional cosmopolitanism and provides the means by which it will achieve a new cosmopolitanism, one that will bring major development. With the possible exception of that of the former Soviet Union, the development of almost all the great powers occurred in open environments. After the disintegration of the Soviet Union, even Russia saw the need to revive overseas trade as the impetus for its economic growth.

At this time, China needs to open itself even more. It should develop its internal markets, overcome regional impediments to trade, and gradually develop a mature market economy. There should be a new strategy involving opening to the outside world and simultaneously developing internal markets. Each element can reinforce the other and compensate for difficulties in one or the other. For example, stability in internal demand can compensate for turbulence in the area of trade.[17]

Marx argued that the absorption of external capital and general opening up are necessary for poor countries that want to skip capitalism and move directly to socialism. In fact, he believed in cosmopolitanism; he saw capitalism in the context of a world system.[18] Lenin expanded the theory of Marx. He believed that socialism had to be built in one country, but he also understood that it was impossible to develop an independent economy without external assistance and, especially, access to the advanced technology of capitalist countries.[19] Later, he identified three factors that made it possible for socialist countries to open to Western capitalism. He showed that the profit motive would overcome any reluctance that Western nations might have to trade with socialist nations. He also showed that socialist nations possess resources needed by their capitalist counterparts. Finally, he noted that capitalist circles were so divided that it would be possible to play each off the other to get favorable terms of trade. By these arguments, Lenin established a theoretical base for Russia to open its economy—and, by extension, for all socialist nations to do the same.[20] Deng Xiaoping understood opening to be an accommodation rather than a basic change and acted accordingly.

China's opening up is based firmly on the Five Principles of Peaceful Coexistence, which means that it does not attempt to make use of conflicts among Western countries as a major strategy. Socialism with Chinese characteristics does not involve the export of revolution. China does not see the Western world as antisocialist, nor does it consider itself to be anticapitalist. It puts national interests as the top priority and regards mutual benefit and cooperation as one of the basic principles of its foreign policy.

In terms of politics, opening up requires a proper redistribution of overcentralized state power to the regions and enterprises so that they can adapt to the changing needs of the world market. While resisting inappropriate Western forms, China should oppose bureaucratism and improve human rights as well as enhance socialist democracy and the implementation of socialist law. Opening also applies to spiritual construction. While China should resist the capitalist lifestyle, it will still need cultural and spiritual stimulation. To open up surely will break down or challenge many old traditions, but this, in turn, can enlarge horizons, renovate values, and change culture in positive ways.

China has begun to enter the world system, and there is no choice except to continue.[21] It is impossible for it to establish another system outside the existing one in the manner of the former Soviet Union. It has neither the military ability to establish a new system nor the economic ability to make it function. This means that its only practical course is to participate in the international system, meet its criteria, and learn its management skills and advanced techniques.[22] Of course, the system will change. In all such cases, there is a process of mutual molding as the two systems connect and promote each other.[23] Of course, China inevitably will experience some conflict. Its insistence on following the socialist road and its position on human rights are bound to cause friction. It will not actively challenge the system, nor will it passively accept its parameters. Rather, it will always emphasize achieving integration into the world system but also seek amendments and alterations to its rules and operations.

The major challenge for China will be to deal correctly with the United States, the leader of the present global world order. By following a strategy of putting integration first while also seeking some amendment and alteration, China and the United States can use cooperation as a basis for managing challenges. Cooperation should be the defining trend of Chinese policies. This policy actually has been in effect for some time. The interaction between China and international society shows that China is willing to abide by the code of conduct of international organizations and that it accepts the norms of international society. When it feels that amendments are appropriate, it makes appropriate proposals according to established rules.

Actions in the economic sector also illustrate Chinese priorities. In economic terms, the rules of international society actually refer to the rules of the market economy, including free trade and following the rules of international trade organizations. In the transition from its planned economy through the mixed planned and market stage to its present socialist market stage, China has clearly accepted and implemented international norms and procedures, despite the considerable costs involved. So too with regard to the principle of protecting intellectual property rights. From 1994 to 1995, the Chinese government took firm steps to close more than fifteen factories and firms that produced pirated CDs illegally and allowed U.S. representatives to supervise the enforcement process. In 1995, the United States finally accepted China's measures on protecting intellectual property rights. Most important, after years of arduous negotiation, China managed to reach agreement with the United States to join the WTO. Its membership began in 2002. Since then, it has been recognized throughout the globe as a responsible and constructive participant in international affairs.

THE MAIN CHALLENGES ARE DOMESTIC

All great powers have faced major development challenges. Some arose from the opposition of other great powers.[24] Such was the case with eighteenth-century France as it was opposed by England. Other challenges were domestic in origin. Russia, for example, suffered several revolutions, which undercut its competitive capabilities. It is necessary to identify the most important challenges and determine when and how to manage them. It is also necessary to anticipate and prepare for the unexpected.

In China's case, the following fundamental questions should be considered: Will China be able to maintain the basically stable political situation? Can it maintain a rapid pace of development? And, in the process of conducting external relations, can it avoid making serious strategic mistakes?

Specifically, there are ten urgent problems in need of proper management and solution: resettling laid-off workers and maintaining full employment; dealing with corruption and establishing an effective legal system; reducing regional disparities; reducing the income gap; improving education and the capacity to innovate; maintaining the pace of economic development; controlling population growth; producing enough energy; protecting the environment; and maintaining social stability.

These questions can be divided into two groups. One includes long-term challenges such as the environment that do not require immediate solution. The other type of challenges, including the income gap and economic disparities among regions, are potentially explosive and must be dealt with immediately lest they lead to economic decline. Fortunately, and contrary to the view of many observers, there is reason for optimism. First, owing to progress in reform and opening, Chinese society is not polarized, as it was at the end of the Cultural Revolution. Radical liberals, dogmatic conservatives, and ideologues of all stripes have all been marginalized. China's government is not likely to face major political challenges. Second, its new social pluralism will reduce the likelihood of discontent crystallizing around any one specific issue. Third, at the highest level, its leadership is in agreement on basic strategies and methodologies. Fourth, owing to the depoliticization of intellectual life, the potential for developing and articulating demands for radical reform is very low. Finally, although widespread corruption has in fact weakened the government's managerial ability, the political system itself retains significant power to mobilize its resources. This, in addition to modern high-tech, transportation, and communication development, strengthens the government's capacity to deal effectively with potential crises.

Accordingly, if the government can innovate, overcome corruption, and distribute the fruits of economic growth more rationally, it can avoid crisis. If the reformers perfect supervising systems by implementing basic-level democratic forms and develop internal checks and balances on Party power, China will move in the direction of democratization with Chinese characteristics. Thus, "China's political future depends on conducting reform in development and seeking stability through change."[25]

3

Relations with the United States

China's Strategic Choices

SIGNIFICANCE OF SINO-U.S. RELATIONS

After the Cold War, the United States became the world's sole superpower. Therefore, the Sino-U.S. relationship became the most important one in China's foreign relations and, arguably, the most important bilateral relationship in the world. The United States is important to China for three reasons. First, as the largest developing country, China needs a peaceful environment. The United States is currently the only country that has strategic conflicts with it. It is also the only country with the ability to launch a large-scale war. Second, the Sino-U.S. relationship has strategic significance with regard to China's modernization. The United States is an irreplaceable source of markets, capital, and technology. Third, the United States is the only world power that is deeply involved in the Taiwan issue. Consequently, the Sino-U.S. relationship directly influences China's ability to maintain its national unity. Ever since the era of Mao Zedong, China has given priority to establishing and maintaining normal relations with the United States. For China, it is a comprehensive strategic issue.

In addition to China's status as one of the five permanent members of the UN Security Council, the United States has several reasons for viewing its relationship with China as of strategic importance. First, although its military will not be competitive with that of the United States for at least fifteen to twenty years, China is one of a few countries possessing nuclear and missile technology. It has the potential to pose a nuclear threat to the United States, and it plays an important role in maintaining the nuclear nonproliferation regime and limiting the proliferation of missile technology. Second, as an influential East Asian power, China shares with the United States a common interest in maintaining peace and stability in the region. Third, as the largest and fastest-growing developing country, it plays an important role in the solution of such global issues as the environment, illegal drugs, smuggling, immigration, and energy. Fourth, after 9/11, the United States and China found a new point of common interest, namely, combating international terrorism.

In general, however, the Sino-U.S. relationship looms larger in China's foreign policy than it does in U.S. foreign policy. This is due to the difference between the two nations' comprehensive national power. China's GNP is only one-ninth that of the United States, its military expenditure only one-twentieth, and its per capita income only one-fortieth, and its soft power, including scientific innovation and management systems, is far behind as well.

Even though China's rate of growth is very high, in recent years the United States has also developed rapidly, with the result that the gap between the two countries in terms of overall comprehensive power has widened rather than narrowed. For instance, in 1980, the U.S. GDP was US$2.599 trillion and per capita GDP US$11,360. This was 9.15 times and 39.17 times that of Chinese GDP and per capita GDP, which were US$284 billion and US$290, respectively. By 2000, however, the U.S. figures had increased to US$9.837 trillion and US$37,836. These were 9.1 times and 42.99 times those of China at US$1.08 trillion and US$880, respectively.

In absolute terms, the U.S. GDP exceeded the Chinese by US$2.315 trillion in 1980, a figure that increased to US$8.757 trillion in 2000. The per capita U.S. GDP was US$11,070 more than the Chinese in 1980 and increased to US$36,956 in 2000. China's trade volume in 2001 was US$500 billion; U.S. trade was US$1.23 trillion in 1990, rising to US$2.503 trillion in 2001, of which US$1.068 trillion represented exports.

The gap in military expenditures between the United States and China is also increasing. U.S. military expenditures were US$298.9 billion in 1991, US$288.6 billion in 1995, US$276.2 billion in 1999, US$291.1 billion in 2000, US$310 billion in 2001, US$343 billion in 2002, and US$379 billion in 2003.[1] By contrast, China's military expenditures were US$7.3

billion in 1993, US$7.6 billion in 1995, US$8 billion in 1996, and US$14.6 billion in 2001, less than one-twentieth of those of the United States.

The position of China in U.S. foreign relations is rising concomitant with the increase in China's comprehensive national power. As former U.S. assistant secretary of state Richard Holbrooke pointed out: "The Sino-American relationship will be the most important bilateral relationship in the world during the next cycle of history, much as the U.S.-Soviet relationship dominated world affairs for most of the last half of the 20th century. Getting it right is vital for our national interests."[2] Nevertheless, we should be clearheaded about the fact that the current Sino-U.S. relationship is not really as important as the Soviet-U.S. relationship was during the Cold War. Yet, as long as China is stable and maintains a relatively high rate of growth, the imbalance in the salience of the Sino-U.S. relationship to the two sides will keep changing, and China's position will rise further.

KEY PERSPECTIVES ON SINO-U.S. RELATIONS

Is Conflict Inevitable?

With regard to Sino-U.S. relations: "It is not only theorists of imperialism who assert that a war between China and the United States is inevitable but also adherents of the realist school of international relations and believers in cultural conflicts."[3] Various and conflicting methodologies are brought to bear in this connection.

Realism and imperialism. Realism, the mainstream of Western international relations theory, holds that every country pursues its national interest to the maximum possible extent and that national interest is determined by available power. The greater the national interest, the greater the power the state requires. The essence of modern international relations is the irreconcilability of interests between powerful states. The irreconcilability of interests leads to conflict and sometimes even to war. Such is the inherent nature of modern international relations. This kind of conflict is most likely to occur between two evenly matched powers. Sino-U.S. relations in essence are those between a newly rising power and an existing hegemonic state. The United States will not allow China to grow into a world power. Therefore, China's growing power will inevitably lead to a severe clash with U.S. containment.

In addition, traditional Leninist theory supports the thesis of an inevitable conflict between China and the United States. The United States is an imperialist and hegemonic state. It represents the acme of imperialist development. The essence of imperialism is aggression and war, pillage and control; it is a war machine to maintain the interests of the nation's monopolistic capitalists and the small ruling elite.

Ideology and liberal idealism. Conflict between a socialist world power and a capitalist world power is inevitable. Socialism and capitalism are two totally incompatible world systems. The socialist political system emphasizes the political leadership of the Communist Party, a dominant state role in the economy, and the elevation of the nation-state and collective interests above individual interests in the realm of human rights. These predicates are incompatible with and antagonistic to capitalist democracy and the tripartite structure of separation of powers, private ownership, and individual freedom. Sooner or later, these conflicts will lead to a strategic confrontation between China and the United States, which cannot help but be enemies.

Some scholars assert that the United States is the leader of the world system and the chief advocate for the expansion of democracy. Therefore: "The primary external challenge to China is, not the United States, but the world system, which combines modern capitalism and democracy. The hegemonic position of the United States in the world system determines U.S. strategy, namely, to exercise hegemony. The logic of Sino-U.S. relations in the administration of George W. Bush is that, since conflict between China and the United States is unavoidable, it is better to acknowledge this and pursue maximum possible cooperation on this basis rather than to seek to paper over the conflicts in the name of cooperation." Consequently, even if China is not an enemy of the United States, the United States still regards it as such. "First, on the U.S. strategic chessboard, China will play the same role as the former Soviet Union did, namely, that of an opponent. In fact, its national power will inevitably grow along with the economy. As it becomes increasingly wealthy, the incompatibility between Chinese and U.S. national interests will expand. Even if China is not actually a competitor of the United States, the United States will perceive it as such. Whether China is an enemy is a matter not simply of fact but also of perceptions, which can be manipulated. Second, the ideological differences between China and the United States and domestic U.S. political factors will exacerbate this situation. Increasing numbers of ordinary Americans believe that China is the main opponent or potential opponent of the United States. As long as communism exists in China, the United States will not stop regarding it as its potential enemy. Taking China's growth into consideration makes Sino-U.S. conflicts even more plausible. The United States can tolerate China's economic growth, but not the challenges caused by its development."[4]

The clash of civilizations thesis. Conflicts between an Eastern, Confucian great power and a Western, Christian great power are inevitable. China and the United States belong to different systems of civilization. Chinese civilization, one of the civilizations of the East, is based on Confucian tradition and Buddhism. The rise of China is the potential root of large-scale civilization wars among core states. China is forming an alliance with anti-Western Islamic countries to oppose the United States. If the United States challenges China's rise as the hegemon of Asia, a big war is likely to break out.[5]

Geostrategic thesis. The U.S. strategic aim of global hegemony ensures that conflict will occur between China and the United States. Current U.S. strategy is a thoroughgoing hegemonic strategy to control the world. It emphasizes control of the Eurasian borderlands, of the strategically important lines of communication, and of key resources. After the Cold War in particular, the United States intensified its military control of territories bordering China and strengthened its strategic deployment. It stations more than 100,000 troops in Japan, South Korea, and the western Pacific. It has expanded the scope of the U.S.-Japan Security Treaty, restored its military presence in the Philippines and Singapore, and signed a new security treaty with Australia. After 9/11, in the name of fighting international terrorism, it attacked Afghanistan, stationed troops there, and propped up a pro-U.S. government in Kabul. During the Afghan War, U.S. military forces entered Central Asia for the first time, aiming at controlling the region's strategic petroleum reserves, which are second only to those of the Middle East, and containing China from the northwest. Washington has stepped up its arms sales to Taiwan, selling a large amount of military equipment to the island, and established a de facto military alliance with Taiwan. The U.S. war in Iraq also aims at controlling the Middle East, the region with the world's largest petroleum reserves. Therefore, the United States has strategically surrounded China. U.S. strategy toward North Korea conflicts with China's strategy of pursuing development and may lead to war.

Another opinion is the following:

The U.S. strategic aim is to split China apart. After the U.S. fin-
ishes fighting Iraq and Yugoslavia, whose turn is next? From the
perspective of its geopolitical requirements in the Asian-Pacific
region, splitting off Taiwan, the Nansha Islands, and Tibet from
China fits the long-term world hegemonic strategy of the United
States and its allies. By controlling a separated Taiwan, the United
States can contain Japan to the north, intimidate ASEAN to the
south, and block China to the east. . . . The Chinese Communist
Party and the Chinese people are left with the choice of forcibly
breaking the chain of containment. This is both a severe challenge and an extremely rare and historic opportunity to break
through the hegemonic blockade.

In other words, China should adopt a strategy of preventive war and strike
before the United States can achieve its goal of splitting China apart. If it
does not, it will have no choice but to accommodate itself to the United
States and relinquish its sovereignty over Taiwan and the South China
Sea. Washington's strategic aim is to solve the European (Russian) and
East European issue first, then the Middle East, next China, and, finally,
India.[6]

Historicism. The history of the rise and fall of world powers demonstrates that conflicts between newly rising powers and existing hegemonic
powers are inevitable. In his 1981 *War and Change in World Politics*, Robert Gilpin said that, in all ages, the first solution to settle the imbalance of
the international system structure and international power distribution
is war, in particular, hegemonic war.[7] In world history, relations between
newly rising powers and existing hegemonic powers are usually full of
conflicts and wars.

Some newly rising countries became world powers by defeating
existing powers. Britain challenged the Netherlands as well as Spain, the
dominant power in Europe, and defeated the Spanish Armada in 1588.
Possessing mastery of the seas, it then vanquished the Netherlands, an
earlier great power, and, thereby, became a European power. During the
eighteenth and nineteenth centuries, Russia, a rising power, challenged
Sweden to its north, the Ottoman Empire to its south, and the Qing
dynasty to its east, controlling the Baltic Sea, and grabbing territory along

the Black Sea and in China. After the Meiji Restoration, Japan challenged the Qing dynasty and Russia and secured victories in the Sino-Japanese War and the Russo-Japanese War. After World War I, the Soviet Union challenged the entire world capitalist system, carried out socialist construction in one country on its own, and presented a model of modernization quite different from the British model.

There are also examples of failures, including the Japanese warlord Toyotomi Hideyoshi's failed invasions of Korea and China in the sixteenth century and the modern aggression against China, Southeast Asia, and the United States in the twentieth century that cost Japan its position as a world power. As an ascending state, Germany seemed to be a natural challenger to the existing international order, but its record of confronting the dominant powers produced mixed results, and its defeat in World War II led to its loss of world power status even though the Versailles system, which Germany had challenged, also collapsed in the process. China, too, cannot escape the laws of history. In *The Tragedy of Great Power Politics,* the U.S. scholar John J. Mearsheimer wrote that international politics is great power politics. Great powers survive by seeking to maximize their power, that is, by becoming regional hegemons. Spurred by its rapid development, China may put forward an Asian Monroe Doctrine and seek to drive the United States out of Asia. Therefore, conflicts between the great powers are inevitable.[8]

The View That Sino-U.S. Conflict Is Not Inevitable

The thesis that Sino-U.S. conflicts are inevitable leaves China with little or no choice. Either it abandons its effort to become a world power, submits to U.S. hegemony, and becomes merely another economically developed country, or it persists in its strategic aim of becoming a world power and faces severe conflict with the United States.

My own view is that a variety of problems undoubtedly exist between China and the United States, but this is not the same as saying that confrontations or clashes are inevitable. Only when contradictions become exacerbated do they rise to the level of conflicts. Therefore, conflict is only one of the possible outcomes, and by no means an inevitable one, of contradictions. Even antagonistic contradictions can be ameliorated under certain conditions. In the early years of New China, Sino-U.S. conflicts were antagonistic, a matter of life and death. Confrontations and wars broke out between the two countries. In February 1972, U.S. President Nixon made his historic visit to China, which resulted in the Shanghai Communiqué. The curtain was lifted on the drama of improving Sino-U.S. relations. This historic event fundamentally influenced and changed the antagonistic character of the Sino-U.S. relationship. Instead of being resolved through large-scale conflict, the antagonism between China and the United States was transformed via a shared understanding concerning the Soviet threat. China and the United States became de facto allies confronting Soviet hegemonism. Similarly, the Sino-Soviet relationship was also an antagonistic one. At one time, China viewed the Soviet Union as its most dangerous enemy, and there were conflicts and even small-scale wars between the two countries. Subsequently, things changed, and China and the Soviet Union became good neighbors, coexisting with each other. The two countries normalized their relations in the late 1980s, and China and Russia established a strategic partnership in the 1990s. These two examples alone clearly show that there are methodological and theoretical problems in the theory that Sino-U.S. conflicts are inevitable. Former foreign minister Qian Qichen pointed out that, although the international relations theory of realism has its merits, it ignores the criticism of the idealist school and that it is largely deduced from Western history and culture. Neglecting the influence of various domestic factors on the external behavior of states, it is extremely one-sided.[9]

The preceding theories regarding the inevitability of Sino-U.S. conflicts reach the same conclusion, but their arguments are contradictory. For example, the methodology of realism conflicts with that of idealism. Idealism, which stresses ideological conflicts, sees ideology as the main root of Sino-U.S. conflicts. Even medium and small countries like Iraq, Libya, and North Korea, which do not practice U.S.-style human rights, democracy, and freedom, are perceived as a threat by the United States. According to the idealist school, China does not present a threat to the United States because of its power. Even if it pursues peaceful policies, it will be unable to alter the U.S. perception of it as an enemy. The main reason is because its ideology differs from that of the United States. If it is successful, Chinese ideas will become increasingly influential and, thereby, pose a challenge to U.S. beliefs. Realism, however, pays scant attention to ideology, which it considers unimportant. Powerful countries, whether China, Germany, the socialist Soviet Union, or a democratic Russia, are perceived as adversaries or enemies by the United States.

Therefore, whether China is a socialist country is of no consequence; what matters is whether its national power presents a threat to U.S. hegemony.

The theories of inevitable Sino-U.S. conflict suffer from five defects. First, they overemphasize the conflicts between China and the United States and overlook the two countries' common interests. Although their conflicts may develop to the point where they outweigh their common interests, the reverse is also possible. If the United States tries to force China to implement Western-style democracy, China might suffer a post-Communist East European–style economic collapse, which would deprive the United States of the economic benefits it enjoys from China. If the United States allows the Chinese economy to develop, there is little chance that the CCP, which guides this development, will fall from power. Therefore, the United States may either seek to contain China's economic development or tolerate the development under the leadership of the CCP. In the latter case, China will not adopt a Western democratic model in the near term, and Washington will have to swallow the bitter pill of coexisting with Chinese economic development and Chinese-style socialism. The United States has still not decided how to deal with the problem. Therefore, there is still breathing space to avert conflicts caused by the differences between social systems and ideologies, that is, the conflicts between U.S. democratic hegemonism and China's socialist system. One cannot conclude that conflict is inevitable.

Second, the theories address the issue in a one-sided way, ignoring possible developments and changes in the Sino-U.S. relationship. They consider the possibility that Sino-U.S. relations may worsen, but not the possibility that they might improve. For example, some adherents of the thesis of inevitable conflict based their position on comments made by President George W. Bush prior to his taking office or at the very beginning of his administration. Subsequently, however, significant changes occurred in his comments. Initially, he regarded China and the United States as strategic competitors; later, he talked about both competition and the possibility of cooperation in the Sino-U.S. relationship. In any case, Sino-U.S. relations have, on the whole, improved, not deteriorated, during the Bush administration. The 9/11 Incident also altered and modified the view of China as an enemy of the United States.

Third, the difference between the Chinese and U.S. social systems should not be regarded as a fundamental element in a supposedly inevitable Sino-U.S. conflict. The biggest difference between socialism with Chinese characteristics and traditional socialism represented by the former Soviet Union is that, domestically, the former stands for the absorption and utilization of the fruits of capitalist civilization and, in foreign affairs, it stands for a peaceful foreign policy and opening to the world. Therefore, the relationship between Chinese socialism and U.S. capitalism is no longer a life and death struggle or a zero-sum game. Chinese socialism is extremely flexible. On the one hand, it strives to achieve social justice, eliminate exploitation, and implement basic socialist values such as social guarantees. In this respect, it learns from and absorbs the successful experiences of European social democracy. On the other hand, in advancing production and establishing a market economy, it learns from and assimilates some of the experiences of U.S. free market capitalism. Chinese socialism advances on a foundation established by absorbing U.S. and other capitalist civilizations and forms a new culture combining the four elements of Eastern culture, Chinese characteristics, the fruits of capitalist culture, and Marxian socialist theory. Although there are, to be sure, fundamental differences between Chinese socialism and U.S. capitalism, these are soft, not hard or antagonistic, contradictions. Particularly with respect to economic and cultural systems, the two countries share many common interests, such as protecting private property, protecting the legal rights and interests of foreign capital, abiding by the rules of the market economy, encouraging the development of scientific and technological education, protecting the environment, and preventing pollution. Even in the field of politics, there are more and more common interests, including the protection of human rights and the acceptance of the principle of the rule of law. Therefore, these differences will not inevitably lead to confrontations between China and the United States. Former U.S. secretary of state Colin Powell once said: "China is no longer in the throes of the Cultural Revolution; it no longer exports Communism; and it is no longer an enemy to capitalism."[10]

Without doubt, the greatest external challenge that Chinese socialism faces is from U.S. pressure. We should distinguish between two kinds of pressure. The first kind is U.S. efforts to change China's basic social system. Even those Americans who advocate cooperation with China still hope to peacefully transform China into a society modeled on the United States. Through sustained intercourse with China and including it in international society, they hope to influence the thought pattern and lifestyle of the Chinese people. In response to this kind of pressure, we must insist on our own principles, on our choice of the path that social development will take, and on our national sovereignty. We must oppose all kinds of U.S. plots. The second type is U.S. efforts during the process of negotiating China's entry into the WTO to impose various conditions, such as revising its economic and legal systems in accordance with international norms. In response to this kind of pressure, China should accept what is reasonable while insisting on the principle of noninterference in its internal affairs. Even on the issue of human rights, while we should criticize U.S. efforts to intervene in China's internal affairs, we should also consider how to better protect the basic rights of the Chinese people through the rule of law. We should transform the external pressure into a force for domestic reform and not simply think of it as part of a plan to change China's sociopolitical system via peaceful evolution.

Fourth, China and the United States belong to different systems of civilization. But such differences have always existed in the world. If the only way to avoid wars is to have only one civilization on earth, I'm afraid that day will never come. Humankind must learn to coexist peacefully in a world with many civilizations developing each in its own way. Today, in the twenty-first century, conflicts have, indeed, arisen between different civilizations, but there is also a cooperative dimension to their relations with each other. In the past, the Chinese civilization embraced Buddhism; later, it assimilated socialist ideology from the West. Now it can absorb elements of Western capitalist civilization. As long as Americans learn to practice tolerance and inclusivity, then there is no inevitability of war between China and the United States, each with its own form of civilization. The fact is that, even though different religions and nationalities fought each other in Bosnia, there is the counterexample of ASEAN, which represents a trend in which countries of various religions and nationalities cooperate with each other. In a pluralist world, many civilizations must coexist. Therefore, between countries with different civilizations, there may be cooperation and coexistence as well as conflict.

Fifth, looking at this issue from the perspective of world history, it is certainly true that many large-scale confrontations and wars did break out between a newly rising country and an existing hegemonic country. "Newly rising countries always are potential strategic threats to the existing powers; the development of their economies cannot but trigger the latter's efforts at containment."[11] In actuality, however, this is not always so.

In the process of becoming world powers, some countries were put under the protection of the existing powers. They adopted the so-called hitchhiking strategy, merged smoothly into the mainstream world system, and achieved world power status. Post–World War II France, Japan, and Germany are prime examples. Such countries, however, have not completely succeeded. Because they remain under U.S. protection, international society does not quite recognize Germany and Japan as independent world powers. Although France is more independent and enjoys greater influence than Germany and Japan, it is not a world power in the true sense. In any case, the point is that the United States, the current hegemonic power, has not suppressed the development of Germany, Japan, and France.

The growth of the United States in the nineteenth century basically took place without interference from or suppression on the part of the European powers. In the eighteenth century, before, and in the early years after, its declaration of independence, the United States had serious conflicts with England. The two countries even fought a war from 1812 to 1814. These conflicts, however, were not between a newly rising power and an existing power because, at that time, no one anticipated what kind of country the United States would become. England was engaged in a war against France and could not muster its main strength in North America. Therefore, the War of 1812 ended with a boundary treaty signed by both sides.

Not until the last half of the nineteenth century, especially after the Civil War, did the U.S. trajectory toward great power status become clear. Some people assert that Americans opposed England's hegemony at that time.[12] This is not quite accurate. If England had really wanted to suppress the growth of U.S. power, the Civil War afforded an excellent opportunity to do so. Suppose that Britain had dispatched its navy, like the United States does at present, to support the independence of the South, declared a policy of neither unification nor independence, neither war nor peace, asserted that unification was acceptable only if the South agreed, reserved the right to sell weapons to the South to fight against the North, and warned the North that, if it tried to solve the issue by force, it would be violating human rights and democracy and Britain would be paying close attention, what, then, would the U.S. government have done? But England did none of these things. Consequently, the growth of the United States in the nineteenth century was a smooth process that occurred with little interference from England. In fact, the United States benefited from the protection that England provided it. Perhaps England was inclined to view the United States, a country much like itself, as its natural successor as international hegemon.

From a methodological perspective, it is a species of fatalism and historical circularity to argue the inevitability of Sino-U.S. conflicts. In *The Tragedy of Great Power Politics*, John Mearsheimer argued that the logic of the old system and past eras remains unchanged. International politics is still great power politics and still revolves in a tragic historical circle. In his view, all powers will inevitably pursue regional hegemony; therefore, conflicts between China and the United States are unavoidable. Such a viewpoint is blind to historical change and human progress as well as to the changes in international politics brought about by the era of globalization. Mearsheimer stressed only the logic of aggressive realism, neglecting the roles of the social system, of history and culture, and of leadership in determining the foreign policy of states. He equated a nation to a Leviathan-like monster devoid of human nature, reason, or progress.[13]

When discussing Sino-U.S. relations, the former Chinese leader Jiang Zemin said:

I don't think China and the United States will confront each other. In the past, China suffered from foreign aggression and expansion. The government and people of China love peace and devote all their efforts to developing the economy and enhancing the people's living standards. We always pursue independent peaceful diplomacy and strive for a peaceful and safe external environment to facilitate our domestic economic development. China's armed forces are purely for self-defense. Compared to the United States and other powers, the level of China's military expenditures and armament is quite low. China never intends to engage in expansion. As for the so-called China threat fabricated by certain people possessing a Cold War mentality, we believe that people of different countries in the world, including the United States, can make the right judgment.[14]

Former foreign minister Qian Qichen also pointed out that the idea of a Sino-U.S. confrontation is mistaken:

Historically, China has no tradition of expansion and never deploys a single soldier overseas. In reality, as a developing country, its greatest desire is to maintain a peaceful international environment. China will remain a developing country for a rather long period in the twenty-first century. It has neither the ability nor the need to threaten anybody. Even when China becomes strong in the future, it will not carry out aggression or expansion or pursue hegemony. This has been written into China's Constitution. China is neither the former Soviet Union nor the old Germany or Japan. China is China. China will never take the old path that other countries followed. Those who disseminate the China threat thesis have no interest in studying history, nor do they desire seriously to understand the present.[15]

This is a real tragedy.

Obviously, there is a lot of space between China and the United States. With regard to Sino-U.S. relations, there are two possibilities, not just one. It may be hard to avoid contradictions, frictions, and even local conflicts between the two countries, and these may even lead to serious conflicts, but it may also be possible to avoid such serious conflicts.

In fact, there are no incompatible conflicts of national interest between China and the United States. China has neither the capability nor the intention of posing a threat to the United States. One need only compare the two countries' national power to see that the idea of China posing a threat to the United States is utter nonsense. That the United States constitutes a big obstacle to China's national security, especially to its unification, is, indeed, a problem. But, from the perspective of U.S. history and the history of Sino-U.S. relations, we can see that the United States likewise does not pose a threat to China. The thirty-five years since the beginning of improved Sino-U.S. relations have confirmed what Mao Zedong pointed out long ago, namely, that the United States will not launch wars against China. At present, other scholars also hold this opinion: "Americans have no intention of attacking China. It is a totally wrong strategic judgment to regard the United States as an enemy or a potential enemy state that threatens China's security. Any strategic choice based on such a judgment is also wrong and could be profoundly harmful."[16] The United States may be a problem to China, and it is the biggest variable in the process of its growing into a world power. In my judgment, however, as long as China does not adopt anti-U.S. policies, the United States will not pose a threat to China.

It can be seen from the earlier discussion of the emergence of new great powers that there are two types of relations between a newly rising power and the existing world powers. One type involves a challenge. A newly rising power challenges the existing powers and tries to break up the original international order and construct a new one in line with its own national interests. Examples of this are Britain vis-à-vis Spain, Japan vis-à-vis China, and Russia and the Soviet Union vis-à-vis the Western capitalist powers. The other type involves a merger. A newly rising country is willing to become a member of the existing international system, and the existing powers encourage this process and possibly even provide support and protection.

How Sino-U.S. Relations Develop Depends on the Two Countries' Policies toward Each Other

As a newly rising power, China has a complicated relationship with the United States. The Sino-U.S. relationship now is different from what it has been in the past. China is not presenting an overall challenge to the United States, nor is the United States supporting, let alone protecting, China. The Sino-U.S. relationship is a brand-new type of relationship between great powers.

China opposes U.S. hegemonism and unilateralism, but it has no intention of posing an integral challenge to the United States. Historically speaking, China has never been a global superpower with influence all over the world. It had little interest in world affairs outside East Asia, and it was always a conservative and defensive power in its region. Contemporary China is continuing this historical tradition. From Mao Zedong and Deng Xiaoping to the present leaders, it has been evident that China will never be a superpower. It was not in the past; it is not now; it will not be in the future. It will never pursue hegemony, great power chauvinism, or power politics. It opposes hegemonism, but it never practices hegemonism itself and has no intention of ever replacing the United States. It opposes U.S. power politics, but it always recognizes the special function and position of the United States as an important country in the international system. It merely hopes that the United States will respect the interests of other world powers and that world affairs will be decided in consultation with the people of different countries rather than by the United States alone. China opposes U.S. unilateralism; it supports multipolarization.

China does not interfere in domestic U.S. affairs, and it hopes that the United States will not interfere in its domestic affairs. It believes that it does not present a challenge to the United States. Rather, it is the United States via its arms sales to Taiwan and its military alliances and military cooperation with China's neighbors that constitutes a challenge to and threat of containment vis-à-vis China. The Sino-U.S. relationship encompasses both cooperation and challenges. As some experts have pointed out, the Sino-U.S. relationship is not the same as the Soviet-U.S. relationship during the Cold War because, unlike the Soviet Union, China does not possess a superior military force that can confront the United States. China has no ambition for hegemony, it does not distinguish friends and enemies on the basis of ideology, and it does not pursue expansionism.[17]

On the other hand, historically China developed its own system. In its own eyes, China was the world, and the world was China. It had its own culture, its special history, written characters, and spoken language. It was a universe unto itself, a country outside the other world systems. Contemporary China, however, has changed this tradition. Since its reform and opening up, it has practiced a universalistic policy, a world policy. Just as Deng Xiaoping called himself "a world citizen," China's orientation is to integrate into the existing international system and pursue its national interests from inside the system rather than remaining on the outside or emulating the Soviet Union by trying to organize a new international system to confront and replace the existing system. This is what China says it is doing and what it is actually doing. It has joined many international organizations that are led by the United States and the West, the most important of which is the WTO. Nevertheless, it insists on maintaining its own socialist system, insists that every country has the right to choose its own values and development model, and believes in a pluralist world in which the international community respects the special histories, cultures, religions, and traditions of different nations and countries and their views regarding national construction and economic development. At the same time, China also recognizes the existence of basic common values, for example, respect for basic human rights, but it insists that every country can choose how to fulfill these basic rights according to its own situation. Therefore, it insists on pursuing the path of socialism with Chinese characteristics, insists on the priority of national development, the priority of national survival, and the priority of social and national interests over personal interests, and opposes the attempts of the United

States and the West to force their values on it. On the other hand, it persists in its goal of establishing a new international political and economic system, reforming the unfair and unreasonable international order and rules set up by the West during the time it enjoyed a historical advantage, and opposes the revision of the existing international order in accordance with Western preferences. China is integrating with the world system while maintaining its own basic system. The United States views only the first part favorably, not the latter part. Thus, a rising China's policy toward the United States can be summed up in one sentence. It is one of limited challenge as well as limited cooperation. That is, it does not pose an overall challenge like the Soviet Union did, but neither does it seek to become a full member of the Western system.

On the U.S. side, there are two opposing views on Sino-U.S. relations. Some people believe that China's growth is a threat to the United States and that China aims at replacing the United States and challenging U.S. hegemony. Since China constitutes a threat, before it has become a fully fledged great power the United States should inhibit its growth and limit its development to a certain degree and scope. Others contend that, since the direction of its development is unclear, the United States should try to pull China into the U.S.-led world system and, through a process of integration, transform it into a Western-style country. At the same time, the United States should accord China a higher status in the world system and acknowledge its position and functioning as a great power.

The U.S. government, which plays the leading role in U.S. China policy, has formally stated on numerous occasions that the United States welcomes an open, prosperous, and strong China, a responsible China that actively participates in the world system. U.S. President Bush said during his 2002 visit to China: "The U.S. welcomes a stable and prosperous China that peacefully coexists with its neighbors. We will complete the great task to establish a prosperous and stable Asia for our future generations together with China." China is not only a trade partner, he continued, but also a great country. "The Sino-U.S. relationship is mature and mutually respected. It is important to the United States, China, and the world as a whole. China has become a formal member of the WTO. It is a partner in the global trade system with the rights and responsibilities to take part in the making of and carrying out of trade rules. In the past thirty years, we see great changes taking place in China, and we believe the same changes will continue happening in future."[18] Then U.S. secretary of state Colin Powell even wished that China would "make decisions and activities suiting the position of a global leader."[19]

In fact, the policies of the U.S. government toward China are always a contradictory and unstable combination of suppressing and welcoming China's growth. As noted above, U.S. policies toward China can be summarized as limited containment and limited engagement and cooperation. As a result, China has a complicated relationship with the United States, one unlike any other in the history of rising great powers. The present Sino-U.S. relationship has not been set in stone, and its future development depends on how China and the United States proceed to construct it. The Western method of constructivism may be used to analyze it. The United States will form its policies toward China in accordance with China's intentions. If China opposes the United States, the United States will treat it as an enemy and seek to contain it. If China wants to establish normal relations with the United States, the United States will tend to adopt policies of engagement and integration. Similarly, China will make its U.S. policy according to U.S. strategy. If the United States regards China as an enemy and contains it, China will have to consider the United States as its main threat; if the United States adopts constructive, peaceful policies of engagement, China will adopt the same policies.

It is not a matter of which comes first and which comes after. It is a mutual and interactive process in which every single step may cause big changes in the Sino-U.S. relationship. Therefore, U.S. analysis and judgment about China and China's analysis and judgment about the United States have vital importance on the future direction that the Sino-U.S. relationship will take.

How Does China View the United States? How Does the World View the United States?

According to some French observers, the U.S. aim since George W. Bush took office is very simple: to defend U.S. interests in the U.S. sphere of influence. Bush's way is obviously different from Clinton's. Bush tried isolationism, but 9/11 changed that. The Americans realized that they could not stand apart from the world, so the neoimperialists and isolationists of the Right and the Left once again gained ascendancy. They wanted to save the United States by applying democratic expansionism on a global scale. They insisted on the Iraq War and aimed at democratizing the Middle East, which they viewed as the source of international terrorism. Such neoimperialism, however, is more likely to stir up anti-Western sentiment in the world and stimulate terrorism than exterminate its roots. The neo-imperialists forgot one thing, namely, that democracy is a process; though important, it must have international legitimacy.[20]

Some Russian observers compare U.S. policies to international totalitarianism. One says: "There has never been a time like now in history that is so convenient for one great power to implement world hegemony. First of all, let's talk about the concept of totalitarianism: the government of one country has all the means for global hegemony and tends to use these means to define the international situation, to force international society to submit to American interests, to impose its standards on other countries, to intervene in the affairs of sovereign countries, and to suppress any resistance against its intervention by force." This approach is very similar to the quests for world hegemony of fascist Germany and Stalin's Soviet Union. Americans are trying to force their democracy on the world, but democracy imposed by force loses its essence and becomes ever more dangerous. There is a high likelihood of an international autocracy dominated by the United States.[21]

Some Americans are also dissatisfied with U.S. actions. Paul Kennedy, the author of *The Rise and Fall of the Great Powers,* pointed out: "Saying that 'we are everywhere; we will prevent any country from becoming a potential dangerous opponent' is ambitious and dangerous. I think the term 'arrogance' applies here. Getting drunk on power is always a challenge facing a 'No. 1.' If the U.S. occupies the seat of 'No. 1' for too long, is intoxicated by arrogance and ego, and regards every disagreeable government in the world as a threat, in my opinion the unpopularity of the 'over-extended empire' will gradually weaken it."[22]

How Far Can U.S. Hegemony Extend?

In 2001, the U.S. author Spencer Johnson wrote a book titled *Who Moved My Cheese?* that became a best seller.[23] "Who moved my cheese?" became a very popular expression among Americans. Another popular expression among Americans in 2002 was "Whose apple is rotten?" which derived not from a best seller but from the successive scandals of big U.S. corporations.

According to U.S. news reports, since the end of 2001 six well-known

U.S. corporations have falsely reported business profits to advance corporate interests at the expense of their investors. On December 2, 2001, Enron, which ranked fifth in the world, applied for bankruptcy and admitted that it had falsely reported US$567 million in income during the preceding five years. On June 15, 2002, the well-known U.S. accounting firm Arthur Andersen LLP was indicted for obstruction of justice. On May 21, 2002, the largest U.S. securities company, Merrill Lynch, admitted to deliberately misguiding investors by issuing false analytic reports. The company paid US$100 million in fines. On June 25, 2002, World-Com, the second largest U.S. long-distance phone company, admitted to falsifying its accounts to the tune of US$3.8 billion. On June 28, 2002, Xerox, the largest U.S. copying equipment company, admitted to falsely reporting US$1.9 billion in income over four years (according to media speculation, the actual amount was close to US$6 billion). Finally, on July 5, 2002, another member joined the false-accounts club when Merck, the world's largest pharmaceutical company, admitted that, although it had collected US$12.4 billion in income from its subsidiaries, this money had never been entered onto its books. Ultimately, some analysts said that about 25–33 percent of U.S. companies had made false reports.

This was a great shock to U.S. corporations. In the wake of President Bush's announcement of severe punishment for false reporting, on July 9, 2002, the U.S. Dow Jones Industrial Average dropped to 8,813, the lowest point since 9/11. Some particularly alarmed Americans declared that the United States was experiencing its most dangerous attack since 9/11.

In fact, the United States was facing a potential crisis. In the view of many domestic and overseas observers, the foundation of the U.S. economy, namely, the credibility of its operations, was at stake. There was widespread fear that the loss of confidence could lead to the eventual ruin of the U.S. economy.

The crisis of confidence in the U.S. economy triggered a debate over whether the decline of the United States had begun. The Yale University professor Immanuel Wallerstein, renowned for his world systems theory, argued that the American eagle was falling. According to Wallerstein: "The United States' success as a hegemonic power in the postwar period created the conditions of the nation's hegemonic demise. This process is captured in four symbols: the war in Vietnam, the revolutions of 1968, the fall of the Berlin Wall in 1989, and the terrorist attacks of September 2001."[24]

In my opinion, however, the critics were off the mark and may actually have misled individuals to adopt an incorrect assessment. In fact, they failed to ground their analysis in a complete understanding of the structure of world power. The United States may be compared to an apple orchard and its companies to apples. If one apple is rotten, it can be discarded, but there will still be many other apples. Similarly, if one basket of apples turns rotten and is thrown away, many baskets will remain.

At that time, the U.S. economy was in a period of transition from high-speed growth to low-speed growth or even stagnation. But it is far too early to say that the United States is declining. The U.S. economy is resilient; it was able to survive the Great Depression of 1929. No one will be able to challenge U.S. military capabilities for at least fifteen years or even longer. The U.S. high-tech economy indeed has bubbles, but it is not a bubble economy. The United States still leads in the development of new technology, and its economy is still stable and growing.[25]

U.S. strength derives from sources that combine in ways found in no other major country: its uniquely advantageous natural environment; its geographic location; and its abundant natural resources. Not least, the ability of the United States to integrate large numbers of immigrants with diverse backgrounds is unparalleled in modern human history. These factors will ensure U.S. strength for a long time. Indeed, even if its power declines by half, the United States will remain a world power.

However, no country can be strong forever. Hence, although it is not wrong to predict the inevitable decline of the United States, such a prediction is of little value. The key is to assess the onset of the process of decline and then to trace its evolution. Over the coming ten, twenty, or even thirty years, the United States will remain the strongest country in the world, and all that other people can do is to work out their respective strategies accordingly. Stated differently, the United States may experience a period of adjustment, but, if we regard the period of adjustment as the beginning of U.S. decline and make that the basis of our diplomatic strategy, we may commit a big mistake.

Between 1918 and 1923, the German philosopher Oswald Spengler published the two-volume *The Decline of the West*, possibly the earliest work on this theme. He gave it as his opinion that, like all other cultures in history, Western culture would inevitably decline. He also boldly predicted that Western culture would complete its decline between 2000 and 2200.[26] Accordingly, 9/11 in 2001 and the U.S. corporate credibility crisis in 2002 seemed to bear out his prediction.[27]

After World War II, there were also those who spoke directly about the decline of the United States. In the 1960s, Arnold Toynbee suggested that it was making the same mistakes that the Roman Empire and Great Britain had made in their time.[28] In *The End of the American Era* (1970), Andrew Hacker stated that U.S. history was coming to an end.[29] Interestingly, this was totally opposed to the view his father expressed in *The Triumph of American Capitalism* (1940).[30] In 1976, the U.S. scholar Richard Rosecrance argued that the *Pax Americana* was over and that the United States had become just an ordinary country, albeit the leading one.[31] Ten years later, the Yale University professor Paul Kennedy claimed that the American century had ended.[32]

Some politicians made similarly incorrect assessments. For example, beginning with Khrushchev, the leaders of the former Soviet Union justified their policy of promoting revolution throughout the globe by referencing the perceived decline of U.S. power. History demonstrated the fallacy of this view. Therefore, it may be a trap to talk about U.S. decline now, and, if we are not careful, we may fall into the trap. We need to consider that, when U.S. decline really begins, it will be, not because of the effect of rotten apples like Enron, Arthur Andersen LLP, and WorldCom, but, rather, because of problems with the orchard itself.

Indeed, there are, arguably, some important indicators of possible troubles ahead. The following examples are illustrative.

The United States possesses unprecedented levels of strength. It also displays unprecedented arrogance. After the Cold War, it emerged as the world's only superpower with a previously undreamed-of comprehensive national strength. Its GNP reached US$9.837 trillion in 2000, accounting for 31 percent of the world total of US$31.492 trillion. Also, U.S. GNP was equivalent to 80 percent of the combined GNP of Japan, Germany, Great Britain, Italy, China, Russia, and India, which was US$12.284 trillion. At the same time, U.S. military expenditure climbed to US$288.8 billion in 2000, accounting for 38 percent of the world total of US$798 billion, and amounting to 1.67 times the total of Chinese, Russian, Japanese, German, and Indian expenditures. In 2002, that figure increased to US$400 billion, equaling 50 percent of the 2000 world total.

On the basis of this strength, the United States pursued unilateralism and hegemonism. In the face of strong Russian opposition, it expanded NATO, and, despite Chinese opposition, it extended the U.S.-Japan Security Treaty. European and Japanese concerns were similarly ignored as

Washington forcefully broke the Kyoto Protocol. Finally, the United States unilaterally withdrew from the Anti-Ballistic Missile (ABM) Treaty and, despite widespread global concern, announced the so-called preemptive strike strategy.

The United States is so strong that none of its enemies will dare to confront it directly. Rather, they will adopt asymmetrical methods to oppose it. The biblical story of David and Goliath is instructive. Because he had never met his match, Goliath was arrogant. He continued to rely on the armor and lance that had served him well. Naturally, he assumed that any challenger would be identically armed and protected. He was, therefore, both surprised and angry when he saw David running toward him armed with nothing but a sling. Because it never occurred to him that David's apparently rash action was an elaborately concocted deception, he failed to notice the young shepherd's sling. He arrogantly walked forward, uncovered his forehead, and, thus, made himself vulnerable to David's stone. He fell before David came within range of his lance.[33] Pride and arrogance were as much a cause of his death as was David's slingshot.

The United States should understand that every country has its vulnerabilities, especially when asymmetrical methods are employed. 9/11 demonstrated these vulnerabilities. Nuclear power plants, electronic communication centers, and hydroelectric power stations provide additional examples. Yet some Americans believe that their overwhelming power enables them to pursue and achieve absolute security.

Some Americans see Russia as a threat and, therefore, insist on expanding NATO to its borders. The United States unilaterally withdrew from the ABM Treaty to build an aerial Great Wall to defend against surprise missile attacks. More seriously, in the eyes of many Americans, China presents a threat to the United States even though bilateral cooperation in the wake of 9/11 proves that this is not the case. Many Chinese analysts believe that the U.S. missile defense system is aimed at China. Hence, China naturally opposes the plan.

Actually, China has no intention of confronting the United States and, perhaps, sparking an arms race. It simply lacks such a capability. If the United States deploys an antimissile system to respond to a nonexistent threat and, thereby, intimidates China, its global standing will be undercut.

U.S. hawks believe that rogue states also pose a threat; 9/11 shows

that this concern is reasonable. However, it is far more likely that terrorists will continue to use the already-proved asymmetrical approach. If
the terrorists knew that the United States had developed an antimissile
defense, they would not attempt nuclear missile attacks. Consequently,
the U.S. quest for absolute security will not really solve problems; on the
contrary, it will cause them. Like Don Quixote, the United States will be
tilting at windmills, but windmills that are, in fact, invisible.

The United States needs to rethink its international strategy. It must
deal with the fact that, despite actions to maintain world peace and stability such as mediating disagreements between India and Pakistan, Washington frequently inspires dislike and even hatred. Americans must learn
that their biggest enemy is not China, not Russia, and not Islamic extremists or international terrorists. Rather, it is the arrogance that arises from
their consciousness of their own power.

Apart from the economy, the United States also faces social problems
related to change and social transformation. In his last address, President Clinton argued that, within fifty years, what is at present a largely
white society will give way to a much more diverse mixture of races and
cultures. One must ask whether, in these new circumstances, the United
States will be able to maintain a unified social system based on freedom,
democracy, and a belief in religion. Also, how will the United States cope
with an influx of people who do not share the values of liberalism and
democracy?

U.S. elites, most notably Samuel Huntington, worry about these questions, but, to date, no solution has been offered. Huntington's solution
is to maintain unity in the United States by upholding present values of
freedom and democracy. However, his critics point out that such values
actually amount to an effort to maintain white supremacy by asserting
the values of the white elite even though it may no longer be numerically
dominant.[34]

The end of the Cold War has not witnessed the emergence of a unipolar U.S. hegemony. Although Russia's comprehensive national strength is
much less than that of the former Soviet Union, its GDP has been increasing steadily since 2000. Chinese success in maintaining high GDP growth
and translating this into enhanced comprehensive national strength is
well documented.[35] For its part, Japan supports the United States on some
issues but also wishes to raise its international status and is, therefore,
not satisfied to act merely as an automatic follower of Washington's lead.

In Southeast Asia, ASEAN runs smoothly and is growing into an important regional force that strives to keep an equal distance in its relations with China, Russia, Japan, and the United States. In the West, the European Union has made profound headway with the rise of the euro and a strengthened independent European defense force. Finally, China and Russia have formed a strategic partnership and founded the Shanghai Cooperation Organization, which has strengthened cooperation among China, Russia, and the nations of Central Asia. Some Russian analysts even cite the possibility of a new center of geostrategic power comprising China, India, and Iran.[36]

Although this trend toward multipolarity has encountered some obstacles, such as U.S. unilateralism, the direction of developments seems to be firmly established. Even Britain, which has the closest relationship with the United States, is concerned about U.S. actions, while, on the Continent, NATO members indicate concern that Washington feels it no longer values their contribution.

In addition, in the United States itself, there are voices, such as Joseph Nye of Harvard University, that oppose unilateralism and favor cooperation. Nye and others point out that the power of the United States depends not only on its military and economic strength but also on taking counsel with allies. The critics argue that, the more Washington relies on unilateral military power, the greater will be the likelihood of an overall decline in its ability to work its will among nations. Multilateralism is in accordance with the true national interests of the United States.[37]

The United States in China's Eyes: Friend or Foe?

Owing to contradictions in U.S. policies toward China and the public acknowledgment of a desire to transform China's social system by a combination of containment and engagement, it is difficult for the Chinese to come to terms with U.S. policies. Some experts note ten contradictions in the U.S. position that puzzle them:

1. Although the United States depends on external capital, markets, and talent, it wants to control globalization.
2. U.S. society emphasizes democracy and openness, but the president has greater power than anyone else and can strongly influence Congress and the public.

3. The United States has the world's most powerful military, but its people are reluctant to take casualties.
4. The power of the United States is unmatched, but it fears becoming the target of all other countries.
5. The United States depends on immigrants, but it is afraid of them.
6. U.S. culture reaches to every corner of the globe, but it is also widely resented.
7. Americans love peace and fear war, but gun violence occurs every day in the United States.
8. Americans are aggressive and ambitious, but now they have nowhere to climb.
9. The United States raises banners of freedom and human rights in spiritual morals, but it is a desert spiritually, filled with violence, pornography, and drugs.
10. As the only superpower, the United States bullies the weak but fears the strong.[38]

This brings to mind the question of whether the term *empire* should replace the phrase *the only superpower in the world* in describing the United States. Although many Americans think that the idea of U.S. imperialism is insulting, sometimes the United States does act like an imperial power. It has extended its military presence globally in an effort to achieve a *Pax Americana.* Moreover, some Americans argue that U.S. imperialism would be beneficial given their country's open, liberal, and democratic traditions. For them, the chief question is, not whether the United States should be a hegemonic power, but, rather, what kind of hegemony it should exercise. On the other hand, other Americans disdain the idea of imperialism on the grounds of elitism, economic wastefulness, and the certainty of eventual moral decay.[39]

Chinese scholars have argued that, initially, U.S. policy was righteous and responsible in the Gulf War. However, things soon began to change. Many Chinese resented the boarding and inspection of a Chinese merchant vessel by the U.S. Navy. Since then, Chinese opinion has come to hold that the U.S. pursuit of hegemony may well challenge Chinese security interests. Basically, most Chinese are suspicious of U.S. strategic intentions in the longer term, especially when they consider the U.S. alliance pattern in East Asia.[40]

In fact, some scholars actually believe that the fundamental U.S.

security objective in Asia is to prevent China from becoming strong. With respect to Taiwan, the bottom line is to give Taiwan de facto but not de jure independence. The United States is most concerned about securing its sea lines of communication. De facto control of Taiwan effectively blocks Chinese outlets to the sea. It also helps control Japan's sea lines of communication. At the same time, however, the United States also wants to reduce its burdens. It does not want China to control Taiwan. Its objective is to thwart China's emergence as a world power: "The U.S. wants China half-dead, to develop unhealthily and to be forced to consume its internal resources."[41] According to this view, the United States is manifestly a traditional imperialist power and a proximate threat to China.

Certainly, anti-China influence is very strong inside the United States. Periodically, the idea of the China threat is used to instigate public hostility to China, to achieve the larger purpose of reversing the one China policy in place since the days of President Nixon. There is reason for the Chinese to maintain vigilance.

On the other hand, we need to look at other U.S. opinion. Although the hope is to change China's social system through engagement, some sectors hold that it is in accordance with the fundamental interests of the U.S. and Chinese people to maintain and develop normal relations.

The U.S. government, though it often vacillates, has generally abided by the one China policy, and bilateral relations have gradually evolved. If China concentrates solely on the anti-China activities of the United States, automatically sees any U.S. action as hostile, and takes diametrically opposed measures, the possibility for it and the United States to become enemies will increase. It is definitely unwise for China to use the idea of a U.S. threat to counter the idea of a China threat.

U.S. policy toward China's rise depends not only on the interaction and struggle of various political influences in the United States, but also on Chinese actions. This is a challenge for China, for it must decide how to harmonize its expanding power and relations with those of the world's sole superpower and hegemon.

There is a process of mutual interaction. Chinese U.S. policy will be influenced by U.S. China policy, and vice versa. If China and the United States take each other's interests into account, they can avoid confrontations; on the other hand, if they are mutually suspicious, there will be more confrontation.[42] The United States has the initiative in bilateral relations. China has few resources available to affect the United States, while the United States has many resources at its disposal for dealing with China.

How should we understand the impact of asymmetrical development on bilateral relations? China is developing economically and, thus, needs a peaceful environment. Its emergence as a world-class power is consistent with maintaining world peace. Why, then, do some countries raise the so-called China threat theory and treat it as a threat to international peace? One of the chief reasons is the idea that the interaction of two nations with different levels of economic development and, therefore, different national interests inevitably leads to confrontation. I argue that China's rise will not follow the traditional path for two reasons.

First, the general trends of development since World War II are different from those in other periods of human history. Basically, the motivation is different. Development since World War II is motivated by a new technological tide of unprecedented depth, breadth, and influence. Contemporary development is a global, as opposed to regional or local, phenomenon. Past patterns had two results: one was that developed countries got richer and richer, and undeveloped countries became poorer and poorer; the other was that asymmetrical development caused a clash of interests, which often led to conflict.

Deng Xiaoping's development theory views this question from a new angle. Deng argues that all countries seek development to overcome backwardness and, therefore, will reconsider their foreign policies to seek peace. Accordingly, the more development is emphasized, the stronger the drive for peace and stability. Also, development in Europe and Asia reduces the absolute advantages of the United States as a superpower and strengthens the positions and functions of China, Europe, and the Third World in the international community. "If the Third World, including China, develops well," he wrote, "and if Europe also develops well, the danger of war can be eliminated. . . . China's development is beneficial to the peace and stability of the Asian-Pacific region and the world, and, the more China develops, the more stability exists."[43]

Second, China will avoid the error of militarism. Although Chinese leaders repeatedly promise that China will never pursue hegemony, other countries remain suspicious. Chinese history, however, demonstrates the groundlessness of such suspicion. When the feudal dynasties of China were strong, they expanded and invaded neighboring countries, including Korea, Vietnam, and Burma. But, in general, after its unification during the Qin dynasty (221 B.C.), China maintained its position by means of a cultural centralism involving a tribute and vassal system rather than by conquest. In the history of its relations with its neighbors, periods of peaceful coexistence were much more common than periods of conflict. Its history also shows that it traditionally has had no interest in areas outside East Asia or in establishing world hegemony.

China's priorities are economic, not military. As Western countries rose, they always regarded armaments as the foremost task. The speed of their military development was much greater than that of their economic development, and expanding military power caused conflicts, especially with existing hegemonic countries. Chinese development has not upset the balance of world political and military forces on the whole. There has been no substantial change in the ratios between U.S. and Chinese economic and military power. The United States is still the only country in today's world with absolute advantages in all areas, and it will not meet real challenges until 2015.

What is more important is the direction of and strategy for development that China has chosen. It has made engaging with and merging into the international community a key element of its development strategy. This will require the constant efforts of several generations to achieve, and, in the meantime, the need to consolidate international peace can only increase.

The history of confrontations between rising countries and status quo powers shows that one of the important reasons for conflict is that rising countries tend to interject new interests into the system and realize them by methods that are not sanctioned by the system. The Soviet Union developed in the context of confrontation between a socialist country and the whole capitalist world. During the period of Soviet-U.S. confrontations, two opposing world systems were established.

China's development as a rising power is, however, different from all those of the past. China will rise by its connection to the core of the world system, that is, the countries of the West. The possibility that it will confront the world system centering on the West in its development process is fundamentally excluded. What it is doing now is trying to become a new center within the system, not trying to expel the existing core or create a new system.

For example, China is working actively to establish mechanisms to ensure peace and security regionally and globally. Between 1982 and 1997, it signed five new international treaties and joined ten new regimes. The latter required submission of seventeen documents and protocols. Additionally, it participated in numerous research programs related to arms control. These related to the Comprehensive Test Ban Treaty, the Chemical Weapon Convention, the nonnuclearization of outer space, nuclear free zones in Antarctica and the South Pacific, and the UN Conference on Disarmament. It is worth noting that it signed the Comprehensive Test Ban Treaty even though doing so is arguably contrary to its interests. In sum, China has chosen the path of responsibility and participation.

China has established a similar record within the region. The Asian-Pacific region provides China with strategic depth, markets, and capital. Continued peace is essential and requires that relations with its neighbors be a high priority for its leaders.[44] China joined both APEC in 1993 and the ASEAN Regional Forum in 1996, even though both were founded partly to restrict the efforts of the major powers. Because of this, its initial participation was tentative and guarded. However, both organizations soon came to be an arena in which China is able to demonstrate its willingness to cooperate, explain and clarify its positions, and participate in constructive dialogue on regional security.

In addition to responsible participation, China is also becoming a leader in regional councils. In April 1997, it took the lead in founding the Shanghai Cooperation Organization. This is the first such organization that it has led and is an important manifestation of its new security concept.

Finally, since 1998, China has regularly published the white paper *China's National Defense*. This publication aims to provide comprehensive explanations of its national defense policies and military power. It is a positive response to the international demand for greater transparency on its part.

The question of how China should view the United States is equally important, but also more complex. U.S. activities actually have two dimensions. Some are frankly the hegemonic acts of a superpower, while others can be seen as the natural and necessary actions of the world's most powerful state.

Therefore, it should be recognized that, although some actions challenge peace and security, others objectively provide a stabilizing function that promotes global economic integration and peace. For instance, in June 2002, U.S. secretary of state Powell and President Bush person-

ally called on Indian president Vajpayee and Pakistani president Mush-
arraf to counsel restraint in dealing with their differences. On the other
hand, the United States has abrogated the ABM Treaty, which may yet
provoke an arms race. In sum, although the United States may at times
act as a self-appointed, arrogant, and arbitrary global policeman, it would
be a mistake to overlook or disregard the positive actions that are also an
important aspect of its foreign policy.

It is essential to recognize reasonable U.S. concerns such as the direction of China's influence once it rises to its rightful position. It is also
appropriate to accept U.S. interests with regard to Chinese conventional
arms sales, the possible transfer of nuclear, biological, and chemical
weapons (especially to nations unfriendly to the United States), dissatisfaction with the adverse Sino-U.S. balance of trade, and the U.S. hope that
China will open its markets. In dealing with these issues, China should
deal appropriately with U.S. arrogance but also attempt to understand
U.S. concerns and resolve differences by negotiation, compromise, and
referral to relevant regimes.

However, such actions as U.S. intervention in China's internal affairs
(especially the Taiwan issue), criticism of its human rights policies, and
efforts to transform its society all overstep the accepted scope of bilateral relations, and China has no choice but to reject them. China can and
should deal with the reality of U.S. power, but it can neither give up its
right to determine the course of its own affairs nor acquiesce to U.S. containment efforts. U.S. policymakers know very well that the unification of
Taiwan and the mainland is one of China's most important core interests.
They also know that reunification does not threaten important U.S. interests or threaten U.S. security.[45]

In other words, if China cannot unify Taiwan, its most important
national interest will be undermined, but, if the United States gives up
Taiwan, it will lose very little. It will still enjoy its leading global position. Its interests in Taiwan are illusory and ideological; they are derived
from its hegemonic interests but not actually involved with its security or
integrity. Of course, it can be argued that U.S. interests in Taiwan actually reflect a kind of potential strategic need. That is, if Sino-U.S. relations
were to deteriorate to the point of conflict, Taiwan could be used as a strategic asset to contain China. Also, reunification might cause the United
States to lose face in front of its Asian allies.

Finally, U.S. policies elsewhere in the region need to be considered;

the U.S. security alliance with Japan is most important in this respect. History shows that the United States has reason to be concerned about Japanese military policy, and it manifests this concern through the security treaty. However, it is unreasonable of Washington to use the treaty to contain China since China has never taken military action against the United States. Similarly, U.S. concern about disputes between China and some of the ASEAN nations arising from territorial claims in the South China Sea is reasonable because those claims have the potential to directly affect important sea lanes of communication. However, this concern also has something to do with maintaining U.S. hegemony in East Asia.

China and the United States clearly have interests in common. However, since the Shanghai Communiqué, political relations have lagged behind economic ties. Although economic relations have steadily grown, the political sphere has been marked by a cycle of stops and starts. Since 1990, China and the United States have experienced several big crises in their political relations: the Tiananmen issue and U.S. sanctions against China, the sale of F-16 fighters to Taiwan, the 1993 *Yinhe* incident, Lee Tenghui's visit to the United States, Chinese military exercises near Taiwan and the subsequent deployment of U.S. ships to the area, the United States linking human rights with trade, the United States raising anti-China proposals in the UN Human Rights Committee, the U.S. bombing of the Chinese embassy in 1999, the aircraft collision issue, and so on.

However, the volume of trade between the two countries keeps increasing. Even the crises described above did not dampen the growth in trade for very long. In the past two decades, the average annual increase in trade between China and the United States has been over 18 percent.

Quantitative development in economic relations may lead to qualitative change in the political arena. China's entry into the WTO, the beginning of normal and permanent bilateral trade relations, removed the most important long-term obstacle to the improvement of Sino-U.S. relations.

Political relations provide a basis for economic relations, but political frictions hinder economic activities. Economic ties are driven by the market, on the one hand, and by the complementarity of U.S. and Chinese economic structures, on the other. In some ways, Chinese exports to the United States are only marginally affected by political factors. Indeed, sometimes economic realities appear to reduce the impact of political differences. When conflict and confrontation increase, economic considerations provide a powerful incentive to both countries to manage their difficulties and to keep the political relationship on track.

In sum, in dealing with conflicts of interests, there is a clear economic imperative for leaders on both sides to recognize the difficulty of compromising on the issues that matter most to each but also to compromise on some issues that are not so important. This, in turn, can provide a basis for cooperation in other areas.

SOME STRATEGIC CHOICES FOR CHINA'S POLICIES TOWARD THE UNITED STATES—THIRD CONFRONTATION, THIRD ALLIANCE, OR SOMETHING ELSE?

The Worst Option: A Third Confrontation with the United States

If it is believed that war is inevitable, China should prepare effectively and maximize its interests. However, this is a bad plan, one that should be adopted only out of absolute necessity. That is, China should act only if, despite its best efforts, the United States defines it as an enemy and acts accordingly or if the United States supports a declaration of independence by Taiwan. But this will harm both Chinese and U.S. interests and should be avoided. China and the United States have clashed twice: once in Korea and once, indirectly, in Vietnam. Both sides paid significant costs in the conflicts, the United States suffering heavier losses in Vietnam than in Korea. But the present situation is different. Today, the United States enjoys an overwhelming comparative advantage in military strength, and, although victory involves far more than superior weapons, China, like any opponent, would suffer grave damage even if it won. Also, with the end of the Cold War, Russia no longer serves to balance U.S. strength, as did the former Soviet Union. Both factors, in addition to U.S.-Japan alliance, put China at a huge disadvantage. In the circumstances, it should strive to avoid confronting the United States.

Best Option: A Third Alliance with the United States

Both sides should recognize that their common interests are best served by acting together, just as when, during the war against Japan and later, they formed a de facto alliance to resist the Soviet threat. For China, such an alliance would support global peace and stability and provide some restriction on U.S. unilateralism. It could also get more capital, greater market access, more technology and military equipment for its modernization, and an easing of U.S. pressure on the Taiwan issue. This is the best choice for China, but it is also unrealistic. Put simply, the two countries lack the basis, in terms of both ideology and national interests, and the will to form an alliance. Any alliance with the United States would require China to subordinate its interests, which, in turn, would degrade its independent status as a world power. It is unacceptable for China to become a U.S. ally at the cost of losing its national self-identity. A third alliance might be possible only if U.S. unilateralism caused a major loss of international support and the United States was to realize the utility of acting on the basis of its common interests with China.

Middle Option I: Peaceful Coexistence with the United States

As some scholars have pointed out, the Sino-U.S. relationship has assumed many different forms, from war to strategic alliance to peaceful coexistence.[46] The "Middle Way" is yet another arrangement in which China would adopt a live-and-let-live attitude toward the United States. It would neither provoke the United States nor allow itself to be provoked. It would maintain a strategic distance.

Skeptical scholars argue that the possibility of peaceful coexistence between China and the United States is remote. The United States is a country with global interests, and many of these interests are in East Asia. China is an important country located on the Eurasian littoral that has been both a friend and a foe of the United States. The two countries have a mixed history, and, at present, if there are common interests, there is also potential for conflict. The United States remains hostile to Chinese ideology, and it has been involved in the Taiwan issue for a long time. Since it continues to intervene in China's internal affairs, it is difficult for China to pursue a policy of peaceful coexistence.

Middle Option II: Neither Alliance nor Confrontation

Consequently, the only strategic choice for China is to try its best to improve ties, enlarge areas of common interest, and accept that the relationship will reflect both cooperation and confrontation. It should use reasonable and restrained means to resist U.S. actions that threaten its interests and try gradually to steer the relationship onto a normal track. This is neither the best nor the worst choice, but it has the best chance of success and should, therefore, be adopted.

This strategic choice synthesizes many possibilities and will be useful in different situations. For example, when conflict seems imminent, China can try to manage the situation to prevent escalation to violence. Also, even if the two nations cannot establish a true alliance, they can cooperate in such key areas as trade, education, the fight against terrorism, and the protection of the environment. Third, peaceful existence is possible with respect to areas in which the two nations do not share common interests, such as those concerning Africa and Latin America. Finally, the two nations should emphasize achieving balance in their relations. When troubles arise, they should manage them and always leave room for improvement. And, when relations are smooth, they should anticipate potential conflicts and adopt preventive measures.

China should work to achieve stable and normal development of Sino-U.S. relations. First, It should not confront the United States on its own initiative. Second, if the United States tries to force confrontation, it should not be afraid of it. Third, it should be prepared for forced confrontation. Fourth, and most important, even when the United States is entirely responsible for a downturn in relations, it should restrain itself from reacting radically and always seek opportunities to change the U.S. position. The United States cannot force its will on China.

To reemphasize my main point, the greatest threat to China is not from the United States but, rather, from the accumulation of internal problems. China has experienced rapid growth and development for over twenty years, but the development is unbalanced, fragile, and unstable. If such problems as corruption, urban and rural unemployment, the widening gap between rich and poor, social security, and social protection are not solved or dealt with properly, they may cause turbulence and slow the historical process of China's rejuvenation and rise.

4

China's Relations and Strategic Choices with Other Developing World Powers

Quasi World Powers and Multipolarization

What Are Quasi World Powers?

Developing or quasi world powers may at times be regarded as the fourth type of world power. They are those powers capable of competing for the position of a world power and on the threshold of becoming one in the near future. In absolute terms, their national power may exceed that of any large powers in the past, but their influence on world affairs does not equal that of such past great powers. For instance, Japan is currently much stronger than, but has considerably less influence than, the Japan of the late Meiji era a century ago. China's present power is greater than that of the Qing dynasty two centuries ago or, for that matter, than any dynasty in Chinese history. But China is less influential in East Asia at present than the Qing dynasty was in its heyday, not to mention the Qin, Han, and Tang dynasties. Germany, France, Great Britain, and Russia are in the same situation.

Quasi world powers may be divided into two groups:

1. The first group comprises those countries that are on the threshold of world power for the first time in their history. This is a stage that all world powers go through. Among the current quasi world powers, that is, Europe, Japan, Russia, China, and India, India may fit into this category. To a certain extent, China, too, may fit in here. Although China was

a great power in East Asia on five occasions in history, its current rise is quite different in terms of the historical context and other conditioning factors from any other time in the past. There is little continuity between the past eras when China was a great power and the present. This is unlike contemporary Japan, Germany, and Russia, all of which are strongly connected to their past as great powers. Russia, in particular, basically inherited the power and potential of the Soviet Union.

2. The second group comprises renascent world powers. These are countries that slipped from their positions as world powers or superpowers or suffered failure and then rebounded to become quasi world powers and may again become full-fledged world powers. Among such countries are the Soviet Union after World War I, Germany, France, and Britain after World War II and the creation of the European Union (of which Germany, France, and Britain are the core), Japan after World War II, Russia after the collapse of the Soviet Union, and China since the 1990s. Some of them may again achieve world power status; others may not.

Among the more than 190 countries in the international community at the beginning of the twenty-first century, only the United States was a genuine world power. All the other large countries were at best quasi world powers. Their influence extends beyond their own regions but is still far from that of a world power.

Relations among Quasi World Powers

Generally speaking, developing countries in the same region at the same time are strongly competitive with each other. This is because world power status is a rare commodity that all the rising powers covet. But, in any given region, there is room for only a limited number of great powers, so not all rising powers will attain the status to which they aspire. Consequently, competition among large countries for world power status is intense and often engenders confrontation and wars. For instance, the Sino-Japanese relationship at the end of the nineteenth century was a typical competitive relationship among rising powers. Both countries sought influence in East Asia, especially in Northeast Asia, and their competition eventuated in war over Korea. Germany, France, and Russia also engaged in numerous wars arising from their competition for influence in Europe. These relationships are complicated because they are influenced by history and the contemporary era and are affected by comparative military power, ideology, national political systems, national characteristics, and religious and cultural factors.

In general, there are several types of relationships among rising world powers. The first type is a competitive relationship. Relationships among geographically contiguous great powers are usually competitive. Examples include those among Britain, France, and Germany, between China and Japan, between China and India, and between Japan and Russia. China's relations with France, Germany, Britain, and Russia are also competitive to some extent, but less so than the former examples. The second type is a good neighborly and cooperative relationship. Examples include those between France and Germany in the framework of European integration, among China, Russia, France, Germany, and Britain, and among Japan, France, Germany, and Russia. Good neighborly and cooperative relationships do not preclude all conflict or competition, but they do restrain the degree of competitiveness. The third type is a hostile relationship. At present, there is no clearly hostile relationship between rising world powers. Strongly competitive relationships may turn into hostile ones if improperly managed. In the past, hostile relationships existed among France, Germany, Britain, and Russia. The current Sino-Japanese relationship could worsen and become hostile. The fourth type of relationship is coexistence. Countries with neither large conflicts nor important shared interests can easily coexist. Examples include China's relations with large regional powers such as Brazil, South Africa, and Egypt.

RUSSIA AND CHINA: RISING POWERS, GOOD PARTNERS, AND GOOD NEIGHBORS

Russia's Potential to Become a World Power

Russia is one of China's largest neighbors, possessing the world's largest territory, abundant resources, and one of the two largest nuclear arsenals in the world. As the major successor state to the Soviet Union, it is still the largest country in the world. Although its population is only around 2.5 percent of the world's total, it possesses one-quarter of the world's timber reserves, one-third of its natural gas, half of its coal, one-quarter of its oil, and 10 percent of its landmass. Russia's landmass is nearly twice that of

China's, its arable land of 132.8 million hectares 40 million hectares more than that of China. Russia has five times as much forest area as China. Its oil reserves are three times greater than China's, its gas reserves exceed China's by a factor of thirty, its water resources are equal to China's but serve a population only one-ninth of China's. Russia's only complaints are that 20 percent of its territory lies in the frigid polar zone and that its access to the oceans is limited.

The collapse of the Soviet Union and the turbulent decade of reform led to negative growth in Russia throughout most of the 1990s, during which time its economy shrank by 55.1 percent. This decade witnessed a collapse of living standards that had risen in previous decades as a result of the hard work of the Russian people. Owing to the constant decline of the value of the ruble and high domestic inflation, half of all Russians saw their savings wiped out and their income steadily decline. Even the low living standards could not be secured. Even very modest pensions were in arrears, and one-third of the population was living below the poverty line. The privatization of state assets at fire-sale prices caused enormous damage to Russia's national assets and inflicted greater losses than those suffered during World War II. Part of these assets was gobbled up by bureaucratic consortia and part escaped abroad, about US$300 billion, according to some estimates, while loans and investments from the West made up only a fraction of this sum. Per capita GNP figures showed that Russia had declined from a world superpower to the status of a medium-developed country. At the time Vladimir Putin took office in 2000, its GNP had fallen by half in the 1990s and was only one-tenth that of the United States and only one-fifth that of China. Its economy rebounded under Putin, but it still faced a long uphill climb to regain even a shadow of its former relative prosperity.

Nevertheless, no matter how low Russia had sunk, one fact stood out. Although it had precipitously declined from the superpower position of the Soviet Union, it had the capacity to regain its status as a world power. Both Presidents Yeltsin and Putin regarded the restoration of Russia's world power position as the basic orientation of their foreign policies. Therefore, the relationship between China and Russia is not only one between two neighboring countries but also one between two rising world powers. Both face the question of how to deal with pressure from the existing world superpower, the United States, and each must figure out how to deal with the rise of the other.

Sino-Russian Relations after the Cold War

Sino-Russian relations developed smoothly after the Cold War, and the prospects for stability are good. The relationship during this period has gone through four stages:

The first stage (1992–1993) saw progress from normalization to friendship and cooperation. After the collapse of the Soviet Union in 1991, China sent a government delegation to visit Russia. The two sides quickly signed a summary of the meeting and reached agreement on Sino-Russian relations. China recognized Russia as the successor to the Soviet Union and a permanent member of the UN Security Council. The two sides agreed to base their relations on the principle of peaceful coexistence and reaffirmed the treaties and diplomatic agreements signed in 1989 and 1991. In December 1992, President Boris Yeltsin paid his first visit to China, during which time the two countries signed twenty-four documents regarding cooperation in such areas as the economy and trade, science and technology, and culture.

The second stage (1994–1995) saw the establishment of a new constructive partnership. In January 1994, Russian president Yeltsin sent a letter to Chinese president Jiang Zemin suggesting "the establishment of a constructive partnership for the twenty-first century" between Russia and China. China responded positively. In September 1994, President Jiang formally visited Russia and signed the China-Russia Communiqué with President Yeltsin concerning future relations between the two countries. The communiqué pointed out: "The two countries have established a new constructive partnership."[1] This relationship is neither confrontation nor alliance, and it is not aimed at a third country. The two sides also signed a communiqué regarding the detargeting of nuclear weapons, an agreement on the western section of their national boundary, and so on. These documents strengthened the mutual trust and security between the two countries; they promised not to use nuclear weapons first and not to use force in any form in their relationship. They proposed to further economic and trade cooperation and stressed closer coordination between themselves in terms of matters involving the international community because neither wanted to establish a unipolar world.[2]

The third stage (1996–2000) saw a developing partnership featuring equality, mutual trust, and strategic coordination looking toward the twenty-first century. In late April 1996, President Yeltsin visited China for the second time. After formal meetings, he and President Jiang issued a communiqué declaring that the two sides had decided to develop a partnership featuring equity, mutual trust, and strategic coordination with an eye toward the twenty-first century. The two countries decided to exchange visits between their leaders on an annual basis, alternating between Beijing and Moscow, and between their foreign ministers and set up a hotline between the two heads of state. In December 1996, Chinese premier Li Peng made a working visit to Russia, initiating regular meetings with his Russian counterpart. Another fruit of Yeltsin's second visit was an agreement on confidence-building measures regarding border issues signed in Shanghai among the heads of state of China, Russia, Kazakhstan, Kyrgystan, and Tajikistan. It was a historic agreement on demilitarizing the eight-thousand-kilometer boundary between China and the post-Soviet states as well as a vivid expression of the determination of the five countries to become good neighbors, good friends, and good partners.

In April 1997, President Jiang visited Russia again and signed a communiqué on world multipolarization and the establishment of a new international order with the Russian leader. During his third visit to China in November 1997, Presidents Yeltsin and Jiang declared that a survey of the eastern portion of the Sino-Russian boundary had been completed and that this section of the boundary (approximately forty-three hundred kilometers long) had been accurately demarcated on the ground for the first time in history. At the same time, the two governments signed a memorandum of understanding regarding the basic principles governing the construction of gas pipelines and developing liquefied natural gas fields, the principles of cooperation between local governments, and the basic orientation of economic and technological cooperation. Jiang's third visit to Russia in November 1998 and Yeltsin's visit to China in December 1999 deepened the friendship and cooperation between the two countries.

The fourth stage can be dated to Putin's election, which signaled the transition of the Sino-Russian relationship to a normal one based on practical considerations. The focus of the two countries shifted to an emphasis on, and the further development of, economic and trade relations as the foundation of their good neighborly friendship. In July 2000, the two heads of state signed the Sino-Russian Beijing Declaration and a joint communiqué on the antimissile issue that affirmed the basic principles of

Sino-Russian relations as they had developed over the preceding decade and reiterated that the relationship was a strategic cooperative partnership based on equality and trust in accordance with the fundamental interests of the people. It played a vital role in promoting a multipolar world and establishing a just and reasonable new international order. The two sides stressed that all the political documents signed and approved by the two countries in the past decade constituted a solid basis for the positive development of their relationship. They reaffirmed their cooperation in international and regional affairs in support of peace, stability, development, and cooperation and their opposition to hegemonism, power politics, bloc politics, and actions that challenged international legal norms such as forceful intervention into the international affairs of sovereign countries. In regional affairs, the two heads of state stressed their determination to encourage cooperation in the framework of the five-power Shanghai Cooperation Organization. In bilateral relations, they reaffirmed their explicit stance on the boundary issues, committed themselves to cooperate on the joint development of certain islands in the boundary river and nearby waters, and to settle the as-yet-to-be-determined section of their boundary through constructive and practical dialogue. In sum, they affirmed the accomplishments of the Yeltsin era with respect to Sino-Russian relations and laid a solid foundation for the development of the Sino-Russian relationship in the new century.

The new stage of Sino-Russian relations was reflected in a number of ways.

1. The strategic partnership opened new areas of cooperation. The Beijing Declaration indicated the two countries' respect for independence, sovereignty, and territorial integrity and opposition to any attempt, domestic or foreign, to foment separatism that threatened national unity. They agreed that ethnic separatism, international terrorism, religious extremism, and transnational criminal activity represented serious threats to the security of sovereign states and world peace and stability and that they would take concrete and effective measures to combat such activities. Such sentiments had not been expressed previously. They embraced global cooperation but emphasized cooperation in Central Asia. China and Russia placed a high priority on promoting military trust and mutual cooperation in border areas and on further strengthening cooperation in these areas.

2. Strategic cooperation will assume more concrete form in the field

of politics as well. The two countries will further develop their political relations while focusing on comprehensive cooperation in economics and trade and in the scientific, technological, and military fields. The Beijing Declaration said that the two countries would expand their cooperation in a number of specific fields and that Russia might participate in China's Western Development plan, specifically in the oil and gas projects. The two governments signed an agreement on continued cooperation in the field of energy, including nuclear power, as well as an agreement between the Bank of China and Russia's Foreign Economic Bank.

3. On the Taiwan issue, the Beijing Declaration and the joint communiqué on the antimissile issue strengthened the consensus of the two sides. Russia not only restated its position that the People's Republic of China is the only legal government of China, that Taiwan is an inseparable part of Chinese territory, and that the Taiwan issue is an internal Chinese affair but also stressed its new stance of "Four No and Two Against"; that is, it did not support Taiwanese independence, did not accept the notion of either two Chinas or one China, one Taiwan, did not support weapons sales to Taiwan, had no tolerance for foreign intervention in the Taiwan issue (which would only increase tension in the region), was against Taiwan's entry into the United Nations or any other international organization limited to sovereign states, and was against involving Taiwan in any foreign missile defense system in any form that would seriously harm regional stability.

4. To further consolidate the Sino-Russia strategic partnership and advance it to another level in the new century, the two heads of state raised the new task of drafting a fundamental document to govern relations between the two countries, that is, a Sino-Russian good neighbor treaty of friendship and cooperation. China and the Soviet Union signed the Sino-Soviet Treaty of Friendship, Alliance, and Mutual Assistance in 1950, but the treaty lapsed in the mid-1960s and was abrogated automatically when its thirty-year term expired. On July 16, 2001, China and Russia signed the Sino-Russian Good Neighbor Treaty of Friendship and Cooperation in order to establish their relations on a solid footing. The treaty states that, on the basis of the Five Principles of Peaceful Coexistence, the two countries will develop a long-term and overall strategic partnership embracing good neighborliness, friendship, cooperation, and mutual trust, that they will solve their disputes only by peaceful means, that they promise not to engage in the first use of nuclear weapons, and

that they support each other's policy of maintaining national unity and territorial integrity. The new friendship treaty provides a more solid legal basis for their relations.

5. The two countries have strengthened their cooperation with Central Asian countries. On the foundation of mutual trust and cooperation mechanisms that the five countries agreed to in 2001 with respect to boundary issues, the Shanghai Cooperation Organization—consisting of China, Russia, Kyrgystan, Kazakhstan, Tajikistan, and Uzbekistan—came into being.

Notwithstanding this positive atmosphere, there are some problems in the relationship that warrant our attention:

1. The development of economic and trade relations has not kept up with political development. The positive political relations between China and Russia provided appropriate conditions for expanding bilateral economic relations. The complementarity of the two economies with respect to product mix, industrial structure, and import-export mechanisms augured well for the expansion of trade and economic relations. But a large gap opened up between what was possible and what actually occurred. In the 1990s, there was considerable fluctuation in the volume of two-way Sino-Russian trade rather than a steady increase, and neither side could be said to be among the major trading partners of the other. In 1998, for example, two-way trade was just US$5.48 billion, accounting for 1.7 percent of China's foreign trade and 5 percent of Russia's. The trade volume increased to US$5.7 billion in 1999, US$8.4 billion in 2000, and US$10 billion in 2001.[3] These figures contrast sharply with Sino-U.S. trade, which was US$80.4 billion in 2001, and Sino-Japanese trade, which was US$90 billion in that same year. The value of U.S. and Japanese trade with Russia also far exceeded that of China's trade with Russia.

2. The Russian scholar Alexander Lukin pointed out: "China is developing vigorously; it is a regional power seeking world status. China has given us reason to suppose that its successful development will enable it to join the ranks of the leading powers."[4] But some Russians are skeptical about China's development, and others even deliberately propagate the China threat theory. Some say that Chinese businesspeople are like a "huge water pump" sucking up Russia's resources and hard currency. The delineation of the Sino-Russian boundary also aroused some controversy. Of the islands in the Heilongjiang River, 538 belong to Russia, while 614 belong to China, and, of the islands in the Ussuri River, 147 belong to

Russia, while 157 belong to China. As a result, Russia had to cede about fifteen square kilometers of territory to China. In addition, China got the right of free navigation in the drainage area adjacent to Heixiazi Island and the right of navigation to the Pacific Ocean via the lower reaches of the Tumen River (the Russia-Korea boundary river). Some leaders in the Russian Far East oppose the boundary treaty because they think that Russia gave away too much. Leaders in Russia's Maritime Province were unwilling to give up even an inch of territory and wanted to abolish or amend the agreement on the eastern sector of the Sino-Russian boundary. Officials in Khabarovsk opposed the clause stating: "The two sides agree that all kinds of ships, including military vessels, can pass freely between Wusuli River and the Amur [Heilongjiang] River near Khabarovsk." This agreement merely restored the boundary line defined in the 1860 Treaty of Beijing and the 1861 Protocol.[5] On numerous occasions, the Russian government expressed its willingness to maintain the provisions of the treaty. Thanks to the common efforts of the Chinese and the Russian governments, the Sino-Russian boundary issue has been basically settled.

The notion that China is a potential threat to Russia has not been articulated officially by Russia, but it exists in Russian academic and political circles and even at the semiofficial level.[6] However, belief in the existence of a China threat is not the mainstream of Russian opinion. According to a public opinion poll conducted by Russian newspapers in May 2002, 66 percent of Russians think that China is a friendly country, while only 4 percent think that it is a threat.[7]

China's Strategic Choices vis-à-vis Russia

A rising China should keep the following points in mind when dealing with Sino-Russian relations. First is that, with respect to China's relations with all the major powers, the Sino-Russian relationship is the best one, based on mutual respect and trust and a model for the relations with other large countries. Second, Russia plays a unique strategic role in the process of China's rise to world power status. It has been the largest supplier of modern military technology and equipment, including Kirov-class submarines, modern destroyers, SU 27-37 fighters, and radar guidance systems to the People's Liberation Army, and has, thereby, made major contributions to upgrading China's military capabilities. In addition, Russia's abundant natural resources, such as oil, gas, and timber, are in great demand in China's economic construction. Third, cooperation with Russia to promote security and stability in Central Asia is vital for the security and stability of China's northwest border. Fourth, settlement of the Sino-Russian boundary has given China a secure northern border for the first time since Russia became China's northern neighbor in 1688. Fifth, the Sino-Russian relationship is a normal friendship not aimed against any third country. Therefore, Russia and China can separately develop their own relations with the United States, Japan, and Europe without undermining their relations with each other. China did not think that Russia would sacrifice the Sino-Russian relationship to attract the United States when Moscow improved its relations with Washington after 9/11, nor does it regard Russia as a potential enemy or threat. It firmly believes that any attempt to undermine Sino-Russian relations would cause equal harm to both countries and would not be in accord with Russian interests as long as the present relations are mutually beneficial. Therefore, China should not respond to the small number of Russians who clamor about a so-called China threat by invoking a Russia threat. China is not a threat to Russia, nor is Russia a threat to China. The strategic interests of the two countries impel them to carry out strategic cooperation. Sixth, the rise of China and Russia points to a multipolar world. It is in the interests of both countries to protect and promote the cause of multipolarization. The rise of only China or only Russia would not lead to a stable multipolar world.

The triangular relations among China, Russia, and the United States merit our attention. An important factor in the historic normalization of Sino-U.S. relations in the early 1970s was the two countries' common strategic interests in opposing Soviet hegemonism. From the beginning, therefore, the Sino-U.S. relationship was embedded in the triangular relations among China, Russia (the Soviet Union), and the United States.

If, initially, triangular relations took the form of cooperation between China and the United States to oppose the Soviet Union in the 1970s and early 1980s, the de facto alliance between Beijing and Washington vis-à-vis Moscow fundamentally changed in the last phase of the Cold War and in the post–Cold War 1990s. After enunciating its independent foreign policy in 1982, China continued to develop its relations with the United States while beginning to normalize its relations with the Soviet Union, a process brought to full fruition after the collapse of the Soviet Union. China and Russia share the strategic goal of opposing U.S. hegemony as manifested in the eastward expansion of NATO, the expansion of the scope of the Japan-U.S. Security Treaty, the Chechen and Taiwan separatist issues, the problem of the former Yugoslavia, and the bombing of the Chinese embassy in Yugoslavia. At the same time, acting on their own national interests, China and Russia both give priority to and seek to improve and develop their relations with the United States.

After 9/11, the interaction of China, Russia, and the United States entered a third stage as Moscow and Washington drew closer to combat international terrorism. Important changes occurred in Russia's policy toward the United States. Although Russia remains vigilant regarding NATO's eastward expansion and the U.S. presence in Central Asia and lays considerable emphasis on its relations with China and India, objectively speaking, it prioritizes its relations with the United States. It views internal separatism as manifested by the situation in Chechnya and terrorism as its major security threat. Putin took advantage of 9/11 to recalibrate Russian policy toward the United States while vigorously asserting Russia's own interests when they differed from those of the United States.

When Russia temporarily drew closer to the United States, this posed no threat to the Sino-U.S. relationship. Later, when Russia pulled further apart from the United States, this likewise had little, if any, effect on Sino-U.S. relations. Despite China's and Russia's shared strategic interests, relations between Beijing and Moscow should not be seen as fundamentally directed against the United States. This would be an unrealistic view. Every country pursues its own national interest. Russia and China are no exceptions. Even when Moscow moves closer to Washington, there is no need to worry that Russia will sacrifice the Sino-Russian relationship to improve its relations with the United States. Of course, within the triangular relationship among China, Russia, and the United States, there will continue to be adjustments, but the possibility of an alliance between Moscow and Washington directed against Beijing is too far-fetched to take seriously. The strategic partnership and cooperation between China and Russia rest on a solid footing, and their good-neighborly relations are in accord with their national interests. In addition, there are broad prospects for further developing Sino-Russian relations, especially in economics and trade. To sum up, the connection between Russian-U.S. relations and Sino-U.S. relations is not a zero-sum game. Russia's development can parallel China's rise, and China should support Russia's efforts to reestablish itself as a world power because this will hasten the transition to a multipolar world that is in the best interest of both China and Russia.

THE DEVELOPMENT OF SINO-EUROPEAN RELATIONS
AND MULTIPOLARIZATION

Europe Has the Greatest Potential to Become a World Power

Europe is the most intensely developed part of the world, containing over half the more than twenty developed countries. The unification promoted by the European Union has made great progress; Europe already has a unified currency, a unified parliament, unified economic policies, and a unified executive committee. After the Cold War, a number of Central and Eastern European countries applied to enter the European Union, bringing new energy into its development. The present member states of the European Union have a population of nearly 400 million, 100 million more than the United States; a territory of 3.11 million square kilometers, or one-third that of the United States; and a GDP in 2000 of US$7.766 trillion, about 80 percent of that of the United States. In 2003, the European Union saw its number of member states increase to twenty-five, its population reach 450 million, and its GDP rise to US$9.30 trillion. At that time, owing to the appreciation of the euro, the depreciation of the dollar, economic recession in the United States, and the accession of new EU members, the EU GDP exceeded that of the United States.

Europe has an advanced economy and technology, possesses a long history of Western culture, and has the all-around potential to become a world power. Among the competitors for world power status, including also Japan, Russia, China and India, Europe is the most likely to achieve this status first.

Several factors will determine whether a unified Europe becomes a power that enjoys world influence. The first factor is the resolve and courage of the larger European powers to achieve unification. At present, France and Germany are in the forefront of unification, while Britain, an important country, has kept its distance from France and Germany. Britain has been willing to play the role of junior partner to the United States and follow its lead in foreign policy, which has somewhat hampered Europe's unification. The war in Iraq, conducted mainly by the United States and Britain, demonstrated that it is not easy for a united Europe to agree on foreign policy. Europe was divided on the use of force against Iraq. Britain and Italy supported the United States, while France and Germany firmly opposed the use of force and proposed to deal with the Iraq crisis within a UN framework. Most of the new Central and East

European members of NATO supported the United States. The whole of the European Union is not equal to the sum of its parts because of its internal fragmentation, different languages, religions, cultures, nationalities, and national interests inhibiting genuine unity. European countries do not need unification to develop their economies, or, perhaps, the impetus of unification has been replaced by the process of global unification. In recent years, European unification has not produced a strong impetus for development. The addition in 2002 and 2004 of ten new EU members, namely, Poland, the Czech Republic, Hungary, Slovakia, Slovenia, Lithuania, Latvia, Estonia, Malta, and Cyprus, increased the population of the European Union to some 450 million people, but the effect of these mostly less developed countries on the development of the European Union was hard to predict at the time.

Germany's development had a huge influence on European integration, and whether the German economy can sustain its high growth rate is of vital importance to continued European integration. After World War II, Germany developed faster than any other European country. In 1950, it commenced its third period of rapid growth. (The first was 1870–1913, the second 1919–1933.) This third spurt lasted thirty years. During this period, Germany's per capita income shot up from US$320 in 1949 to US$10,837 in 1979—an increase of over thirtyfold in thirty years— to a point higher than the U.S. per capita income, which in 1979 was US$9,595.

Germany was divided during the Cold War. East Germany and West Germany were the front line of the Cold War. The two countries were hostile to each other for a long time, but the spirit of national unification endured. When the Cold War ended, the two German states were reunited as West Germany swallowed up East Germany. After 1990, Germany resumed its place among the great powers of Europe, and its strength far exceeded that of Britain, France, or Italy.

Following World War II, Germany became one of the two locomotives of European integration after it had made a clean break with militarism, anti-Semitism, and Nazism and engaged in a process of national introspection. It has engaged in profound self-criticism regarding its role in unleashing two world wars and bringing disasters to humanity; it has admitted its culpability and apologized to the European countries that suffered as a result of its actions and, thereby, earned their forgiveness and trust. Its state constitution excludes the possibility of reversing the verdict on German war crimes; it has educated its young people in a spirit of "Europeanism" and achieved a popular consensus. It has repudiated its past dream of dominating Europe and now sees itself as a constituent of Europe rather than its master. It is no longer the source of European wars but a keeper of the peace and an engine of European growth. Germany first became reconciled with France and then promoted the European integration process together with France. Its development became the impetus for European economic development.

Germany's second unification in the twentieth century took place in the 1990s. The collapse of the Soviet Union made the unification of the two German states unexpectedly easy, like manna falling from heaven with no expenditure of force, albeit lots of money, making this manna very expensive. Germany was the greatest beneficiary of the end of the Cold War. Its power was enhanced; its population and territory were greatly increased on unification. It had already been the strongest country in Europe prior to unification; unification further strengthened its position.

Unification brought to Germany not only joy but also trouble. Contrary to expectations, instead of promoting stronger economic growth, reunification was a brake on the economy. In 2002, according to German economic statistics, the unemployment rate reached a new high of 11.3 percent, 37,700 companies went bankrupt, and the economic growth rate was a mere 0.2 percent, the lowest in Europe. Some scholars even thought that Germany might become the second Japan, with a stagnating economy. Since it had been Europe's engine of development, this downturn in its economy was a cause of great anxiety.

How Europe manages its relations with the United States is key to whether it will become an authentic world power. The United States exerts a huge influence on political and military affairs in Europe via NATO and its eastward expansion. Europe's actions during the Yugoslav Wars and the Kosovo War show that, by itself, the European Union cannot solve problems arising in Europe without U.S. help and participation. In contrast, the issues emerging in Europe, such as the rise of the right wing, xenophobia, and the increased problem of unemployment, have not disappeared in the process of European integration but have become exacerbated and likely to persist for a long time. Moreover, most of the medium and smaller countries in Europe have little interest in competing with the United States for the position of superpower. They are concerned with practical interests rather than investing more money in building a stronger European army. They are not keen on establishing a European military force and apparently have no objections to the United States playing a leading role in Europe. They do not want to free themselves from the United States. Britain had significant disagreements with France and Germany over European defense issues. France and Germany preferred an independent European defense, while Britain insisted on coordination with the United States.[8] As long as Europe remains in the shadow of the United States, it will be unable to exert much influence in the world or become an independent pole of power, let alone a superpower. Therefore, some critics charge that the United States wanted to enlarge NATO to expand its own influence in Europe and that an enlarged NATO would become even more dependent on U.S. leadership. The strong military and political presence of the United States in Europe is detrimental to the prospect of Europe becoming an independent pole of world power, notwithstanding its great power potential.

After two rounds of post–Cold War expansion, NATO has absorbed ten Eastern European countries. These new member states mostly followed the lead of the United States on the Iraq War and criticized the antiwar standpoints of France and Germany. U.S. secretary of defense Donald Rumsfeld intentionally exaggerated the divergence among European countries by dividing the continent into new and old Europe. Americans paid little attention to Europe and believed that the United States would have more freedom of action with the albatross of Europe removed from around its neck. The Afghan War demonstrated this point. The U.S. plan to attack northern Iraq from Turkey, a NATO member, was frustrated by Turkey's refusal to allow its territory to be used for this purpose. Decisions like this exacerbate mistrust between the United States and European members of NATO.

Some analysts expressed pessimism about the trend of U.S.-European relations. For instance, the U.S. scholar Charles Kupchan wrote in *The End of the American Era* that conflicts between the two sides went beyond trade, that the traditional alliance partners were changing into strategic competitors, and that the European Union was bound to become an opponent of the United States and would challenge its hegemony. He predicted that the next clash of civilizations would occur between Europe and the United States, a clash that could spell the end of the West.[9] Another U.S. scholar, John Mearsheimer, even supposed that Germany might become a competitor of the United States.[10]

The aforementioned three issues have an enormous influence on the prospects for European integration and Europe becoming a world power. If they are not effectively managed, then Europe may forfeit its position as the most likely candidate for world power status.

Sino-European Relations and China's Strategic Choice

Among China's relations with other emerging world powers, the Sino-European relationship is unique. China has no significant conflicts of national interest with Europe apart from the fact that a few European countries openly criticize it on matters of ideology and human rights and sometimes equivocate over Taiwan. It enjoys good trade relations with Europe, and Europe is one of the focal points of its economic opening up. Common interests outweigh any divergences of opinion, and cooperation trumps any conflicts and confrontation. As emerging world powers, China and Europe are not in competition with each other. Each sees the other's emergence as a world power as natural and inevitable.

Compared with Russia, Japan, and India, Europe is the least influenced by the China threat theory. European countries are more at ease with the prospect of China becoming a world power. In the eyes of many European countries, China's strength is a good thing rather than a threat to the world; a weak and unsuccessful China would pose more of a threat.

The Sino-European relationship is stable. China should continue to cooperate with Europe in promoting multipolarization. Although the conflicts between the United States and France and Germany over the Iraq War were temporary and subsequently subsided, they demonstrated that multipolarization is in accord with China's interests as well as Europe's. Both China and Europe want to maintain the authority of the UN Security Council, oppose U.S. unilateralism, and advocate world peace and stability. China should firmly grasp this point and further develop substantial political and economic relations with Europe.

One Mountain Can Accommodate Two Tigers: Improving Sino-Japanese Relations via Multilateral Cooperation

Is China a Threat to Japan?

Japan and China are the two most important countries in East Asia; their relations directly affect the stability of Asia and the world. Japan is among

China's neighbors with a population of over 120 million people and a territory of 380,000 square kilometers. It was the only Asian country among the world powers in the nineteenth century. It was also one of the fastest-developing countries after World War II. It created the Japanese miracle during the 1960s–1980s, and its GNP surpassed that of the Soviet Union within twenty years to become the world's second largest economy after the United States.

In Japan, people were discussing not only whether China posed a threat to Japan but also how to deal with a strong China. Japanese newspapers and magazines refer to three forms of the China threat. First is that China's remarkable economic development will soon make it a world economic power. Second is that its products are strongly competitive and that China is becoming the factory of the world. Third, growing imports from China will hollow out Japanese industry. An important research report published in 2002 indicated that Chinese manufactures at the time were mostly in the processing industry and that China still lagged behind in the fields of capital-intensive and high-technology manufacturing industries. Its processing industry depended on imported parts and equipments, so most of the added value was produced outside China. It had no advantage in design, marketing, planning, research and development, and management in manufacturing industry, so its economy was only one-quarter that of Japan and its per capita GDP only one-fortieth of Japan's. Its advantage lay mainly in its abundant labor force. Therefore, its economy did not present a threat to Japan's; the two countries' relations were overwhelmingly complementary rather than competitive. China-Japan economic relations, therefore, were a win-win situation.[11]

Other Japanese experts also dismissed the notion of a China threat. There are many medium and small countries in China's neighborhood. Among all these countries, why are there so many people in Japan who view China as an economic threat? Which part of the China threat—the real or the illusory—should be given greater weight? These experts concluded their analysis by saying that whatever threat existed came not from China alone but from the global corporations that were using China as a stage for competing in the global market. The real question, they argued, was what strategy should Japan employ to respond to these challenges? The real threat came not from China but from Japan's domestic problems.[12]

In 2002, when for the first time since World War II China surpassed the United States as the number one source of exports to Japan, even though some Japanese believed that imports from China would intensify Japan's deflation, the trade volume between the two countries, which soared to US$100 billion, signaled that Sino-Japanese economic relations had entered a new stage. Trade with Japan accounted for one-sixth of China's foreign trade, and Japan became China's largest trading partner, accounting for 13 percent of Japan's trade. China became Japan's second largest trading partner.

Some Americans think that China is not only a large exporter but also a large importer with roughly equal volumes of exports and imports. The key point is that, when the U.S., European, and Japanese economies are depressed, China's economic progress inspires hope throughout the world. Its development in the last decade has been more significant for the world economy than even Japan's rapid rise after World War II. The U.S. economy benefits at least as much as it loses from China's economic development. To sum up, China's development is both an opportunity and a threat.

Twenty-first-Century Japan: In Decline but Capable of Being a World Power

Japan has experienced significant domestic political changes and suffered economic stagnation for most of the past decade and a half. Its GDP stagnated or declined for ten consecutive years; Japanese corporate bankruptcies increased, and unemployment became a growing problem, rising to 6 percent in 2003, the highest since World War II. Nonperforming loans of Japanese banks equaled 36 percent of GDP. During the 1990s, the Nikkei Index dropped precipitously, Japan's national debt soared, and the yen depreciated in value. Japan's standing in the global competitive index plummeted from the top spot in 1989–1992 to twenty-sixth in 2001. Its future prospects with regard to competitiveness looked equally bleak. According to a 2000–2001 survey of seventy-five countries conducted by Harvard University, Japan, which had always been regarded as a leader in applied technology, ranked twenty-first in the application of information technology; the Japanese ranked tenth in ownership of personal computers and twentieth in Internet use.

With regard to politics, the party system, formerly dominated by the Liberal Democratic Party with the Socialist Party and others in opposition, has changed to one in which right-wing conservative parties that seek to amend Japan's peace constitution, deny past war crimes, and support sending troops overseas to enlarge its international influence have emerged. Since the 1990s, the Japanese government has accomplished little with respect to systematic reform and has taken only palliative measures, alleviating the symptoms rather than getting to the roots of problems. The effect has been to exacerbate an already bad situation instead of solving the problems that brought about further economic depression, political turmoil, more unemployment, worsening public security, and higher crime rates. The roots of these crises lie in the Japanese system itself. The model, which created the economic miracle, has been unable to adapt to post–Cold War changes and the challenge of globalization.

Japan has not abandoned its hope of regaining its position as a world power; rather, a species of Japanese chauvinism has emerged that resulted from efforts to stir the pot of Japanese nationalist sentiment. It differs from the militarism of the past because the Japanese people have keenly felt the pain of war and most Japanese oppose resort to war as a means of upgrading their country's international position. Yet the rise of chauvinism is an indicator of dissatisfaction with Japan's current international position. On the one hand, it is a means for people who are unhappy with the way things are to let off steam; on the other hand, it is an attempt to stir up the Japanese national spirit by appealing to a crisis mentality with the end of changing Japanese psychology to demand an enhancement of Japan's international position. Right-wing elements in the country add fuel to the fire by trumpeting the so-called China threat, while some others propose that Japan should say no to the United States. They hope to find a way out of the current crisis by explicitly defining the goal of transforming Japan into a world power.

Moreover, Japan has the capability of achieving this. It remains the second largest economy in the world, has the second largest military expenditures, and was the second largest trading country in the world at the beginning of the twenty-first century. It also had enormous foreign currency reserves, exceeding the combined total of the United States, Canada, Britain, France, and Italy. In addition, its overseas net capital reached US$1,157.9 billion at the end of 2000, first in the world, and its Office of Development Assistance was also the largest in the world. In 2000, Japanese per capita GDP calculated in terms of the exchange rate was US$37,000; the technological level of Japan's manufacturing industry is on the top worldwide. Japanese products that dominated the world market included CD players, MD players, DVD players, camcorders, digital cameras, and vehicular guidance systems, among household electronic equipment; silicon materials, semiconductor resin package materials, ceramic tubes for integrated circuits, liquid crystal monitors, lithium batteries, CD-ROM drives, floppy disk drive, etc., in the fields of electronic materials and components and parts; and machine tools, industrial robots, semiconductor manufacturing equipment, semiconductor abrading and cutting equipment, duplicators, shipbuilding equipment, motorcycles, limousines, etc., in the fields of machinery and equipment. Japan is the third largest producer of steel in the world, behind only China and the United States, but its output of high-grade steel exceeds that of China, and it was the largest exporter of steel in the world at the end of the twentieth century. It also ranked at or near the top in motor vehicle production, digitally controlled machine tools, industrial robots, and shipbuilding. It was also one of the largest creditor nations in the world, while the United States was the largest debtor nation. Japan is still the wealthiest large nation in the world, although its people are reluctant spenders. Though its overall competitiveness has declined a great deal, its scientific and technological competitiveness is still second after the United States. It invests a lot in scientific research and development, next only to the United States, and more than France, Germany, and Britain combined, including the second largest amount of government spending in this area. It has the second largest number of researchers in the world, behind only the United States. It has the highest average national education level of any country, the most precious resource for it economic and social development. It also boasts the longest average life expectancy—77.10 years for men and 83.99 years for women in 1999. As the world's second largest economy, it is much stronger than other developed countries, apart from the United States, in economic scale and power. For instance, in the early twenty-first century, its GDP was 4.4 times, and its per capita GDP 44.4 times, that of China's. Though China's economic growth rate is much higher than Japan's, the economic comparison of China and Japan can be described only as relations between a rising developing country and a stagnant developed one. Japan is still the leader in many high-tech fields.

Like China, Japan is seeking to become a world power. The strategic aims of Japan are not only to keep its position as an economic power but also to strive for the position of a political and military power and then to become a world power in line with its overall strength. Now it is at the crossroads of development, and its future depends on the results of its reform and the choice of which road it takes. Again like China, it has an opportunity to reemerge as a world power. As long as it can draw the proper lessons from its painful history and properly manage Sino-Japanese as well as Sino-U.S. relations, it is positioned to become a world power faster than China. Therefore, it is China's neighbor as well as one of its rivals for world power. It is also the most important of China's trading partners, with the largest volume of total trade.

Nevertheless, Japan lacks four things to become a world power: (1) Quite a few of its right-wing politicians entertain the wild ambition to establish hegemony over East Asia. It lacks the courage to face up to what it did in the past and only tries to cover up its historical misdeeds. It lacks the political courage to become a world power. (2) It has thousands of politicians but lacks leaders with vision as well as a grand strategy to guide it into the future. (3) It is good at imitating, but it lacks the necessary cultural creativity to become a world power. (4) Its goods and capital circulate all over the world, but it is not well liked in East Asia.

Competition or Cooperation: Strategic Choices in Sino-Japanese Relations

Properly managing Sino-Japanese relations is one of the tasks facing China on its path toward becoming a world power. We should not regard the process of China and Japan becoming world powers as a zero-sum game. If China becomes a world power, this is no obstacle to Japan likewise becoming a world power, and vice versa. Some people are accustomed to invoking the old saying that one mountain cannot accommodate two tigers or to seeing things as a zero-sum game when they consider the geopolitics of the Sino-Japanese relationship. They think that China and Japan cannot live side by side and that their relationship is necessarily antagonistic. In reality, the two countries enjoy cooperative and complementary relations. They are interdependent, and their cooperation is essential if the goal of unifying East Asia is ever to be achieved. East Asia will flourish if the two countries cooperate and be weaker if they do not. East Asian unity is dependent on Sino-Japanese cooperation, and only via such cooperation can unity be realized. Indeed, the goal of unity can serve as a new foundation for Sino-Japanese cooperation. China's population constitutes 60 percent of the total population of East Asia, and, without China, East Asia cannot be strong. Japan's GDP accounts for roughly two-thirds of East Asia's total; therefore, without Japan, East Asia will not be prosperous.

The Sino-Japanese relationship rests on four pillars, namely, economic cooperation, historical issues, security protection, and Japan's domestic political system. At present, the domestic political system has changed a lot since the early 1990s. The previous consensus regarding Sino-Japanese relations shared by the Liberal Democratic Party, the Social Democratic Party, and Komeito has largely eroded. The older generation of Japanese politicians committed to maintaining normal relations with China has retired from the stage of history, and the rise of right-wing politicians has complicated Sino-Japanese relations. Meanwhile, Japan's left wing is less committed than hitherto to Sino-Japanese cooperation. Japanese policy toward China has hardened, and historical issues and security issues have become more prominent and problematic. The remaining pillar—economic cooperation—though still operative, is weaker than it was a generation or so ago. After China and Japan established formal diplomatic relations in 1972, their trade and economic relations developed very rapidly, including exchanges of personnel. Japan became China's largest trading partner and second largest source of FDI after Hong Kong, Macao, and the Taiwan area.[13] It also provided the largest amount of government preferential loans to China, more than the Asian Development Bank and the World Bank combined.[14]

The present state of Sino-Japanese relations, however, is unsatisfactory. The problems that exist between China and Japan have seriously affected public attitudes in both countries, as demonstrated by numerous polls revealing the low level of esteem and high level of antipathy in which the Chinese hold the Japanese, and vice versa.

Japan and China face the critical task of devising new ways to promote the Sino-Japanese relationship in the twenty-first century. This relationship has stagnated since 1992 owing to numerous disturbances. These disturbances include disputes over sovereignty of the Diaoyu Islands as well as the U.S.-Japan Security Treaty, the Taiwan issue, and Japan's culpability for its aggressive war against China in the 1930s and 1940s. China and Japan hold opposite views on these issues. China thinks that the Diaoyu Islands have always been Chinese territory, while Japan thinks that these islands belong to it. China views the U.S.-Japan Security Treaty as a product of the Cold War that should have been dissolved rather than expanded once the Cold War was over. Enlargement of the scope of the treaty to include areas adjacent to Japan was clearly aimed at China and constitutes an important part of the U.S. strategy to contain China. By acquiescing to treaty revision, Japan partnered with Washington's hostile anti-China policy. There are actually a range of views in China regarding the U.S.-Japan Security Treaty, but the key area of concern is whether Japan interferes in China's internal affairs should an incident occur in the Taiwan Strait.

The Japanese assert that the treaty is directed against regional instability, not against China, and is intended to guarantee East Asian stability. At the same time, some senior Japanese officials contend that the treaty applies to "the situation in Japan's periphery," including Taiwan. Other Japanese speak evasively and say that China need not concern itself because Japan would consider intervening in the Taiwan issue only if China first resorted to military force and the United States responded in kind. Because these are such remote contingencies, the issue should not be emphasized in Sino-Japanese relations.[15]

China thinks that it has displayed a very lenient attitude toward Japan's past war of aggression against it. It was magnanimous in its treatment of Japanese prisoners of war; it declined to exact war reparations, and its leaders adopted a forward-looking attitude rather than dwelling on the past. But Japan has been unwilling to reflect deeply on its actions during its war of aggression against China. It has attempted to reverse the verdict on the war and even to deny its crimes, something that is intolerable. Even the Americans, who see Japan as an ally and want to promote U.S.-style democracy in Asia, think that the biggest problem in Asia is that "Japan, the most powerful and successful democratic country in this region, has difficulties in becoming a prototype because of its cultural peculiarity and its reluctance to confess its colonial evil doings in the 20th century."[16]

Though quite a few Japanese believe that they should reflect deeply on their country's war responsibility, many others cannot face up to that history, for a number of different reasons. First, they say that the situation has changed and that China should understand that Japan's failure to acknowledge war crimes is largely due to changes in the international situation over the more than six decades since the end of World War II. Second, Japan itself was a victim of war as the only country ever subjected to atomic bombing. Third, as a matter of national pride and self-respect, Japan should not publicly admit to and apologize for its war because it is trying to stress its glorious national history and should not condemn the activities of earlier generations who died in the war. A distinctive feature of Japanese society is not laying blame on the dead. Confessing war crimes would be detrimental to the task of fostering a new generation of young Japanese who can take pride in their national identity. Fourth, what is past is past. Japan has corrected its past mistakes, and its Constitution guarantees no further aggression against other countries. Therefore, Asian countries should trust it and stop making trouble. Fifth, the war with China was a war of national liberation for Asia. This perspective completely denies the historic facts of Japan's invasion of China and demands that information about the so-called comfort women, the Nanjing Massacre, etc. be purged from textbooks because it promotes a kind of national masochism.[17] All these ideas are unacceptable to the Chinese people. An overwhelming majority of Chinese think that Japan's attitude toward its past aggression is the biggest obstacle to Sino-Japanese relations. Some Japanese scholars also think that the root question lies in the ambivalent attitude of the Japanese to World War II. Although the Japanese people were also victims of the war, the Chinese people suffered the most. Moreover, the key point is that Japan launched the war, something that the Japanese should reflect on. This obstacle can be eliminated only through Japan's sincere understanding of history.[18] Japan's attempt to cast aside its status as a defeated nation embodies a serious risk in that some leaders want to deny its past aggression and propose to amend Article IX of the Peace Constitution, which would only exacerbate the divergence and mistrust between China and Japan in the post–Cold War era.

This change reflects Japan's altered strategy toward dealing with China. During the 1970s and 1980s, especially during the 1980s, when it had serious conflicts with the United States because of economic friction, Japan had a positive view toward China. Quite a few Japanese wanted to help China become prosperous in order to create a counterweight to U.S. economic hegemony. As long as Japan held to this notion—despite having, under pressure from the United States, occasionally had to adopt some anti-China policies—it pursued a prudent China policy. For instance, on the Taiwan issue, it made no clear commitment to come to the aid of the United States should it become involved in a military confrontation with China over Taiwan.

Even in the early 1990s, when the United States imposed sanctions on China, Japan maintained normal relations with China. But its decade-long economic recession and stagnation beginning in 1991 undermined its leading position in Asia and shook its strength and confidence regarding its interchanges with China. The early 1990s was also the time when the so-called China threat first surfaced in Japan. Some scholars pointed out many Japanese had become fearful of a rising China as a potential threat to its neighbors even though China had no intention of expanding. Another issue arising from Japan's economic recession and China's economic development was the view that Japan should pare its economic assistance to China and adopt stricter measures regarding economic and trade issues to limit Japanese imports from China. For example, this led to disputes over Japanese agricultural imports from China in 2001.

In 1995, China conducted a nuclear test. In 1996, it engaged in military exercises in order to defend its national unity and oppose Taiwanese independence. In 1997 and 1998, when the countries of East Asia confronted a financial crisis and hoped that Japan would assist them, Japan felt that it lacked the wherewithal to do so, while China acted positively. Instead of feeling pleased, Japan experienced a sense of loss and thought that China would replace it as the leading country in East Asia. Its mistrust of China gradually took the upper hand. Meanwhile, its military expenditures exceeded 1 percent of total GDP for the first time, and it approved the revised draft U.S.-Japan Security Treaty in 1995, adding the ambiguous clause regarding its expanded zone of interest to the communiqué regarding the treaty in April 1996. This gave it the flexibility to support the United States in the future. At the same time, it declared that it would reduce and then terminate its aid to China at the end of the 1990s.

Owing to mistrust of China, Japan's strategy toward China has changed from the 1970s and 1980s policy of aiding it and promoting its development as a way of reducing U.S. pressure to one of strengthening its alliance with the United States and using bilateral and multilateral mechanisms to balance or restrict China.[19]

Problem solving within the original framework is difficult when Japan's China strategy has changed so much. Therefore, policies and strategy regarding the Sino-Japanese relationship must be reconsidered.

When adopting a new strategy toward Japan, China must take into account Japan's own changed China policy. In essays published in 2001, a number of U.S. scholars pointed out that Japan sees China as a rising power whose development trajectory is still unclear. Therefore, it behooves Japan to cultivate friendship with China and be on guard against it at the same time. Japan should promote greater transparency with China regarding national security issues and resort to peaceful negotiations to solve problems, but it should also keep a sharp eye on China and pursue a policy of soft containment via multilateral engagement, multilateral economic contacts, and multilateral cooperation with China. These scholars further supposed that China would surpass Japan economically by 2010 and become an economic superpower able to control its own future development. Therefore, while maintaining a friendly attitude toward China, Japan had to prepare itself for a range of unknown future contingencies.[20] Japan was also conducting covert nuclear weapons research. In April 2002, Ozawa Ichiro, a member of Japan's Liberal Party, asserted that the country's nuclear power plants have enough plutonium to make three to four thousand nuclear warheads in a very short time and that its military power is not inferior to China's.[21]

The policy of the soft containment of China involves strengthening the U.S.-Japan alliance and cooperating with countries such as South Korea and Australia to keep an eye on China's future development. Japan asked for unambiguous U.S. support in case of a confrontation with China over the issue of the Diaoyu Islands, and it emphasized the anti-China content of the U.S.-Japan Security Treaty. But it failed in its attempt to enlist Southeast Asian countries in containing China. Though ASEAN countries are on guard against China, they do not seek confrontation with it. Meanwhile, we should note that Japan's soft containment policy by no means views China as a serious threat and that Tokyo has not adopted any measures that might jeopardize Sino-Japanese relations with respect to such sensitive issues as Taiwan. It basically abides by the one China principle.

In addition, another major aspect of Japan's new strategy toward China is to promote contact with China on security and economic issues within a multilateral context. Japan initially supposed that China would not attend multilateral conferences or make use of multilateral dialogues such as the ASEAN Regional Forum, but it soon learned that China was even more actively interested in such multilateral security dialogues than it itself was. Moreover, it supported China's application to join the WTO as early as September 1997, well before the United States and Europe.

Naturally, we must pay attention to how far Japanese right-wing politicians will go along the road of military confrontation with China. For instance, Ishihara Shintaro's article calling for the defeat of China as the way to reconstruct Japan is a dangerous signal. This Japanese lunatic publicly proposed this idea. He desires to stir up Japanese nationalism to confront the United States in the east and China in the west and revive the old militarist dream of establishing a Greater East Asian Co-Prosperity Sphere with Japan as its core. He even picked up some clichés from the dustbin of history, like H. G. Wells's idea from his 1933 *The Shape of Things to Come* of achieving world unification centered on Japan in order to evoke the dead "Nippon Spirit" and rejuvenate Japan. In this article, Ishihara displayed the Japanese psychology of utter dejection by saying that Japan "may be the hypocenter of world economic collapse" and sounded the alarm that it would either become the fifty-first state of the United States or be swallowed up by China. On the other hand, Ishihara savagely criticized the jungle law mentality of U.S.-dominated global capitalism, saying that not only the Islamic countries but also all Asian countries, including Japan, "will be caught up in the whirlpool of the U.S. strategy of globalization." At the same time, he suggested that Japan should confront China and establish an Asian network centered on Japan. He expressed the hope that domestic problems would cause China to splinter, which would enable Japan to draw Shanghai into its orbit. Sadly, many despairing Japanese regard this madman as their savior and think that he alone can extricate Japan from its crisis. If the Japanese elevate Ishihara to the prime minister's office, not only would this fail to solve the crisis, but it would also put Japan on the dangerous path toward confrontation with China. Not only would there be no New Japan, but Japan would sink even deeper, along with the hope for a New Asia.[22]

Obviously, if we think we can advance Sino-Japanese relations only after we have solved these three problems, the Sino-Japanese relationship may continue to stagnate or even retrogress. With regard to the territorial issue, it is impossible to expect either China or Japan to abandon its claim to sovereignty over the Diaoyu Islands. Should either side try to solve the dispute by force, this would have an extremely deleterious effect on Sino-Japanese relations. With regard to the U.S.-Japan Security Treaty and the associated Taiwan issue, China cannot agree that the treaty should cover Taiwan, nor can it force the disbandment of the U.S.-Japanese military alliance or demand that Japan renounce the treaty. It is likewise impossible to ask the Chinese people to forget the crimes that Japan committed during its war of aggression, but Japanese civilization has not advanced to the level where it could engage in deep reflection on past history.

It is difficult to improve Sino-Japanese relations, but we cannot retreat in the face of difficulties. As one Japanese scholar has pointed out: "The Japan-China relationship is important and indispensable to both countries. No matter how many conflicts may arise, we should build a foundation that will survive any attempts to harm friendly and cooperative relations. Even when China's and Japan's economic strengths are equal, neither side can afford to ignore the other."[23] Against this background, both China and Japan should think creatively about how to rescue the Sino-Japanese relationship from its present stagnation and raise it to a new level in the twenty-first century.

The Diaoyu Islands issue concerns national dignity, but it is not an urgent issue for either country. They can exercise restraint, maintain the status quo, refrain from taking any action to occupy the islands, and seek ways to pursue joint development and utilization.

Historical issues are a basic problem in Sino-Japanese relations. China insists that Japan reflect deeply on the past. It is also on guard against and resists any Japanese attempts to reverse the verdict on its crimes of aggression during World War II, but it does not regard this point as a prerequisite for developing Sino-Japanese relations. It can keep mum and wait as long as Japan does not do anything to provoke the Chinese people's emotions. In essence, this is an emotional issue and should not be an obstacle to achieving the important political and economic interests of the two countries.

The negative influence that the U.S.-Japan Security Treaty exerts on Sino-Japanese relations is more complicated than the previous two issues insofar as it mainly involves the U.S. containment policy toward China, the issue of Theater Missile Defense, and the Taiwan issue. But neither is it a serious obstacle to Sino-Japanese relations. It is only a theoretical possibility that Japan may follow the United States and join Washington in intervening in the Taiwan issue. Since neither side of the Taiwan Strait plans on taking any definitive action in the near future, the possibility of Japan participating in a U.S. intervention is remote. China will remain vigilant regarding any new developments surrounding the U.S.-Japan Security Treaty, but it can also look for opportunities to promote Sino-Japanese relations in the existing circumstances.

The way out of the present impasse in Sino-Japanese relations lies in preventing the three problems from worsening and damaging the over-all Sino-Japanese relationship rather than in solving them. The main point is to find common political and economic interests and construct "a friendly cooperative partnership toward peace and development in the twenty-first century" based on common interests.[24]

New thinking regarding Sino-Japanese relations may be summarized as follows: (1) Find a common denominator of bilateral political and economic interests and seek a breakthrough in bilateral relations. (2) Pursue common interests within a multilateral framework and promote new bilateral progress in the process of establishing a new political and economic order in East Asia. (3) Establish a system in which China and Japan play equally important roles based on cooperation instead of competition for leadership in East Asia.

Many discussions have addressed the problem of how to advance Sino-Japanese bilateral relations, so, here, I intend to emphasize multilateral cooperation. There are broad prospects for developing Sino-Japanese relations by means of seeking common interests via multilateral cooperation and promoting Sino-Japanese relations in multilateral relations. Regional multilateral cooperation is a new trend after World War II, and regional integration is a worldwide tendency that has occurred simultaneously with globalization. For a long time, regional multilateral cooperation has exerted great influence on the solution of economic, political, and security problems in the region and attracted considerable attention. At the same time, it has played a unique role in fostering bilateral relations.

Franco-German bilateral relations within the EU framework are a successful example of such cooperation. Conflicts between France and Germany arising from geopolitics can be traced up to recent times and became exacerbated to an unprecedented degree owing to the two world wars of the twentieth century. Such conflicts between contiguous countries are difficult to solve bilaterally. From the very beginning, post–World War II European integration involved French attempts to restrict Germany via this process. By subsuming bilateral relations within the framework of regional multilateral cooperation, it successfully solved Franco-German conflicts and promoted friendly Franco-German relations. European integration and Franco-German relations are an example of how to solve bilateral relations through regional multilateral cooperation and provide a model for developing Sino-Japanese relations. Of course, the Sino-Japanese relationship is not the same as the Franco-German relationship, but the two share some similarities in geopolitical terms. Objectively speaking, if the France-Germany axis is the core of European integration, the China-Japan axis could serve as the core of East Asian integration.

East Asia, home to China and Japan, is the fastest-growing and most vigorous region in the world. As the two major powers in this region, China and Japan play leading roles in the regional multilateral cooperation framework and have many common interests and many shared understandings that are the chief factors promoting the development of their relations. Therefore, regional multilateral cooperation can be a powerful impetus to the Sino-Japanese relationship. Regional multilateral cooperation does not mean bypassing bilateral relations or avoiding conflicts and problems in bilateral relations. On the contrary, it is based on Sino-Japanese bilateral relations and aims at further developing Sino-Japanese relations. China and Japan have an objective basis on which to strengthen regional multilateral cooperation as well as practical regional multilateral cooperation mechanisms. Although these are still in a rudimentary stage and have not yet been formalized, they provide a basis for development, for setting directions, and for advancing toward standardization and model building. At present, these mechanisms involve various fields, such as politics, economics, and security affairs, and form a multilevel structure in which formal and informal, official and unofficial complement each other. In addition, there is complementarity between regional and subregional mechanisms. The following three regions are of vital importance to Sino-Japanese relations.

Northeast Asia. Northeast Asia is the center of Sino-Japanese geopolitical relations, the locus of the two countries' direct interests. The Northeast Asian region embraces China, Japan, Russia, South Korea, North Korea, and Mongolia and is home to many complicated conflicts. The United States has a strong interest in this region. China and Japan play leading roles in this region, and their relationship influences peace, stability, and prosperity.

The process of multilateral cooperation in Northeast Asia has developed slowly, and the mechanism has not been completed yet, but the direction has become clearer with time. This helps to clarify the key issue areas in which China and Japan can engage in regional multilateral cooperation in the future.

From an economic perspective, the Northeast Asian region contains about 800 million people, has a GDP of US$5–US$6 trillion, and includes vast areas of China (the northwest, the north, and the east), Japan, the Russian Far East, South Korea, North Korea, and Mongolia. Various regional cooperation schemes have been proposed, including the establishment of a Bohai Gulf economic zone, a Yellow Sea economic zone, and a Japan Sea economic zone, but none of these have been formalized as yet. To date, the Tumen River economic development plan was the most attractive. It was started in 1992 and involved the zone where China, Russia, and North Korea intersect with Japan and South Korea, from which capital and technology were expected to flow. If this multilateral cooperation were to come to fruition, this would further strengthen economic complementarity and reciprocity among Northeast Asian countries. Such cooperation could yet develop, but it has been inhibited by a number of political and security conflicts, especially the situation on the Korean Peninsula. We should further discuss the possibility of cooperation among China, Japan, and South Korea in the Northeast Asian region. These three countries have close economic relations: Japan is China's largest trading partner, China is Japan's second largest trading partner, China is the biggest recipient of South Korean investment, and Japan has close economic relations with South Korea as well. These factors constitute the foundation for further cooperation among these three countries in Northeast Asia.

Since it is not easy to construct a regional security system, dialogue mechanisms can first be established among the countries concerned. China and Russia have already established confidence-building measures. Russia has said that it will soon reach agreement on the Northern Territories issue with Japan, which would help improve Russian-Japanese relations. Japan should make more of an effort to establish diplomatic relations with North Korea, and it should try to initiate security dialogue mechanisms among China–Japan–South Korea, China-Japan-Russia, China–Japan–Russia–South Korea, and China–Japan–South Korea–North Korea as the foundations for a future Northeast Asian security system. The new trend that emerged in 1997 is the ASEAN Plus Three forum, which serves as a coordinator of cooperation between the ASEAN nations and China, Japan, and South Korea and undoubtedly further promotes the connection between China and Japan in multilateral cooperation.

To be sure, the multilateral cooperation machinery for Northeast Asia needs further development. The present focus is on politics and security, whereas economic cooperation is still relatively undeveloped, a sharp contrast to the "hot-economy/cold-politics" situation of the Sino-Japanese bilateral relationship. Multilateral cooperation obviously promotes the development of bilateral relations.

Southeast Asia. Southeast Asia is another subregion where Chinese and Japanese interests intersect. The region's main multilateral cooperation organization is ASEAN, which plays the leading role in multilateral cooperation in the fields of politics, economics, and security, and whose influence even extends to all of East Asia. As indirect participants, China and Japan play influential roles in the multilateral cooperation of this region.

The systematic development of multilateral cooperation in Southeast Asia, beginning with the adoption of common standards, is inseparable from the successful development of ASEAN. In economic terms, regional multilateral cooperation took the form of efforts to develop the ASEAN free trade zone and also facilitated the development of APEC. China and Japan began their multilateral cooperation with ASEAN through APEC. In 1990, then Malaysian prime minister Mahathir put forward a plan for an East Asian economic group comprising ASEAN, China, Japan, and South Korea that smacked strongly of East Asian regionalism. Unfortunately, this plan encountered U.S. opposition and Japanese ambivalence, which hindered the development of multilateral economic cooperation.

The focus of Southeast Asian regional multilateral cooperation has been on dialogue and cooperation regarding political and security issues. The ASEAN Regional Forum, established in 1993, is the only multilateral dialogue machinery in place for politics and security. It centers on ASEAN and attracts many countries, including China, Japan, South Korea, and the United States, and is of vital importance in promoting mutual trust and reciprocity as features of the security environment. The informal East Asian summit, that is, ASEAN Plus Three, constitutes a multilateral political and security dialogue mechanism with ASEAN, on one side, and China, Japan, and South Korea, on the other. It forms the basis for consensus on regional politics and security issues. As such, both Chinese and Japanese leaders pay a lot of attention to it.

China and Japan are involved in various aspects of Southeast Asian multilateral cooperation, to a greater degree even than in Northeast Asia. The development of Southeast Asia is directly connected to various interests of China and Japan, especially their political and economic interests.

Multilateral cooperation in Southeast Asia promotes closer Sino-Japanese bilateral relations and is an important way to enhance mutual understanding between China and Japan.

East Asia. The broadest region for the cooperation between China and Japan is East Asia. At present, APEC is the only multilateral cooperation mechanism that covers all East Asia. It is the fruit of the economic integration of the Asian-Pacific area via multilateral economic cooperation. Since its founding, it has held annual ministerial-level conferences of its member states and, since 1993, has organized informal summit meetings that have served to promote economic cooperation and trade liberalization in the Asian-Pacific region. As two major APEC members, China and Japan enjoy important influence within the organization, partly because of their immense economic interests. The Southeast Asian financial crisis of 1997 provides the best example of why improving Sino-Japanese cooperation is necessary and urgent. APEC provides a favorable venue for the development of bilateral Sino-Japanese relations, promotes dialogue and cooperation at various levels between the two countries, and directly affects the development of their bilateral relations.

APEC's current problems derive from the diversity of its member states, the huge spread in the development levels of its members, and its extraordinarily broad scope. Yet regional multilateral cooperation is essential and has great potential. As such, it will be an important focus of future development for both China and Japan. This raises the issue of whether it is worth considering the establishment of an East Asian multilateral cooperation mechanism that would encompass both the Northeast Asia and Southeast Asia subregions.

The East Asian region comprises China, Japan, South Korea, North Korea, and the ASEAN countries. These countries have long historical and cultural connections as well as practical common interests in the areas of politics, economics, and security. Strengthening multilateral cooperation in East Asia is increasingly their common demand. In 1988, Japan advanced the idea of an East Asian economic circle, intended to encourage the economic integration of East Asia and establish a system of economic cooperation under Japan's leadership. But this proposal evoked little interest from within the region because it was manifestly too obvious a mechanism for advancing Japanese leadership. Yet, in the absence of economic regionalization and integration, the countries of East Asia have difficulty competing with the European Union and NAFTA inasmuch as economic globalization is closely connected to economic regionalization. East Asia must find a road to regional integration. The East Asian economic crisis of 1997 once again placed this issue front and center.

Constructing a system of multilateral cooperation in East Asia requires leadership. As the two largest countries in East Asia, China and Japan should play the leading roles in such an enterprise. Apart from the China-Japan axis, a China-Japan-Indonesia axis and a China–Japan–Indonesia–Malaysia–South Korea axis are also possible sources of leadership. Conditions for developed mechanisms for economic cooperation in East Asia are more mature. The 1997 financial crisis showed that it was time to establish an Asian development bank, an Asian currency system, an Asian trading system, and an Asian economic cooperation organization. Without such mechanisms, Asian countries may pay a greater price when facing a new crisis than they did in 1997. Additional areas of potential East Asian cooperation include science and technology, economic development, ecological and environmental protection, antismuggling and anticrime measures, and antiterrorism. China and Japan share a growing awareness of these issues. To conclude, China and Japan should manage their relations with East Asian countries from the long-term perspective of promoting multilateralism and an East Asian system. As the two largest East Asian countries, they should shoulder the responsibility for promoting and, eventually, establishing an East Asian political and economic order led by East Asians.

In exploring new ways to promote Sino-Japanese relations, both China and Japan have to adjust their mind-sets. They should adopt measures to limit words and actions that undermine Sino-Japanese relations. China has always cherished its friendship with Japan, paid much attention to Japanese reactions to its domestic dialogue and actions, and fully respected reasonable Japanese views. It is normal to publish writers' remarks in newspapers and magazines. As soon as Japan expressed dissatisfaction with a certain article on Sino-Japanese relationship by a Chinese author, China immediately took appropriate measures. In fact, the intention of the article was not at all to undermine Sino-Japanese relations, and its thesis was in line with the goals of peace and friendship between China and Japan. The only problem was that the title of the article was a bit sensational,[25] and it was this title that sparked Japan's unhappiness. Compared with anti-China articles in Japanese newspapers and magazines, this particular problem counted for little, and it certainly bore no comparison to public denials of Japan's historical actions. Nevertheless, the Chinese government criticized the newspaper that had printed the offending article. From this incident, we can see that the Chinese government places considerable emphasis on maintaining Sino-Japanese friendship and tries to limit remarks that may exert a negative influence. On the other hand, China has not devoted sufficient resources to publicizing Japan's positive contributions to China's process of reform and opening up. For example, the Japanese government has loaned 2.26 trillion yen to China, helping promote China's modernization. Japan also played an important role in ending Western sanctions against China imposed after the Tiananmen Incident, but China said little about this. China should increase positive publicity surrounding Sino-Japanese relations in the future.

Japan should also take measures to stabilize Sino-Japanese relations, check the rise of domestic anti-Chinese forces, and curb any further actions to reverse the verdict on the history of Japan's war of aggression. Since the two countries have different political systems, they must take different measures to restrain words and actions that undermine Sino-Japanese relations. The Chinese people can understand these political differences, but they should not be used as excuses for allowing anti-China remarks and action to flourish in Japan, nor should the Japanese government abdicate its responsibility. Serious offenses like denying the Nanjing Massacre and attempts to reverse the verdict on Japan's invasion of China, offenses that not only seriously hurt the feelings of the Chinese people but also undermine Japan's national interests, absolutely must be restricted. It is a fundamental responsibility of Japan to develop Sino-Japanese relations. The Chinese people can wait for Japan to engage in serious reflection on its history, but they cannot tolerate insults to the tens of millions of people who died in the Japanese war of aggression against China. As long as Japan takes appropriate measures, historical issues will not be serious obstacles in the progress of Sino-Japanese relations. Similarly, Japan should take some measures on the Diaoyu Islands issue, restrain the words and actions of the anti-China people that damage Sino-Japanese relations, and prevent incidents that provoke the ire of the Chinese people.

A prerequisite for the development of multilateral cooperation is to ensure that Sino-Japanese bilateral relations do not retrogress from their present position. Multilateral cooperation would be very difficult in such circumstances.

For Japan, the most important issue is how to cope with the reality of China's rise. Several Japanese prime ministers from Koizumi on have rendered positive judgments on the rise of China, which, they have said, contributes to the well-being and security of Asia. These judgments are quite at variance with the alarmist right-wing Japanese rhetoric about the China threat. Former Japanese prime minister Nakasone also voiced a positive view regarding China's rise. He said:

I have a negative attitude toward the China threat theory. China is undoubtedly a big country. Its economy will develop, and its strength will grow in the future, and we cannot deny the natural increase of its power. At present, it is stressing economic development, social stability, and western regional development and tackling environmental issues, especially the water problem in the north. It needs peace to solve these issues. I think its will for peace has been clearly expressed by its access to the WTO and its hosting of the 2008 Olympic Games. It will be a world power and is advancing along this road. It will realize this aim through economic development rather than overseas aggression. Therefore, China and Japan have mutually cooperative relations. The Japanese worry that the huge investments by Japanese companies in China will cause the hollowing out of Japanese industry. This is Japan's responsibility, not China's. It is a natural rule of economics. I think that, as long as China does not suffer serious insults, it will continue practicing peaceful diplomacy. . . . Top state leaders on both sides must tell their people that the two countries have established firm, cooperative, and complementary relations.[26]

If someone like Ishihara Shintaro were to come to power, Japan might take the road of confrontation with China. China and Japan should review their East Asia policies and adopt more positive standpoints to establish an East Asian multilateral cooperation system.

Owing to U.S. policies of containing and blockading China, past multilateral systems in East Asia were all intended to encircle and blockade China. China was also highly suspicious of the Asian security model proposed by the former Soviet Union. As a result, it always had a negative attitude toward or opposed establishing a multilateral system in East Asia. Since the 1980s and 1990s, however, it has significantly altered its policies in this regard, mainly because its relations with East Asian countries have generally improved and it has adopted more open policies toward these countries. In the future, it will have even more positive and proactive views on East Asian multilateral cooperation. As one Japanese scholar put it: "If China does not agree with Japan's concept, it should propose its own design."[27]

Japan should reconsider the issue from the perspective of Sino-Japanese cooperation. The main point is that Japan should not slavishly follow the United States or seek to establish a system of East Asian multilateral cooperation centered on the Japanese-U.S. relationship. By the same token, it should not try to establish a system of East Asian cooperation centered on itself, nor should it seek to utilize an East Asian international order as a means for promoting its own power or establishing itself as a so-called normal nation. Finally, it should not use an East Asian multilateral system to target China.

Asian countries, including China, will find it impossible to accept its proposals for a multilateral East Asian security cooperation system if Japan does any of the following: It talks about promoting East Asian security cooperation and maintaining peace, on the one hand, while seeking to reverse the verdict on Japan's war of aggression against East Asian countries, on the other. It calls for the unity of Asian countries to cope with challenges from North America and Europe, on the one hand, yet tries to build an East Asian security system on the basis of U.S. leadership, on the other. It proposes opposition to nationalism, on the one hand, yet emphasizes its own position as a great power and its centrality, on the other. It stresses the importance of the Sino-Japanese relationship, on the one hand, yet attempts to cope with China as a potential threat through many bilateral security systems and an East Asian multilateral system, on the other. China opposes the United States playing the role of world policeman; it likewise opposes any country acting as a policeman in East Asia.

Neither China nor Japan should seek the leadership of an East Asian multilateral system, either alone or in partnership with countries outside the region. Instead, they should play the leading roles together as East Asian powers on the basis of mutual trust and respect. China has expressed time and again that it will never be the leader, form alliances, or seek to become a superpower. The major issue for China is not becoming the leader but fulfilling its function as an East Asian power more actively.

The following principles should govern the establishment of an East Asian multilateral cooperation system. First is the principle of Asianism, namely, that Asian issues should be solved by Asian countries. Second is the principle of regional openness, namely, that an East Asian multilateral cooperation system should not target or exclude any non–East Asian country. Third is the principle of equality of interests, mutual trust, and consensus through consultation, namely, the idea that the multilateral system does not target any East Asian country and that no East Asian country should join a group or alliance aimed at other East Asian countries. Fourth is the principle of antihegemonism, namely, that East Asian powers such as China, Japan, and Indonesia should play the leading roles in establishing a multilateral cooperation system and should coordinate with each other but that no country should intervene in the internal affairs of another.

Japan should become a genuine Asian country with sincere intentions to be friendly to and cooperate with other Asian countries, rather than a Western country that happens to be located in Asia. For a long time now, Asian countries have regarded Japan as a Western country, but, in recent years, Japan has given consideration to the idea of returning to Asia. Some Japanese believe that Japan should leave Europe and return to Asia. This process is not complete. Some people contend that Japan thinks only about the United States, not about any Asian countries, and that its only desire is to become a military power.[28] Some people even think that Japan's activities in recent years, such as the depreciation of the yen, have betrayed Asian countries and that Asia should abandon its illusions regarding Japan.[29] Japan must play a greater role in and become one of the leading countries of East Asia. Japan and China should respect each other's standpoint, cooperate with each other, and explore a social system that is appropriate to countries with a high population density and that enables people to live and work in peace and contentment. One Japanese social activist, Kimuraka Zumi, wrote that Japan and China can contribute to the peace and stability of Asia. In contradistinction to the Western, particularly U.S., theory of "rule by force," China and Japan should, on the basis of equal sovereignty, mutual trust, and nonintervention, establish a new variant of the Asian "kingly way" with virtue as its essence.[30] In any case, if Japan is to play a key role in establishing an Asian multilateral system, it must first become an Asian country.

Some experts contend that China's growth in East Asia not only presents no obstacle to Japan's own growth but may also even provide a new impetus for Japan's development and help catalyze its economic reform. Moreover, since China is the most populous country and largest market in the world and Japan is an economically developed world power, the two can complement each other and even form a perfect economic partnership.[31]

China and India: No Mutual Threat but Common Development

India Aims at Competing for World Power Status

India is China's most important neighbor to the west. Like China, it is an ancient civilization in the East with a long history. It was under colonial and imperialist domination. It has the second largest population in the world and passed the 1 billion mark in 2000. Its birth rate is higher than China's, so some experts predict that it will surpass China to become the world's most populous country in at most a few decades. Its territory is 2.97 million square kilometers, or seventh in the world. Although its territory is less than one-third of China's, its arable land is 165.31 million hectares, almost twice the size of China's 92.82 million hectares. It ranks second in the world in irrigable land. Its forest cover is, at 22.5 percent, much higher than China's 13.4 percent, and it has abundant deposits of iron, bauxite, and copper. It is richer in resources than China. It is better situated than China with regard to ocean access. It faces the vast Indian Ocean, which provides a sixteen hundred kilometer defensive buffer. It also enjoys a better security environment than China; no South Asian country can threaten its security. Thirty-five million Indians are fluent in English; the country's scientific and education levels are higher than China's. India ranks third in technical personnel; its software industry ranks first in the world and accounts for 30 percent of the world market. In 2000, its GDP was US$456.9 billion, ranking thirteenth in the world, and its per capita GDP was US$491. If calculated according to PPP, its GDP reached US$2.5 trillion, or fifth in the world.

In addition, India possesses a strong military force and is one of the few Asian countries with aircraft carriers. It considers itself the fourth strongest military power and the largest democracy in the world. Consequently, many people think that it is not only a South Asian power but also a potential sixth pole among world powers, along with China, the United States, Japan, Russia, and Europe. India set itself the goal of becoming a first-class world power.[32] It has expressed its ambition of becoming a world power ever since the Nehru era. Although it has developed more slowly than China, it has quickened its development pace since the 1990s.

Not only does India want to be a permanent member of the UN Security Council and a political power, but it also wants to be a military power. In order to pursue the goal of becoming a first-class world power and a regional military power, it has adjusted its military strategy and the pace of army construction in recent years. It has 1.14 million soldiers; its armed forces number twice that of all the other seven South Asian countries combined and rank fourth in the world. Its objective of becoming a world power is indicated by its rapid growth in military expenditures over the past decade, more than doubling from 1990 to 2000, and continuing on a rapid upward trajectory thereafter. It has made great efforts to develop the "Blue Sky" ground-to-air guided missile and the "Earth" ground-to-ground guided missile. In addition, it has successfully researched the "Flame" middle- and long-range missile with a range of two thousand to twenty-five hundred kilometers. Now it is developing a long-range missile with a range of five to ten thousand kilometers. In addition, it emphasizes offensive operations theory and stresses systematic adjustment to bring its armed forces up to full strength and to beef up the navy, air force, and technical services. It places equal stress on research and development, the introduction of new weapons systems, and military modernization as the core of its military strategic adjustment. In its twenty-year plan for defense modernization, it set the goal of becoming one of the world's leading military powers by 2015.

India possesses nuclear weapons and is actively developing strategic deterrent forces centering on nuclear weapons. Some foreign observers estimate that it already has 20–60 nuclear weapons and enough plutonium to produce 70 nuclear warheads, 100 nuclear bombs by 2005, and 120–160 nuclear bombs in total. Meanwhile, India is pursuing ballistic missile research and development with the goal of establishing in the near future a tripartite strategic deterrent force consisting of land-based ballistic missiles, submarine-launched missiles, and strategic bombers. On August 17, 2000, the Indian National Security Consultant Advisory Committee published a draft of the country's nuclear weapons policy. It asserted that India will adopt an effective minimal nuclear deterrent strategy and use nuclear weapons only to retaliate against an enemy first strike. This was India's first nuclear weapons policy statement.

India has expressed its wish to become a world power more clearly than has China. Indian deputy prime minister Advani even said that the twenty-first century belongs to India. The Indian president also expressed the wish that his country be on an equal footing with the G-8 countries.

The Sino-Indian Relationship in Transition and China's Strategic Choice

After the founding of the People's Republic of China, India was the first nonsocialist country to recognize it. It supported China's effort to join the United Nations, and, during the Korean War, it maintained neutrality and sympathized with China. It proposed the famous Five Principles of Peaceful Coexistence with China and Burma in 1954 and, together with China, called for a spirit of Asian-African unity at the Bandung Conference of 1955. At one time, Nehru had profound feelings toward China. In the preface he wrote for the translated edition of *India and the World,* which was written in 1937, he said: "India and China are huge countries, but the problems they face are bigger than their areas: their problems are the number one problems in the world. Therefore, we must understand and make allowances for each other because, in the future, we will have many things to decide on together."[33] The two countries enjoyed an intimate friendship in the 1950s. From 1954 to 1957, Premier Zhou Enlai visited India three times, and Prime Minister Nehru visited China in 1954. The two countries formed a fraternal partnership. At that time, Mao Zedong wrote a poem that likened China and India to two clay Buddhas. After they had been broken and mended, their parts were intermixed, and it was impossible to tell them apart. Mao Zedong esteemed Nehru highly, which was hardly the case when it came to his feelings toward Soviet leader Khrushchev. He always regarded India as a friendly neighbor and was at ease with India. Even when the relationship between the two countries became tense in 1959, he still insisted that China and India had no geopolitical conflicts. China would not be so stupid, he said, as to confront the United States to the east and make enemies with India to the west. In his opinion, it was China's national policy to avoid two points of stress; the quarrels between China and India were just incidents in their eternal friendship. China had to focus on the threat from the east. In order to repair the relationship, Zhou Enlai took political risks and visited India for the fourth time as prime minister during a period of worsening Sino-Indian relations. He tried in vain to restore relations with India. In 1962, India, ignoring China's warnings, sent troops into Sino-Indian border areas that had always belonged to China and provoked military confrontations that seriously undermined relations between the two brotherly countries. In 1976, China and India exchanged ambassadors and moved partway to restore their relations. In 1988, Indian prime minister Rajiv Gandhi visited China and accelerated the process of restoring relations. When meeting with Gandhi, Deng Xiaoping repeated Mao Zedong's words from thirty years before. China and India have no big conflicts between them apart from the boundary issue, and, as long as China and India are tolerant of and considerate toward each other, they will not threaten each other.

Recent history has shown that India, however, tends to compete against China for world power status. In May 1998, then Indian defense minister Georges Fernandes, prattled about the China threat, which he invoked as an excuse for India's nuclear tests that month. A report by the Indian National Security Committee even listed China as a chief potential threat and argued that China and India represented different cultures, adhere to different ideologies, compete for leadership in Asia, and have fundamental conflicts of interest.[34]

Objectively speaking, the Sino-Indian relationship is characterized by both conflicts and the existence of common interests. Among the common points shared by China and India are their similar Eastern cultural and historical traditions. Indian Buddhism greatly influenced ancient China. Both countries have opened up to the world, and, inasmuch as they are undertaking economic development, they need a peaceful environment. India and China have basically the same views on the structure of world politics and insist on peace and development. They invoke the principles of peaceful coexistence as the basis of a new world order, and they call for a drastic reduction in stockpiles of nuclear weapons. On human rights, they oppose Western intervention into the internal affairs of developing countries on the pretext of concern about human rights, favor multipolarization, and oppose terrorism. It is worth noting that India has consistently upheld the one China principle, supported China's efforts to regain its legal seat in the United Nations in 1971, affirmed that Tibet and Taiwan are parts of China, supported China in the UN Human

Rights Commission, and opposed Western intervention into China's internal affairs.

The two countries, however, also have points of conflict in the following three areas. First is the Sino-Indian boundary dispute. The Sino-Indian boundary is about 2,000 kilometers long, divided into eastern, middle, and western sections, and involves 125,000 square kilometers of disputed territory. During the Qing dynasty, the reign of the Guangxu Emperor in 1903, the British governor-general of India, Lord Curzon, planned to send troops to invade Tibet. At the Simla Conference in 1914, Britain proposed dividing Tibet into Inner Tibet and Outer Tibet. British and Tibetan delegates, behind the backs of the Chinese delegations, secretly drew a line that pushed 80–130 kilometers into Chinese territory and grabbed 90,000 square kilometers of Chinese territory. This treaty has never been recognized by any Chinese government. After the peaceful liberation of Tibet in 1950, India inherited the illegal MacMahon Line of 1914 and formally raised territorial demands vis-à-vis China. Adopting the standpoint that disputes should be solved peacefully, the Chinese government suggested that the boundary issue should be solved through consultation and negotiation. The principles that the Chinese government applied to the Sino-Indian boundary were that the boundary has never been formally drawn but that there is a traditional boundary line; that the two countries should maintain the status quo and avoid escalation before they reach a solution; and that China and India should be tolerant of and considerate toward each other.

The Tibet issue is a second area of conflict between China and India. Britain once used Tibet as a buffer area between China and India. After the peaceful liberation of Tibet, the Indian government acknowledged China's sovereignty over Tibet. In 1954, the Nehru government signed the Sino-Indian Agreement on Commerce and Communication between the Tibet Area of China and India with the Chinese government, which relinquished British privileges and withdrew Indian guards from Tibet. After Tibet's dalai lama fled to India, the Indian government expressed sympathy toward him and provided support to the 100,000 Tibetans. In reality, this made India the de facto headquarters of the Tibetan separatists. Sometimes, Indian officials and senators, such as Indian Prime Minister Rao in 1994, go so far as to say that India has never acknowledged Tibetan independence and that, as long as Tibet remains China's colony, Indian independence and security are not assured. The Chinese government naturally insists that Tibet is China's internal affair and opposes Indian intervention.

Another troublesome issue is the Indian-Pakistani relationship and Kashmir. As a close neighbor of both India and Pakistan, China is unintentionally involved in the Indian-Pakistani dispute over Kashmir. India and Pakistan have fought three wars over this territory: in 1947–1948, in 1965, and in 1971. China reached a boundary agreement with Pakistan in the 1960s, including that portion of Kashmir under Pakistani control. In the India-Pakistan wars in 1965 and 1971, the Chinese government announced its support for Pakistan. Consequently, India thinks that China favors Pakistan and is dissatisfied with China.

Overall, except for the period in 1998 when India invoked the China threat to justify its nuclear weapons tests, the Sino-Indian relationship has improved since the 1990s. After Prime Minister Rajiv Gandhi's visit to China in 1988, India stopped talking about chasing every Chinese from every square inch of disputed territory and agreed to solve the dispute peacefully and not alter the status quo by force. Both sides agreed to stop regarding a solution of the boundary issue as the prerequisite for improving bilateral relations, and they decided to advance their political and economic relations. A delegation from India's National Defense College visited China in 1990; Chinese premier Li Peng visited India in 1991, the two sides agreed to solve boundary disputes through consultations, and India reiterated its view that Tibet is part of China. New Delhi forbade Tibetans from engaging in anti-China activities on Indian soil. The Indian national defense minister and some Indian generals visited China in 1992; Indian prime minister Narasimha Rao visited China in 1993 and signed the Agreement on Maintaining Peace and Tranquility along the Lines of Actual Control on the Sino-Indian Boundary. When Jiang Zemin visited India in November 1996, he signed the Agreement on Strengthening Military Trust along the Lines of Actual Control in the Border Area, and he proposed the establishment of a constructive cooperative partnership with India. The president of India visited China in 2000 and repaired the damage to Sino-Indian relations that had occurred in the aftermath of India's nuclear tests. Generally speaking, China has given up its previous policy of supporting Pakistan and opposing India with regard to the Indian-Pakistani relationship. Instead, it has adopted a policy of befriending India while strengthening and developing its traditional friendship with Pakistan. It has adopted a stance of neutrality regarding disputes between India and Pakistan and hopes for their peaceful resolution. At the same time, India has altered its previous position that it will develop Sino-Indian relations only after it regains control of the territories it claims along the Sino-Indian boundary to one of negotiating peacefully with China on the basis of maintaining the status quo while moving forward with other aspects of the relationship. Against this background, China's growth serves to promote the Sino-Indian relationship, particularly in the area of trade.

In 2002, Chinese premier Zhu Rongji's visit to India had a positive influence on developing Sino-Indian economic cooperation. China and India have strong complementary advantages in information-technology cooperation; China has advantages in hardware, while India has advantages in software. Thus, China can promote India's development in the process of becoming a world power. Many people regard India as a rival to China in its process of becoming a world power. In reality, cooperation outweighs competition in the Sino-Indian relationship.

The Sino-Indian relationship is not, as some people suppose, one of mutually threatening competition. As one Chinese observer has pointed out: "Some scholars are pessimistic about future Sino-Indian relations and believe that competition and even confrontation between China and India are inevitable as their national power increases. Some scholars think China will pose a threat to India because it is developing at a faster pace than India. This concept may be called the theory that power comparisons are decisive. It is worth discussing whether this theory is in accordance with objective facts."[35] Actually, China has never regarded India as a threat. Both Mao Zedong and Deng Xiaoping shared this view. It was a practical and realistic conclusion based on history and the record of traditional friendship.

There are also those who believe that the U.S.-Indian relationship has advanced considerably in recent years and that the increasing closeness of the two countries is motivated by a mutual desire to contain China. Such a view is also not necessarily correct. It is normal for India to develop relations with the United States that are in accord with Indian national interests, but the United States and India will not form an alliance directed against China. On welcoming Premier Zhu Rongji to India, then prime minister Vajpayee expressed his wish to develop friendship with China, saying: "Although we have different political systems, the challenges we face together compel us to make efforts together and learn from each other. The rapid development of globalization provides bright prospects for us . . . and our bilateral relations keep improving steadily and have recently made headway."[36] Moreover, India must preserve its independent stance if it wants to become an authentic great power. Becoming part of a U.S.-inspired anti-China strategy would harm its prospects for becoming a world power.

Then Indian prime minister Vajpayee made a formal visit to China from June 22 to June 27, 2003, that greatly promoted Sino-Indian relations. During his visit, the two countries issued the Declaration of Principles of Relationship and Overall Cooperation between the People's Republic of China and the Republic of India. This document put forward several new principles as a foundation on which to develop their relations:

1. *The principle of developing common interests and not posing a threat to each other.* India and China have broad common interests in maintaining peace, stability, and prosperity in Asia and the world, and both hope to enhance mutual understanding in regional and international affairs and to achieve wider and closer cooperation.

2. *The principle of peacefully settling boundary disputes.* The disputes should not violate the overall development of the bilateral relations.

3. *The principle that India-China relations are not aimed against third countries and that, in developing relations with third countries, neither India nor China is aiming at the other.* This principle relates mainly to China's and India's relations with Pakistan, Russia, and the United States.

4. *The principle that priority should be given to trade and economic complementarity.* Economic complementarity provides an important basis for the further improvement of economic relations and opens great prospects. In order to promote their economic cooperation, the two sides will adopt necessary measures to eliminate the obstacles in trade and investment according to their national laws and norms and international responsibility.

5. *The principle of one China and agreement that Tibet is a part of China.* For many years, the Tibet issue was a thorn in the Sino-Indian relationship, but it is no longer. India recognizes that the Tibet Autonomous Region is the territory of the People's Republic of China and reiterates its ban on Tibetans undertaking anti-China

political activities in India. It reaffirms the one China principle, which China much appreciates.

In addition, the recent economic cooperation of China and India shows that the prospect for cooperation is bright. In 2002, China surpassed Japan to become the major destination for Indian exports. The two countries have much room for cooperation in the information-technology industry.

Marx and Lenin had high expectations regarding the future of China and India, the two most populous countries in the world. They thought that the success of the Chinese and Indian revolutions would greatly influence the entire world. The great Indian writer Rabindranath Tagore also said that the fates of China and India are linked to each other and that, when China stood up, this would benefit not just China itself but all of Asia. Prime Minister Nehru said that both China and India were major countries in the world and that their problems were of the utmost importance. How they developed would exert an important influence on the whole world, and they must, therefore, know and understand each other.[37] If China and India can deal with their problems from a strategic vantage point, their relations can, not only advance, but also make a significant contribution to establishing a multipolar world characterized by coordination and cooperation among all the great powers.

5

China and Its Neighbors

Geopolitical and Strategic Choices

As recent trends indicate, China's development into a global power is occurring in conjunction with the development of its neighboring countries. In many ways, its growth can benefit them by creating an East Asian economic cooperation system. For example, the lifestyle of the Chinese people has changed significantly thanks to economic development. More and more Chinese citizens are choosing to travel abroad. Singapore, Malaysia, Thailand, the Philippines, Australia, South Korea, Japan, Vietnam, Cambodia, Burma, Nepal, Brunei, Indonesia, and Laos have all been listed as tourist destinations by the Chinese government. China's overseas travel expenditure ranked ninth in the world and second in Asia as early as 1999. Chinese travelers spent US$20 billion in Southeast Asia, South Korea, and Japan in a single year. It was estimated by the World Travel Organization that, by 2020, around 100 million Chinese will travel abroad, putting China fourth after Germany, Japan, and the United States.[1]

China's growth will surely contribute to the development of and peace in East Asia and a new period of prosperity. This will be in stark contrast to the history of expansion and military conquest, wars, confrontation, and blood that marked the rise of Western powers and Japan in world history. Developing together with its neighbor states is one of China's fundamental strategies.

How China's Neighbors Influence Its Growth
into a World Power

Characteristics of China's Neighboring Countries

China has many neighbors, large and small. It is surrounded by many major powers in the world, including Russia, Japan, India, and Indonesia.

China is situated in the most densely populated part of the world. Most of the nations with populations of more than 100 million lie in this region. Twelve of China's neighbors have populations of over 40 million and account for more than half the world's total population, that is, over 3 billion. China is also in the world's most complicated region politically, economically, and culturally. All the socialist countries except Cuba are located there, along with the most developed country (Japan) and the newly industrializing nations (South Korea and Singapore), the richest nations (Japan and Brunei) and the poorest nations (e.g., Laos, Burma, and Bangladesh). Most of the world's religions and cultures are represented in this region, including Eastern Orthodoxy, Catholicism, Protestantism, Buddhism, Islam, and Hinduism. As world-famous cultural giants, China and India are endowed with rich heritages.

In the post–Cold War era, China has enjoyed generally good relations with its neighbors. Since the 1990s, it has established diplomatic relations with Singapore, Brunei, Kazakhstan, Tajikistan, Kyrgyzstan, Turkmenistan, Uzbekistan, and South Korea. Normal relations have been resumed with Indonesia; Sino-Russian relations have smoothly evolved to the point that they are mutually beneficial. China has established a strategic and cooperative partnership with Russia, the best in the three-hundred-year history of the bilateral relationship.

China has made considerable progress in terms of cooperation with neighboring countries in the past few years. First, an agreement has been signed in Shanghai to solidify the military trust in bordering areas among China, Russia, and three Central Asian nations. China has signed border treaties with Russia, Tajikistan, Kazakhstan, and Kyrgyzstan. For the first time since the Qin dynasty, more than two thousand years ago, China has tackled the biggest geopolitical problem in the north, thereby making the once turbulent northern border the safest of all its borders. Second, China's relations with the the ASEAN nations have been greatly improved since 1996. In 2002, a Sino-ASEAN accord on establishing a free trade zone in Southeast Asia was signed. Third, the Sino-Vietnamese relationship has been revitalized and is advancing rapidly. In the year 2000, the fundamental principles to be used in settling the land and water borders between China and Vietnam were agreed on bilaterally. Fourth, Sino-Indonesian relations are greatly improved; former president Wahid chose China as the object of his first official visit. He publicly expressed his wish to improve the bilateral relationship and to exchange ideas about the Indonesian Chinese issue. His successor, President Megawati, furthered this trend and pushed Sino-Indonesian relations to a new stage. That positive trend is continuing. Fifth, the summit among China, Japan, and South Korea within the framework of ASEAN negotiations has proved useful and successful. Therefore, China is enjoying a period of unprecedented friendly relations with its neighboring countries.

Difficult Issues in China's Relations with Neighboring Countries

The danger of nuclear proliferation. Technically speaking, for many countries it is not that difficult to develop nuclear weapons. There are many nuclear-capable countries in China's neighborhood. India and Pakistan tested nuclear weapons in 1998 and developed missile delivery systems. Japan has long possessed the knowledge to manufacture nuclear weapons, and many right-wing Japanese figures frequently push for it to produce its own nuclear weapons. The nuclear crisis on the Korean Peninsula has attracted a great deal of world attention. Not all the nuclear-capable states in its neighborhood perceive China as a potential adversary, but the increasing trend toward nuclear weapons capability is hardly a good thing, and the situation is becoming more complicated. India is accelerating its drive to achieve major power status by intensifying its nuclear-oriented military efforts. It is estimated, as we have seen, that India possesses twenty to sixty nuclear weapons and has the potential to produce seventy more. At the same time, it has been researching and developing its missile delivery systems. Its aim is to possess a tripartite strategic deterrence capability, including land-based missiles, submarine-launched ballistic missiles, and strategic bombers, in the early twenty-first century.

The potential for disruptive and injurious regional conflicts. A Cold War environment persists on the Korean Peninsula. Both the North and the South station heavy forces along the truce line, and occasional military clashes over territorial and boundary issues have occurred. On

August 31, 1998, North Korea launched an artificial satellite that soon aroused suspicion and antagonism on the part of South Korea, Japan, and the United States. In mid-June 2000, the three countries proclaimed that they detected another North Korean missile launch. On June 15 of that year, a collision between North and South Korean warships led to a sea battle. In November 2002, North Korea withdrew from the framework it signed with the United States in 1994 and declared that it would resume work toward producing nuclear weapons. In January 2002, U.S. president George W. Bush called North Korea, Iraq, and Iran the "axis of evil" and asserted that the United States might launch preemptive strikes against them to avert the threat to the United States and the international community. Then, on March 20, 2003, the United States launched its war against Iraq without justifiable reason or UN permission. After the collapse of Saddam Hussein's regime, it repeatedly threatened to use force against North Korea, but Pyongyang reacted vigorously to this warning by proclaiming its intention to develop nuclear weapons to deter or retaliate against any U.S. attack.

Kashmir is another Pandora's box. India and Pakistan fought two wars over it (in 1947 and 1965), and the United Nations soon brokered a cease-fire and an armistice line. Both parties, however, have carried out continuous military exercises against each other since then. On July 10, 2002, India and Pakistan reached a bilateral armistice, but the complicated questions of nationality, religion, and territory will impede for a long time the normalization of relations between them.

It is worth noting that China's neighboring countries are among the main markets for arms sales. According to the annual reports of the London-based International Institute of Strategic Studies, world arms sales in 1998 were around US$55 billion, slightly lower than in 1997, but the share belonging to East Asia increased significantly. In the world arms markets, the biggest buyers are all from Asia; Saudi Arabia occupies first place with US$10.4 billion, followed by Taiwan's US$6.3 billion, Japan's US$2.1 billion, South Korea's US$1.4 billion, and Singapore's US$900 million. In 1999, India's military budget increased 11 percent to US$10.7 billion, and Pakistan's defense expenditure increased to US$4 billion.

Challenges to China's territorial sovereignty. China has settled border issues with Burma, Nepal, Mongolia, North Korea, Laos, Russia, Kazakhstan, Kyrgyzstan, and Tajikistan. However, territorial disputes with Bhutan, India, Vietnam, and some Southeast Asian countries, especially the South China Sea dispute with the Philippines, have been casting a shadow over China's security and stability.

The South China Sea issue between China and the Philippines has recently been intensified owing to the U.S.-Philippine Visiting Forces Accord. This accord mandates that large-scale joint military exercises will be resumed, thereby introducing U.S. forces into Asia to a much greater degree. The Philippines attempted to make full use of this accord to secure special economic benefits as well as security guarantees. Following the South China Sea clash in 1995, Manila has viewed China as the most significant potential threat. The return of U.S. forces is intended to improve the position of the Philippines. The accord will certainly help in the modernization of Filipino military forces.

In Northwest Asia, China has achieved good relations with bordering countries, but separatist forces in Xinjiang have received assistance from sympathizers in neighboring countries.

China should elevate its relations with bordering countries so that they become a key part of its overall diplomatic strategy. It should view its relations with its neighbors not in a purely bilateral perspective but in a comprehensive fashion. Its diplomatic strategy should contain two cores and two basic points.

The first core is to serve the overall interest of modernization through creating a peaceful and stable environment, securing international space for China to become a genuine world power by the middle of the twenty-first century. The second core is to sustain and solidify national unification and territorial integrity and create conditions for ultimate reunification, again by the middle of the twenty-first century.

Two basic points in its diplomatic strategy function like two wheels to carry China forward toward becoming a world power. They are the relations with major powers and relations with neighbors. Relations with the United States, Russia, the European Union, and Japan play a vital role in China's efforts to construct a new world economic and political order, to nurture the process of multipolarization, to promote world peace, to open itself up to the outside world, to absorb technology, capital, talent, and experience, and to achieve national unification and security. Relations among the major powers determine the international situation as a whole, so they must also be the key aspect of China's diplomatic strategy. The other emphasis is the relation with neighboring countries. This is not because these include Russia and Japan but for the following reasons.

First, China has important interests in regional security, economic construction, and international politics in East Asia. The bordering countries exert a direct and vital influence on China's unification and territorial integrity. In order to ensure the return of Taiwan, to strengthen the linkage between the outer provinces of Xinjiang, Tibet, and Inner Mongolia and the inner provinces, and to counter separatism, China must have good relations with its neighbors. Moreover, it should not be forgotten that there are still unresolved territorial disputes with India, Japan, and the ASEAN countries. Second, East Asia is of prime importance with regard to China's economic construction, national modernization, and policy of opening up since it represents three-fifths of its foreign trade. Many of China's Asian neighbors are among its top ten capital providers and trade partners. Third, East Asia has great significance with respect to China's development into a world power. East Asia, a rapidly growing region, will be the central stage for China's prosperity. The increasing importance of East Asia in the world arena will greatly help China cultivate its world image. There is no exception to the rule that all world powers have first gone through the stage of being the leading power in their own region. China, of course, will follow this precedent. It needs to become a major power first in East Asia, then in Asia, and finally in the world. Fourth, regional relations in East Asia may contribute to the balance between China and other world powers. The Sino-U.S. relation has been fragile and unstable for a long time. To a great extent, good regional relations can minimize the negative consequences of Sino-U.S. relations on China, especially when it is forced to take some reactive measures to unite the country. On the other hand, only an East Asian system can neutralize the negative influence of the U.S.-Japan Security Treaty and promote a multipolar world by showing the way in East Asia.

FROM SELF-RELIANCE TO EAST ASIAN MULTILATERALISM

In the past, for historical reasons China emphasized bilateral relations, such as Sino-Russian and Sino-U.S. relations, as well as a tradition of self-reliance. Since the world has evolved to an unprecedented degree, it is necessary to advance our understanding of this strategy. We can categorize China's handling of neighboring relations under two headings, namely, *self-reliance* and *multilateralism*.

China's tradition of self-reliance is quite unlike the U.S. tradition of using force to compel other nations to bend to its will. Rather, on the one hand, China focuses on self-reliance; in other words, it develops according to the path it has chosen regardless of what other countries do. On the other hand, it defines its own interests in world affairs. For example, during the East Asian financial crisis of 1997, it did everything possible to maintain the value of the yuan at a time when all other Asian countries devalued their currencies. Its tradition of self-reliance is determined by its interests, yet, if we continue to adhere strictly to this tradition and neglect the importance of multilateral diplomacy, we may face two questions.

On the one hand, we may arouse suspicion if we still cleave to self-reliance. As a major power, China's rapid development will naturally cause anxiety and suspicion at least on a regional scale. Even though China has demonstrated that the development of its comprehensive national strength is oriented toward self-defense, that it will never aspire to be a superpower or to exercise hegemony, and that its growth will enhance world peace and development, still no country bases its national policy on promises from other countries, so it will be difficult to eradicate these suspicion or overcome the China threat theory. The continuous increase in military expenditures in East Asia is one example of suspicion and jealousy.

On the other hand, given that we have already experienced the first East Asian financial crisis, we must face the possibility that other crises will occur in the areas of economy, trade, and so on. If so, will China again play a lone hand? Even if it does, will it be willing and able to afford such a high price once more?

Bilateralism is a supplement to self-reliance. It means that China negotiates and settles problems with other countries through a bilateral mechanism. It has proved to be extremely fruitful in many cases, especially with neighboring countries. It will still occupy a place in China's diplomacy. We have managed to develop good bilateral relations with Russia, Pakistan, Burma, and Thailand; we may do the same with Vietnam and Indonesia. Nevertheless, neither self-reliance nor bilateralism accords with the tendencies of globalization and regionalization. The rapid development of multilateral cooperative mechanisms in North America and Western Europe provides successful examples as well as a challenge to East Asia. East Asia has not yet developed such an integrated system to compete in the near future. Therefore, while developing both self-reliance and bilateralism, China must place its relations with neighboring states in both multilateral and regional frameworks.

Mao Zedong repeatedly pointed out that Asian people should be responsible for Asian affairs: "The people in every country should be in charge of their own national affairs, Asian people should manage their own affairs; it is not for the United States to manage."[2] Zhou Enlai voiced the same point of view. On March 28, 1950, he refuted U.S. secretary of state Acheson's assertion that the United States has gained nothing from Asia. Did it not gain control of the Philippines through war, and, after World War II, did it not likewise control Japan and South Korea? Moreover, it helped the reactionary forces in the Chinese civil war, attempted to control Indonesia, Vietnam, Thailand, Burma, and India, and sowed dissension among Asian nations by saying that China was interfering with Asian affairs. Zhou said that the United States should stick to its own business and let Asians take care of their own affairs.

Zhou's visits to India, Pakistan, Nepal, Sri Lanka, Burma, Vietnam, Afghanistan, and Cambodia in 1957 reinforced his views of Asian unity. With its long-standing cultures and civilizations, Asia has contributed greatly to world civilization, and China enjoyed time-honored and historical connections with Asian countries. Yet the era of Western colonialism reduced almost all Asian nations to the status of colonies or protectorates except Japan. Asian countries struggled long and hard to achieve their independence. Speaking of China's policy toward Asia, Zhou said: "Friendly cooperation is the common interest of the peoples of Asia. . . . We should oppose the divide-and-rule conspiracy of Western countries who try to set Asians against Asians."[3]

The East Asian regionalism espoused by Mao Zedong and Zhou Enlai remains valid today. As a major power, China should combine multilateralism and East Asian regionalism as vital elements of its strategy for conducting relations with its neighboring countries. In addition, it can employ multifaceted multilateral relations to serve its national security interest. With the goal of constructing a Greater East Asian multilateral security system and obtaining collective economic cooperation, it should promote subregional collective cooperation in the four subregions of Northeast Asia, Central Asia, Southeast Asia, and South Asia.

East Asia is generally thought to consist of Northeast Asia and Southeast Asia, but, if we view China as the center, Central Asia and South Asia may be included as parts of Greater East Asia. As one of the key actors in Greater East Asia, China should and can play an increasingly important role in this region. The East Asian financial crisis of 1997 witnessed the emergence of China as a leading actor in this area. Faced with the sharp devaluation of Asian currencies, including the Japanese yen, China shouldered the responsibility of maintaining the value of the yuan in order to avert further deterioration of the situation. Moreover, it provided economic assistance to several Asian countries to help them out of their crises. Through its efforts in this crisis, China demonstrated the utility of multilateral diplomacy, in which it played a major role.

Under present conditions, China can demonstrate its leadership to a greater extent in East Asia by adjusting its diplomatic strategy. In geopolitical terms, it has never been the center of the world, but it is the natural center of East Asia. There has been a long history of close ties between China and Central, South, Southeast, and Northeast Asia. China is the largest market and has the biggest population. The rapid growth of its economy over the past twenty-odd years has brought with it increasing influence in the economic affairs of East Asia, an influence that will grow if China can put multilateralism and regionalism into full play in its various relations in the region. China will make a great contribution to the Greater East Asian system of collective cooperation while enhancing its own stature as a major power.

On the foundation of improved all-around relations with its neighbors, China, along with Japan, India, Russia, and Indonesia, will play the lead in the integration of Greater East Asia. It can play a vital role stabilizing its relations with its neighbors by focusing on its relations with Russia, Japan, India, Indonesia, ASEAN, and South Korea.

From a Strategy of Independence to a Strategy of Coprosperity

Independence was China's diplomatic practice for a long time and will continue to be the basic policy pursued in the construction of an all-around moderately well-off society. Nevertheless, there are many people who misinterpret the changing and multilayered meaning of independence as it has evolved over the past fifty years.

The Fundamental Meaning of Independence: Four Dimensions

Independence literally means a policy whereby a state or government excludes influence from other states or governments and isolates itself from outside servitude, domination, and interference. Independence as a foreign policy, however, implies a lot more than this. In fact, it contains four unifying as well as contradictory meanings:

1. First is the opposition of small or medium-sized countries to oppression, exploitation, invasion, interference, dominance, and enslavement by major powers. The two sides of this relationship are the influence of major powers seeking control and the small- and medium-sized countries that do not develop any relations with the major power or isolate themselves entirely. There are many points on the continuum between these two extremes.

2. Second is the relationship between large, powerful countries and small- and medium-sized countries. Independence means that one country does not interfere in the internal affairs of other countries. There are also two ends to this spectrum. One is that a given country interferes in and controls the affairs of other countries; the other is that it takes no interest at all in the affairs of other countries. There are also many points along the continuum between these two extremes.

3. The third meaning is that a state manages its domestic affairs entirely on its own. It refers to the relationship between internal and external factors in resolving domestic issues in any given country. It touches on the degree to which a given country relies on external forces to resolve its own problems. Again, there are two sides to this. At one end is a situation in which the main problems in a given country are decided by external powers; the other end is a situation in which external powers play no role at all in the resolution of a given country's internal problems. Yet again, there are many points along this continuum.

4. The fourth meaning relates to world affairs and global issues. All countries deal with world affairs according to their own norms and judgments. The relationship here is between a given country and the world system. That country may involve itself wholly in world affairs, or it may stay completely aloof or have an antagonistic attitude toward the rest of the world. Therefore, China's independent foreign policy has multiple meanings and implications. It contains both changeable and immutable aspects. As for the immutable aspects, according to Jiang Zemin's speech at the Sixteenth Party Congress in 2002: "No matter what changes may occur in the world, we shall adhere unswervingly to an independent and peaceful foreign policy."[4] What does this really mean? There are four aspects to this policy. The first is to protect and develop China's national

interests and maintain world peace and prosperity. Second is the assertion that China will not yield to any form of interference from superpowers when its national interest is threatened. Third is the fact that China does not interfere in the internal affairs of small and medium countries, particularly its neighbors. It does not seek to become a superpower, to expand, to control its neighbors, to carve out a so-called sphere of influence, or to engage in extraneous criticisms. Fourth, with regard to international affairs, China's position is determined by whether a given policy serves the interests of the Chinese people and the people of the world, whether it benefits world peace and stability, or whether it is just or not. These are the immutable aspects of China's independent foreign policy.

The changeable factors include the following: First, the aforementioned four points of China's independent foreign policy have continuously evolved during the three eras of Chinese foreign policy. Second, between the endpoints on the continuum of policy there are many intermediate points or policy choices. Therefore, China's independent foreign policy is based on immutable principles, but it advances with time, changes in different situations, and evolves in relation to China's main domestic tasks and the development of its comprehensive national power, but its essence remains the same. For instance, although China rejects interference and control by major powers, it maintains contact with them. There are many points along the continuum between cooperation and struggle, and which of these is dominant at any particular time is subject to change. The same is true with respect to alliance formation. Each of the several generations of CCP leaders who have pursued an independent foreign policy have done so in their own distinctive ways but within a common framework.

Mao Zedong's Alignment Strategy and Independent Foreign Policy

The distinctive feature of Mao Zedong's views on foreign policy was adherence to the principle of independence on crucial issues. Mao believed that one of the most important dimensions of independence was that a given country manages its own domestic affairs without foreign interference. At critical moments during the Chinese Revolution, he clearly pointed out: "China is an independent country; the Chinese people and their government are responsible for the affairs within China. If any foreigners suggest that one or more foreign governments should act as mediators in China's civil war, they will surely be rebuffed." Later, he said that independence means that "all countries should manage their own affairs": "This is a fundamental truth. Americans should take care of their own affairs. We do not interfere in their affairs, but now the United States is butting into too many places."[5]

Mao's independent foreign policy had several distinctive features. First, given the history of foreign aggression against China, Mao emphasized China's independence and sovereignty and strongly resisted U.S. and Soviet attempts to interfere in and control China. Second, his strategy of alignment was designed to maximize China's independence. Third, with respect to the role of foreign powers in China's economic development, in the early 1950s, he initially opened China to cooperation with the Soviet Union sand Eastern Europe, but then, in the 1960s, he pursued a closed-door policy of self-reliance. Fourth, he insisted on a policy of nonexpansion, noninterference, and nonaggression with respect to medium and small neighboring countries; nevertheless, he maintained an active interest in their affairs. China became involved in the Korean War, fulfilled its internationalist duty to support Vietnam in its war of resistance against U.S. aggression, provided support to a number of Communist parties in the 1960s and 1970s, and spent 5–7 percent of its state budget on foreign aid, which was more than it could afford. Fifth, for a long period owing to objective reasons, China adopted a passive position with respect to world affairs and, on some issues, simply followed the Soviet Union without considering its own national interests. For example, Yugoslavia was always friendly toward China, but China just adopted the Soviet position of criticizing it.

The Evolution of Nonalignment during the Deng Era

Although, in practice, Mao Zedong pursued an independent foreign policy, it was Deng Xiaoping who officially proclaimed a peaceful and independent foreign policy as the essence of Chinese diplomacy. In his opening speech to the Twelfth Party Congress in 1982, Deng solemnly put forward the concept of an independent foreign policy, one of genuine nonalignment. In subsequent speeches, he pointed out that it is crucial for China to uphold real independent diplomacy because it is a manifestation of Marxism. The second phase of his independent foreign policy differed significantly from Mao's policy in the following aspects.

With respect to great power relations, Deng sought a balance between the United States and the Soviet Union. Mao's version aimed at fighting first the United States and then the Soviet Union. Deng opposed neither the Soviet Union nor the United States. Concurrent with the growth of its comprehensive state power, China shifted its focus from the consolidation of sovereignty, the hallmark of its first period, to the development of its national economy. This shift led to a rethinking of the Sino-U.S. coalition against the Soviet Union from the mid-1970s. Deng's decision to change this strategy was based on several considerations.

First was the power imbalance in the bilateral relationship; China was much weaker than United States. Opening up to the United States might facilitate modernization by improving access to capital, technology, equipment, talent, and experience, but, at the same time, it threatened China's capacity for self-reliance. Therefore, Deng determined to put some space between China and the United States in order to preserve independence.

Second was that, in the early 1980s, the United States began to behave in an unfriendly manner toward China. It put pressure on China and acted like a hegemonic power with respect to the issue of Taiwan. From 1981, Deng closely observed four trends in U.S. views of China, namely, that China was too backward to merit U.S. attention, that China needed the United States but that the United States did not need China, that the United States could get concessions on the Taiwan issue from its support of China vis-à-vis the Soviet Union, and that Chinese ideology remained antagonistic toward the United States. Deng realized that it was harmful for its international image if China was too close to the United States and that the international status of China might be misunderstood. Even though U.S. assistance was important in its modernization program, China had to prepare for the unexpected, for turmoil in the world and U.S. intrigues on the Taiwan issue. To take proper precautions was better than having to engage in damage repair. Deng was well-known for being circumspect and farsighted; he concluded that China must adhere to a truly independent foreign policy.

Third was the unfriendly turn in U.S. policy. Deng had in mind here the Taiwan Relations Act, passed by the U.S. Congress in 1979, and the Reagan administration's policy of expanded arms sales to Taiwan. Adopting a hegemonic and interventionist position, Reagan repeatedly asserted that China must not solve the Taiwan problem by force. Since the United

States, a hegemonic power, was unfriendly to China, why should China continue to support it against the other hegemonic power?

Fourth was the world balance of power and the world's perception of China. If, as a major power, China was too close to the United States, this would harm the global balance of power and world peace as well as damage China's position in the world and weaken its influence. By the 1980s, the Soviet Union was bogged down in Afghanistan, and its influence had declined. Under Reagan, the United States had adopted a hard line toward the Soviet Union and strengthened its position vis-à-vis its rival. Generally speaking, there was a strategic balance between the two superpowers, resulting in a stalemate. China's global position had improved, but, if China continued to support the United States, this would produce an imbalance of global power and encourage U.S. hegemonism. While the United States continued to pressure China on the Taiwan issue, for China to maintain a quasi-alliance relationship with the United States was neither appropriate nor beneficial for world peace.

Fifth was the weakness of a one-line strategy that limited the flexibility of Chinese strategy and did not promote the national interest. Like the strategy of leaning to one side, it meant that we categorized countries according to their relation with the superpowers. During the period of leaning to one side, China developed friendly relations with allies of the Soviet Union. During the period of the one-line strategy, it was precisely the reverse. China manifested antagonism toward the Soviet Union and its East European allies. It supported the United States in opposing Soviet hegemony, but this stance made it difficult for it to oppose U.S. hegemony and hindered the process of reconciliation between China and the Soviet Union. The price of this hostility was high on both sides. In both the period of leaning to one side and that of the one-line strategy, China was put in a subordinate position. Its diplomatic flexibility was severely limited, and its international image suffered as a result.

The independent foreign strategy proposed by Deng Xiaoping can be summarized as the Four No's and the One All, namely, no alignment, no isolation, no confrontation, no targeting third countries, and an all-directional diplomacy based on nonalignment. In fact, nonalignment was the main form of Deng's independent foreign policy. This policy is quite different from that of Mao Zedong.

Deng believed that a diplomatic stance of nonalignment could better serve the goals of antihegemony and maintaining world peace. In September 1985, he pointed out that not only Western Europe but also some countries in Eastern Europe had to an extent adopted an independent foreign policy and that this reality had changed the structure of the international political system. His diplomatic strategy firmly adhered to an omnidirectional form of diplomacy. In concrete terms, this meant that China had to adjust its relation with all major powers, transform its quasi alignment with the United States into a normal state-to-state relationship while preventing the United States from overreacting to this shift, convert what had been a hostile Sino-Soviet relationship into a normal one along pragmatic lines, and enhance relations with Europe in a way that would advance the antihegemony goal. Taken together, these elements in Deng's nonalignment strategy enhanced China's diplomatic flexibility, strengthened its global status, and added greater authority to its voice in international affairs.

Deng's independent foreign policy prioritized national interest in the quest for world power status. Mao's policy had been largely formulated on the basis of ideology, the primacy of Sino-Soviet relations, historical heritage, and the idiosyncratic factor of the leader's personality. Deng was determined to oppose any attempts by others to impair Chinese national interests and was cognizant of the fact that the advanced countries had not changed their policy of bullying less developed countries. He insisted on staying on high alert and standing firm in the face of potential adversaries who look down on those who exhibit any signs of weakness.[6] In sum, the strategy of independence was aimed at countering any forms of anti-China forces and protecting Chinese dignity. In the late 1980s and early 1990s, the international situation experienced drastic changes, but, thanks to its independent diplomacy, China was an island of relative stability amid the turbulent changes. It enjoyed a comparatively favorable position in the post–Cold War era.

Deng's independent diplomacy provided for a policy of opening in all directions while maintaining independence during the process of opening to the world. It was very different from Mao's policy, which often closed China's doors to the world. The questions of how to balance between opening to capitalist systems and persisting in building socialism and how to balance between self-reliance and autonomous development while utilizing foreign capital in economic construction have long been thorny issues in Chinese diplomacy. In stressing self-reliance to counter external interference, Mao achieved some results, but he failed in making use of the capitalist world to benefit the Chinese economy. This isolated China from the mainstream of development.

Deng emphasized a policy of opening up to the world as the only possible path of Chinese development. At the same time, he insisted on resisting decadent foreign ideologies and rejecting capitalist lifestyles. He emphasized the importance of upholding the Four Basic Principles in order to maintain political stability. The Third Plenum of the Eleventh Central Committee in December 1978 resolved that China would open up to the outside world while ensuring that development proceeded in accordance with specific Chinese conditions and requirements. Opening to the world must not and would not compromise China's independent foreign policy.

In China's relations with small, medium, and neighboring countries, Deng's independent foreign policy also introduced significant changes and developments in comparison to Mao's policies. On the one hand, Deng continued Mao's Third World policy, which stated that China belongs to the Third World. On the other hand, he extended his diplomacy of non-alignment to the Third World. China abstained from any involvement in the domestic affairs of other countries and ceased supporting a number of Communist parties it had previously aided. It also forswore any leader-ship role in the Third World. Deng said that China should practice self-restraint and never stand in the front of the line. In the past, China often spoke out on behalf of the Third World. Deng amended this practice and adhered to the principle of not criticizing or condemning others, avoiding excessive verbiage, and concentrating on China's own modernization project.

Cooperative Development: China and Its Neighbors in a New Era

The third generation of Chinese leaders continued the independent diplomacy inherited from the time of Mao and Deng but introduced innovations in content and practice to advance with the times.

As its comprehensive national strength has increased, China has acted more confidently in its relations with the great powers. Mao started from the fact that the newly founded People's Republic of China was weak and vulnerable. He believed that China had to remain vigilant and on guard to maintain its independence. In Deng's time, China was stronger, but, as the weakest side in the Sino-Soviet-U.S. triangle, it had to seek normal relations with both the United States and the Soviet Union. To guarantee its independence, it had to do a good job of balancing between the superpowers. Yet this policy, which was based on the reality of relative weakness, naturally harbored suspicion toward the more powerful countries and was a reactive rather than a proactive policy.

In the post–Cold War era, especially in recent years, what in the past had been an unequal relationship between a weak China and a powerful Russia has qualitatively changed into a substantially equal partnership. Therefore, China no longer needs to worry about Russian interference in China's domestic affairs. Since there is still a power imbalance favoring the United States in Sino-U.S. relations, there is still the possibility of the United States interfering in China's domestic affairs. Yet the nature of Sino-U.S. relations is also changing.

What in the past had been a relationship between a weak China fighting to maintain its self-respect and defend itself in the face of a powerful United States has changed into a relationship between the sole superpower and the largest developing country. China has adopted a proactive policy in its relations with both the United States and Russia. China and Russia have developed a strategic partnership and have signed a treaty of friendship that precludes the possibility of Russian interference in Chinese affairs. There are still contradictions, however, between Beijing and Washington. China must be on guard against anti-China forces in the United States and be prepared to struggle against the United States. But China seeks good relations with the developed countries (especially the United States) and views its main task as establishing and broadening the area of common interests.

The new version of China's independent diplomacy is no longer restrained by questions of alignment or nonalignment. The sole criterion of Chinese diplomacy is the question of whether a given policy or action serves the interests of the Chinese people and the people of the world, whether it benefits the maintenance of world peace and stability, and whether it fosters world development. China, along with Russia and the Central Asian states, initiated the Shanghai Cooperation Organization, a political and security alliance designed to fight against international terrorism, religious extremism, and national separatism. China and ASEAN are working for the establishment of a Sino-ASEAN free trade zone. Meanwhile, conventional and nonconventional security cooperation between the two sides is being strengthened. After 9/11,

China cooperated with the United States in efforts to fight international terrorism, thereby earning President George W. Bush's praise as an ally in combating terrorism.

There have also been changes in China's relations with small, medium, and developing countries. During the era of Mao Zedong, China occasionally intervened in the internal affairs of some countries and devoted disproportional resources to support the Third World at the cost of national interests. During the era of Deng Xiaoping, it focused exclusively on domestic development and paid little heed to the affairs of others. Its current independent diplomacy pursues a win-win strategy in line with the goals of safeguarding its national interests defined in terms of the changing world situation and China's present state capabilities. China neither interferes with nor ignores the domestic affairs of other countries. While protecting its national interest, it provides appropriate assistance to developing countries without trying to be the leader.

With respect to global issues and the nature of the international system, the present independent foreign policy contains elements that were absent in the era of Mao and Deng. In general, China adopts a more positive and proactive stance, promoting global integration and cooperative development. Mao kept China on the sidelines of the international system with the objective of maintaining its independence, but he did rail against the United States and the Soviet Union. For example, China opposed the Nuclear Test Ban Treaty that the United States and the Soviet Union signed in 1963. Deng began to change this position but was still rather negative toward multilateral issues in the 1980s and early 1990s. For example, China was quite cool toward Japan's proposal in the 1980s for a system of Asian economic cooperation. Since the end of the Cold War, while maintaining its independent foreign policy, China has introduced many new elements into its diplomacy. On the foundation of its policy of opening to the world, it adopted a policy of integration with the international system, entered the WTO in 2001, and won the right to host the 2008 Olympic Games in Beijing and the 2010 World's Fair in Shanghai. Now it acts as a conscientious member of the world community, working with other countries to counter international terrorism and the proliferation of nuclear and biochemical weapons. It plays a responsible role in addressing a whole range of global issues. It played a major role in helping resolve the East Asian financial crisis. It is now cognizant of the importance of taking other countries' interests into consideration along with its own in addressing important regional issues. This is a significant departure from the past. Its recognition of a common interest in development is a key aspect of its current policy.

THREE DIMENSIONS OF CHINA'S GEOPOLITICAL STRATEGY

Post–Cold War Geopolitical Changes in East Asia

Significant change took place in the traditional geopolitical heartland. After the collapse of the Soviet Union, the traditional geopolitical heartland became a contested space with uncertain prospects. In traditional geopolitical theory, the Central Asian lands of Russia were viewed as the strategic heartland, greatly influencing geopolitics throughout the world. The collapse of the Soviet Union sharply devalued the influence and importance of this region in world geopolitics. The Soviet Union, a former superpower, splintered into fifteen countries, and what had been unified was now fragmented. The other fourteen independent countries besides Russia developed four kinds of links with Russia itself. Some, like Belarus, allied with Russia; others, like the Central Asian republics, tried to achieve a balance by keeping close ties with but preserving a certain distance between themselves and Russia. Turkmenistan declared itself a neutral nation. A third group included the nations of the Caucasus and Ukraine and Moldova. Of these, only Armenia is close to Russia; the other nations, like Azerbaijan, Georgia, and Ukraine, try to keep their distance from Moscow. Finally, the three Baltic nations attempted to shake off Russian influence entirely. The Baltic states, Ukraine, Moldova, Georgia, and Azerbaijan aspired to join NATO and the European Union.

As the successor of the former Soviet Union, Russia saw its comprehensive national power sharply decline and its geopolitical status change from that of a world power to that of a regional power. Its influence declined commensurately. Prolonged economic crisis and domestic political turmoil degraded its international status. Its nuclear arsenal was all that sustained its image as a great power, but its military expenditures were only a tiny fraction of those of the United States.

At the beginning of the twenty-first century, according to then president Putin, even under ideal conditions with the economy growing at an annual rate of 8 percent, it would take Russia fifteen years to catch up to the economic level of a small European country like Portugal. If it wished to catch up with Britain or France, its growth rate would have to rise to at least 10 percent.[7]

Its diminished comprehensive national power is the starting point for how Russia deals with global issues. Russia must act with restraint and avoid direct confrontation with the United States and the West. It has no choice but to retreat from Latin America, Africa, and Asia. It can do little, if anything, to stop former Warsaw Pact members from joining NATO. Serbia was once an ally of Russia, but Russia was unable to stop NATO's war against Serbia. At the nadir of its power, Russia had to stand by and watch the Caspian region being converted into an U.S. sphere of influence. It was one of the initiators of the Middle East peace process, but it saw its influence in the region steadily wane.

The involvement of the United States brought about momentous changes in the Eurasian geopolitical situation. Traditional geopolitics was based on a relative power balance between continental powers and maritime powers. On the Eurasian continent, a dominant maritime power or group of maritime powers struggled for dominance against a dominant continental power or group of continental powers through any means, including wars, to upset the existing balance of power and establish a new one. Whatever changes occurred in the past, the dominant power or coalition was one based in Eurasia itself, and none could maintain dominance for a long time. At one time or another, Britain, Germany, France, Russia, and Japan, individually or in combination, dominated the continent, but none of them were able to bring about a fundamental change in the geopolitical structure of power.

By becoming deeply involved in Eurasian geopolitics, the United States shattered this traditional system. The world geopolitical balances tilted sharply toward the United States, which has occupied the dominant position. This is evident in the following ways.[8]

For the first time, a non-Eurasian power has come to dominate the Eurasian geopolitical sphere. After World War I, the United States completely withdrew from Europe, but, after World War II, it became involved in the Cold War geopolitical struggle for dominance in Eurasia. With the end of the Cold War, it became the sole superpower and enjoyed an unprecedented degree of influence in Eurasia. No country on the continent can counterbalance the United States, and, to one degree or another, almost all countries on the continent are under U.S. geopolitical influence. The likes of this have never been seen before, not even when the Mongolian Empire swept across Eurasia many hundreds of years ago.

For the first time, both ends of Eurasia are controlled by an extraregional power. In the west, the United States built up NATO under its leadership and enmeshed within it the three great European powers of Germany, France, and Britain. In the east, it established military alliances with Japan and South Korea and bound Japan to it via a security treaty. In this way, it became the first country in history to control both ends of Eurasia. In addition, it thereby displayed its strategic intention to contain China and Russia via the aforementioned military alliances.

For the first time, a maritime power is deeply involved in the heartland of Eurasia. In the past, the struggle for the geopolitical dominance of Eurasia often took place at the two ends of the continent, but U.S. geopolitical strategy is changing this now. The United States strengthened its position in the heartland via two wars in the post–Cold War era. The Gulf War in 1991 brought it the right to station forces in Saudi Arabia. On the pretext of enforcing sanctions against Iraq, it kept a permanent military presence in the Persian Gulf. The Kosovo War in 1999 demonstrated its military power in Southern Europe and the Balkans. These two wars solidified the U.S. impact on what Zbigniew Brzezinski called the Balkan southern front of Eurasia. At the same time, the United States penetrated the heartland from both ends of Eurasia via military and political means. Under the rubric of constructing peaceful partnerships, NATO expanded eastward, enabling the United States to establish such partnerships with five Central Asian countries. The United States helps them train military officers and regularly conducts joint military exercises.

The other action the United States has taken is in the Caspian Sea region in connection with oil. On November 18, 1999, the United States, Azerbaijan, Turkey, Georgia, Kazakhstan, and Turkmenistan signed a treaty to lay an oil pipeline for the Central Asian oil producers. This pipeline circumvents Russia and Iran but goes through pro-U.S. Turkey. 9/11 provided the United States an excuse to station forces in Afghanistan and Central Asia. All these actions demonstrated its ambition to tie together the separate pieces of Eurasia.

Four Unchanging Geopolitical Elements in East Asia and Eurasia

The Globalization and Information revolutions have exerted significant influence on geopolitics, but the importance of traditional geopolitics has not diminished in international politics and may even be increasing.

Eurasia remains the center of geopolitics. In classical geopolitical theory, Eurasia was the center of world geopolitics. The British scholar Halford Mackinder pointed out: "Who rules East Europe commands the Heartland: Who rules the Heartland commands the World-Island: Who rules the World-Island commands the world."[9] The "world island" is Eurasia. Eurasia was and remains the core concept for scholars of geopolitics. For instance, Brzezinski's *Grand Chessboard* takes it as the strategic background and main arena for geopolitical struggles. The author put it as follows: From Lisbon to Vladivostok, Eurasia is regarded as a grand chessboard. The chessboard determines world stability and prosperity and is the central stage on which the United States must maintain its world dominance. Therefore, in order to maintain its geopolitical strategic interests on Eurasia, the United States must "establish alliances, selectively admit new members, and make skillful use of its political capital."[10] It was according to this principle that the United States framed its global strategy after the end of the Cold War. It started the eastward expansion of NATO and strengthened the Japanese-U.S. military alliance. NATO's eastward expansion killed three birds with one stone, namely, compressing Russia's strategic space, preventing Western Europe from becoming an independent pole in a potentially multipolar world, and amplifying the U.S. voice in European affairs. After the end of the Cold War, even though the United States laid claim to global leadership, it still placed strategic emphasis on Europe. It will not allow the emergence of a European rival. The eastward expansion of NATO naturally strengthens its leading position in this region. In Asia, the United States solidified its military alliance with Japan, expanded the spheres of their defense cooperation, and initiated the Theater Missile Defense program. It intervenes in the Taiwan issue and uses human rights and trade disputes to pressure China. We can see that it attached great importance to Eurasia from all these indicators: the eastward expansion of NATO, the Kosovo War, the Middle East peace process, sanctions against Iraq, joint military exercises with Central Asian countries, Caspian oil projects, criticism of India and Pakistan for their clashes and their nuclear tests, viewing China as neither an enemy nor a friend, intensifying the military alliance with Japan, and overreaction to the nuclear question on the Korean Peninsula. The double-headed eagle strategy that Russia proposed to respond to the U.S.

challenge also emphasized the Western world, which was the target and the end result. In sum, from the strategies of both the United States and Russia, it is not difficult to judge that Eurasia is still the center of geopolitical struggle and that Eurasia's importance in the world geopolitical structure has not diminished.

The global geopolitical power structure is basically unchanged. There are five powers in the global geopolitical structure: the United States, Russia, China, Japan, and Europe. Although, in the post–Cold War period, there have been economic changes that affect the geopolitical power structure, the overall geopolitical situation has not fundamentally changed. In the past, Western countries controlled the main power resources; they continue to do so today. On balance, the United States and Western countries occupy the dominant and leading position as they did in the last century. Nowadays information technology has become the main means for geopolitical contention, the United States and Western countries controlling most of the major information technologies and dominating the Information Revolution. Its extremely strong and comprehensive national power will enable the United States to continue its world leadership and guarantee its global interests.

The United States pursues the following strategy: In Europe, it encourages cooperation between Germany and France and attempts to construct a politically vital Europe, a Europe that is linked to the United States and is part of an expanding international system of democracies. It carefully manages the issues of leadership within NATO and NATO's and the European Union's eastward expansion. In Asia, the United States views Japan as a partner in dealing with the new agenda in global affairs. China as a major power should become the anchor of U.S. policy in East Asia. Washington seeks to achieve a balance of power in Eurasia.[11] The United States also vigorously supported the process of political democratization in Russia and extended limited aid to Russian economic reform but energetically urged Russia to cut its nuclear and conventional militarily capability. It also tried to promote the trend of geopolitical diversification in the sphere of influence of the former Soviet Union in order to contain Russia. In sum, it strives to contain Russia and China but simultaneously construct economic, political, and military ties with them.

Russia, China, Japan, and the European Union have responded in various ways to U.S. geopolitical strategy. Under the rubric of a *double-headed eagle* strategy, Russia has resisted the eastward expansion of

NATO, strengthened its ties with European countries, and bound CIS members to itself as a means of ensuring its geopolitical security. In the east, it initiated a strategic partnership with China, maintained cooperative relations with India, and was an active player in Southeast Asia. Russian-U.S. geopolitical strategies exhibit a combination of cooperation, containment, and countercontainment.

The European Union accelerated eastward expansion and the process of internal integration with an eye toward embracing all of Europe and extending toward the Middle East and Asia. It has established a comprehensive partnership with China to strengthen its voice in Eurasian affairs. Japan has put forward its "Eurasian Concept," solidified its alliance with the United States, and at the same time improved relations with South Korea and Russia. It strengthened its ties with Central Asia, South Asia, and Southeast Asia and sought to restrain and make use of China in its quest for a leading role in the Asian-Pacific region. China has focused on developing its economy while pursuing an omnidirectional foreign policy that bolsters its status as a major power in Asia and the world.

In sum, the structure of post–Cold War geopolitics is as follows: the United States strives for global leadership and seeks to contain possible rivals; the other powers endeavor to occupy favorable positions in the multipolar structure by rejecting U.S. hegemony and advocating multidirectional diplomacy. Therefore, the structure of global geopolitics has remained virtually unchanged.

Geopolitical strategic thinking still centers on neighboring countries. Geostrategic thinking is a mode of thought in which a state makes use of its geopolitical relations with others to seek its own national strategic interests. Bipolarism ended with the Cold War, and a process of multipolarization commenced. In order to secure a favorable situation in the coming multipolar world, all countries sped up their economic construction, built up their comprehensive state power, and elaborated their own geopolitical strategies. Some of the strategies are global, some are regional, but in all cases they are based on the neighboring areas. This is because the security and stability of one's neighbors is the most important guarantee of one's own security.

Relations with one's neighbors are the number one concern in the geostrategy of many countries. China's way of thinking about its neighbors is different from that of the West, something that reflects the difference in geopolitical culture. China is situated in a relatively enclosed physical environment, and its agricultural civilization centered on the

Yellow and Yangtze rivers prospered for a long time. Possessing a self-sufficient economy and far-flung borders, it developed a mode of strategic thinking that was inwardly focused and that emphasized continental rather than maritime concerns. Its dominant Confucian culture exalted peace over war. With regard to relations with its neighbors, it advocated peaceful coexistence and strived for a security zone that buffered it from any direct threat. The West, especially Europe, is surrounded by seas and is situated in a relatively open environment rich in islands, peninsulas, and ports. This environment favored the emergence of an outward-looking commercial civilization that was vulnerable to external threats. Thus, Europe's geostrategic thinking was oriented toward the outside and to the maritime world. European countries were inclined to think of their neighbors as enemies. These two very different geostrategic cultures produced different kinds of relations among neighbors. The well-known Five Principles of Peaceful Coexistence were the foundation on which from the outset China based its relations with its neighbors. They emphasized mutual respect, noninterference, equality and mutual benefit in developing relations, and peaceful coexistence. Therefore, China enjoyed good relations with its neighbors both during and after the Cold War. Because the dividing line of ideology was deleted, its relations with its neighbors have made even further progress in the post–Cold War era.

The core of Russian geopolitics is the Commonwealth of Independent States and the Baltic countries. Neighboring countries like China and North Korea are next in importance.

Concerned above all with survival and security, Western countries tend to regard neighboring countries as enemies or potential rivals and usually adopt a zero-sum stance in relations with them. In the post–Cold War era, interdependence among countries has grown greatly, and peaceful means are used with increasing frequency to resolve problems. Nevertheless, from a geopolitical perspective, neighboring countries are still considered as potential rivals or enemies. This is the rationale for the eastward expansion of NATO and the European Union as well as a series of new strategic measures in the U.S.-Japanese security relationship.

China's Contemporary Geopolitical Situation: Its Tri-Level Geostrategy

Increasing numbers of scholars have studied China's post–Cold War geopolitical position.[12] During the Cold War, the geopolitics of China had three main characteristics. The first was the threat from the north. From the late 1960s, China and the Soviet Union confronted each other militarily. The Soviet Union once deployed 1.5 million soldiers on its border with China, including more than 100,000 on the Mongolian border, posing a direct threat to China's heartland. Second, China's relations with neighboring countries were tense, as attested to by the border wars with India and Vietnam. There were also territorial sea disputes between China and Southeast Asian countries. Third, during the struggle against Soviet hegemonism, China forged partnerships with the United States, Japan, and West European countries, all states with maritime interests. After the Cold War, there remained some constant elements in China's geopolitical situation, namely, its friendly relations with Pakistan, the Indian-Pakistani conflict over Kashmir, and the military confrontation on the Korean Peninsula. Apart from these, however, there were great changes in China's geopolitical situation. Among these were the following:

The main threat from the north disappeared, but new unstable elements arose. In Chinese geopolitics, importance has always been attached to defending against aggression from the north. Historically speaking, more than half of the dynastic changes came about because of alterations in the balance of power in the north. Since Russia became China's neighbor more than three hundred years ago, it has been a great threat on its northern border. This situation fundamentally changed, however, after the end of the Cold War. As the Soviet Union disintegrated and Russian power decreased dramatically, China's power increased significantly. Along with the improvement in Sino-Russian relations, these changes made the northern border relatively stable and peaceful. Although Russia's military force remains one of the strongest in the world, its overall national power was surpassed by China's for the first time in recent history.

At the same time, the disintegration of the Soviet Union created a geopolitical belt of fragmented states in Central Asia. China acquired three new neighbors, namely, Kazakhstan, Kyrgyzstan, and Tajikistan, all formerly parts of the Soviet Union. In the northwest, where China had formerly had relations with one country, it now had them with four. Moreover, the national religion of the Central Asian countries is closely connected to national minorities in China's northwest, and this introduces a new element of instability into that region.

Despite improved relations with Southeast Asia, the South China Sea issue persists. After the Cold War, China and Indonesia resumed diplomatic relations, and China established diplomatic relations with Singapore. At the same time, it developed friendly relations with Burma, Vietnam, Laos, and Cambodia and further enhanced its relations with Malaysia, Thailand, and the Philippines. It formed a dialogue partnership with ASEAN and joined the ASEAN multilateral mechanism. However, its conflicts with the Philippines and Vietnam over South China Sea territorial waters intensified.

After the Cold War, the Taiwan issue became increasingly prominent. After the Cold War, China reasserted its sovereignty over Hong Kong and Macao without any difficulties under the policy of one country, two systems. These were great strides along the road to unification. The Taiwan issue is an old one in China's geopolitics, but it has acquired a different significance in the post–Cold War era. Because of a growing trend in Taiwan of support for independence, the issue of Taiwan has changed from a dispute over which side represents China to a dispute over whether there is one China and one Taiwan or two Chinas. This has led to an exacerbation of the conflict. The 1995 visit to the United States of Lee Teng-hui and China's 1996 military exercises directed against Taiwanese independence underlined this change in China's geopolitical strategy.

Important changes took place in Sino-U.S. relations after the Cold War. Sino-U.S. relations developed with twists and turns. U.S. globalist policy created conflicts with China's geopolitical interests. During the Cold War, because of their common interest in opposing Soviet hegemonism, disputes over Taiwan were put on the back burner in Sino-U.S. and Sino-Japanese relations. In other words, the Taiwan issue was subordinated to global strategy. China aligned itself with the maritime powers to oppose the Soviet plot to dominate Eurasia. With the disintegration of the Soviet Union, China and the United States no longer shared a common geostrategic interest, and their quasi partnership ended. The United States interfered in China's domestic affairs and imposed sanctions on China. Thanks to the efforts of both sides, Sino-U.S. relations have moved forward, albeit along a road filled with twists and turns. Nevertheless, it remains true that the globalist geostrategy of the United States conflicts with China's multipolar approach to world affairs. For example, China sharply criticized the United States for launching the war in Kosovo. Not only does NATO's eastern expansion intrude into Russia's strategic space, but the NATO/U.S. infiltration of Central Asia is also of considerable

202 INSIDE CHINA'S GRAND STRATEGY

concern to China. The enlargement of the scope of the U.S.-Japan Security Treaty is obviously aimed against China. On the Taiwan issue, the United States plays a double hand: it claims to oppose the independence of Taiwan, yet it not only sells weapons to Taiwan but also exerts pressure on the Chinese government and winks at the development of the pro-independence forces.

In sum, China's geopolitical situation after the Cold War is indeed the best since the establishment of the People's Republic of China, but it is also extremely complicated. The question, then, is, Under these circumstances, what sort of geostrategy should China pursue?

In the near and medium term, China's geostrategy should be to stabilize the west, rely on the north, and contend for influence in the southeast. What this means specifically is that, on its western border, China's major relations are with South Asia, India, and Pakistan in the first instance. China enjoys a traditional friendship and normal relations with Pakistan, a situation that may be further developed in the future. The most important country on China's western flank is India. Apart from the border dispute, India has no conflicts with China over core national interests. China has never regarded India as a threat and does not think that it will become a threat. India generally acknowledges that Tibet is Chinese territory. Although some Indians regard China as a threat, their numbers are diminishing, as is their influence.

Qualitative changes have taken place in the relationship between China and Pakistan. While developing its traditional relationship with Pakistan, China attaches importance to the development of its relations with India. Its improved relations with India in recent years indicate that it will likely be able to maintain a relatively stable situation on its western borders.

There are six countries to the north of China, including Russia, Mongolia, Kazakhstan, Kyrgyzstan, and Tajikistan. With the exception of Mongolia, all these countries have joined with China in the Shanghai Cooperation Organization. Border issues between China and all those countries have been settled, and the borders are now peaceful. The settlement of these issues acted as a powerful force in facilitating a strategic partnership between China and these other countries and promoting China's multipolarization strategy. Although there are East Turkistan separatists and terrorist elements fomenting trouble in China's northwest, its neighbors cooperate in opposing terrorism. There is mutual trust on both sides of the border, founded in a common interest in opposing terrorism and maintaining stability and peace in Central Asia.

China's geostrategy is mainly directed toward the southeast, including the southeast coastal area and the South China Sea. In this area, clashes and conflicts persist, and cooperative mechanisms are absent. Among the hot spots are the Korean Peninsula, the Taiwan issue, and the disputes over the South China Sea and exclusive economic zones. Consequently, China must pay more attention on this area.

At the same time, looking at the near, middle, and long term, China should pursue a tripartite geostrategy including the following:

A maritime strategy focused on the China Sea and the Taiwan Strait. This includes the Bohai Sea, the Yellow Sea, the East China Sea, and the South China Sea. This area is separated from the Pacific Ocean by features such as the Korean Peninsula, the Japanese island chain, the Philippines, Malaysia, and the Central-South Peninsula. These four coastal waters define a long, relatively closed arc, a maritime territory that is closely related to China's geostrategy and constitutes China's maritime strategic zone. Some comrades define three zones along China's coastal area, namely, one zone consisting of the Bohai Sea and the Yellow Sea, another consisting of the East China Sea, and a third consisting of the South China Sea. We are accustomed to organizing our naval forces on the basis of this strategic concept, but it is actually better to think of them as a whole.

In China's maritime strategy, the Taiwan Strait is an area of great strategic significance. Should Taiwan fall into enemy hands, sea communications between the South China, Yellow, and Bohai seas would be severed, and China's southeast coastal area would be under grave threat. This would be extremely harmful to China's geostrategy. In economic terms, the Taiwan Strait is also an important channel for China. A substantial portion of its imports and exports pass through it. It can never afford to lose Taiwan. After the return of Hong Kong and Macao in 1997 and 1999, respectively, the reunification of Taiwan with the mainland has risen higher on the government's agenda. Unfortunately, proindependence sentiment on the island is a serious obstacle to unification, while support for this tendency from the United States and Japan further complicates things. Great efforts must be undertaken to find a peaceful method to settle the Taiwan issue under the policy of one country, two systems. At the same time, preparations must be made to unify Taiwan with other than peaceful methods should the preferred peaceful method fail to yield results. Consequently, study of this question must include the perspective of geostrategy. Most likely, the Taiwan Strait will long remain a focal point in China's overall geostrategy.

The South China Sea is another strategic area of interest in China's maritime geostrategy. While the Taiwan Strait is important with respect to the issue of unification, the South China Sea is important for the present and future development of China. China has a population amounting to 22 percent of the global population but possesses only 7 percent of the world's arable land. Thus, it must develop its marine economy, and a China that is open to the world must become an important maritime state. The South China Sea occupies an important strategic position. It contains abundant oil, natural gas, and tropical ocean resources that make it a prime area for exploration in China's future development plans. Since the 1970s, there have been contending claims to the South China Sea on the part of China, Vietnam, and the Philippines, each of which has asserted its sovereignty and occupied one or more of the islands, reefs, and shoals that dot the sea. As time passes, the importance of the South China Sea becomes increasingly evident.

Whether one thinks of Taiwan or of the South China Sea, it is clear that China must shift the focus of its geostrategy from the land to the ocean. In the twenty-first century, it should change from its historical position as a large continental power to that of a major power with both continental and maritime interests. The traditional historical preoccupation with defending against enemies from the north should shift to a geostrategy that focuses on the southeast frontier of the South China Sea. Such a change will be truly historic in nature.

A continental geostrategy focused on stabilizing the periphery. China's geostrategy is still concerned above all with the neighboring states on its borders. The countries that share a common border with China are Russia, Mongolia, and Korea in Northeast Asia, Kazakhstan, Kyrgyzstan, Russia, and Tajikistan in Central Asia, Afghanistan, Pakistan, India, Nepal, Sikkim, and Bhutan in South Asia, and Burma, Laos, and Vietnam in Southeast Asia.

Generally speaking, whether a given country enjoys stable relations with its neighbors depends on two factors. First is whether there are frontier disputes; the other is whether there are transnational ethnic and religious issues. Using these criteria, we may say that the settlement of the

Sino-Russian and Sino-Vietnamese boundaries has brought considerable stability to China's periphery.

China has formed a strategic partnership with Russia, maintains friendly relations with Pakistan, and enjoys normal relations with neighboring Mongolia, Nepal, Burma, Vietnam, and Laos. Although North and South Korea deploy roughly 1 million troops along the thirty-eighth parallel and a conflict between them would affect China's security, this situation does not pose a very big threat to China. If the situation is properly managed, China will not get involved militarily in Korean affairs, as it did in the 1950s.

There are three issues in the broad expanse of East Asia that still affect the question of stability along China's borders. First is the still unresolved Sino-Indian boundary dispute. The second is instability along China's northwestern border because of nationalism and religious trends in the Central Asian states. Finally, there is the possibility of a war in Kashmir because of the clash between India and Pakistan. Since these two countries possess nuclear weapons and missile delivery systems, the threat that war poses to the areas adjacent to China is considerable. Nevertheless, despite these potential points of conflict, the influence of all these elements on China's geostrategy should not be exaggerated. They cannot be compared to the importance of the maritime strategic area focusing on the Taiwan Strait.

A Eurasian geostrategy focused on promoting multipolarization. Accelerating the process of multipolarization is an important aspect of China's global strategy after the Cold War. Multipolarization is a global phenomenon, but it is noteworthy that the main poles are in Eurasia. Multipolarity generally involves five poles, namely, the United States, China, Russia, Europe, and Japan. (Traditionally, Japan belongs to the Eurasian periphery.) Except for the United States, all the poles are countries in Eurasia. (India, which may also be regarded as a pole, is also in Eurasia.)

The core of China's strategy of promoting multipolarization is to smash the U.S. intention to dominate the world and oppose its geostrategy to control Eurasia. Toward this end, China opposes not only the eastward expansion of NATO but also the enhancement of the scope of the U.S.-Japan Security Treaty. China's strategy of multipolarization involves developing its strategic partnership with Russia, encouraging Europe to become a pole, and helping Japan escape from U.S. control and become an independent pole. In other words, the multipolarization strategy means enabling Eurasia to play a more important role in global affairs and defeating the U.S. intention to be the only superpower.

During the Cold War, China occupied a subordinate position in Eurasia. The heartland of Eurasia was the focus of the strategic competition between the United States and the Soviet Union. To check the power of the Soviet Union, the United States established an arc of containment around its borders. After the end of the Cold War, China's position in the geopolitics of Eurasia greatly improved, even though its geographic position in Eurasia obviously remained unchanged. Its policy of reform and opening and changes in its foreign policies jump-started its economy. By 2002, its GDP of more than US$1 trillion already put it among the top six countries in the world, and it became a major player in global geopolitics. Other major players, like the United States, Russia, and France, now must take China into account as it has made the transition from a marginal to a central and independent player in managing global issues in its capacity as the largest of the developing countries.

CHINA AND ASEAN: COOPERATION TRUMPS COMPETITION

According to Singapore's renowned statesman Lee Kuan Yew, the rise of China will change the balance of power in the world since China possesses the potential to become a superpower. Tension between China and the United States will ensue since the United States wishes to maintain its position as the lone superpower. China has the advantage of high national morale and unity. When China's GDP approaches that of the United States, the world will be very different than it is today.[13]

Different Attitudes toward China

There are essentially three different attitudes toward the growth of China's power among the countries of Southeast Asia.

Suspicion: Indonesia. Either because of territorial disputes, ideological differences, or problems concerning overseas Chinese, among the ASEAN nations Indonesia is generally suspicious of China's growth toward world power status. As the largest and most important country in Southeast Asia, Indonesia exerts significant influence on ASEAN's policies toward China. Indonesia and China established diplomatic relations in July 1950. As such, Indonesia was one of the People's Republic of China's earliest diplomatic partners in East Asia.

From 1950 to 1965, notwithstanding certain conflicts and clashes between them, China and Indonesia generally enjoyed close relations. Their relationship peaked in the mid-1960s after Indonesia, because of its disputes with Malaysia, in January 1965 announced its intention to withdraw from the United Nations and establish a new world organization in its place. At that time, Indonesian president Sukarno was eager to establish an anti-imperialist axis comprising such countries as China, Indonesia, Vietnam, and North Korea. However, following the September 30 Incident in 1965, relations between Indonesia and China nosedived. In 1967, China withdrew its diplomatic personnel from Indonesia, and, until relations between the two countries were resumed in August 1990, their relationship was tense and hostile. Even after the normalization of relations, three problems persisted to one degree or another in China's relations with the ASEAN states.

The first problem concerns historical disputes, including some from the distant past as well as some from the 1950s and 1960s. Some Indonesians believe that China invaded Java early in the thirteenth century and view Zheng He's maritime explorations as having a great influence on that area. More recently, China's support of the Indonesian Communist Party in the 1950s and 1960s was also regarded as interference into Indonesia's domestic affairs. China's past support for the Communist parties of Thailand and Burma likewise generated disputes and clashes between China and these two Southeast Asian neighbors.

The second problem concerns Chinese Indonesians and overseas Chinese in Indonesia. Ethnic Chinese, who account for 3 percent of the total population of Indonesia, play an important role in Indonesia's economy. The Chinese cannot forget the numerous instances of large-scale anti-Chinese pogroms that have scarred Indonesian history. They view the persecution and bloodletting carried out against Chinese in Indonesia as a manifestation of hostility to China that arouses their indignation. In the past, these events were seen as the domestic affairs of Indonesia. Starting in the 1990s, however, more and more Chinese and the Chinese government, too, began paying attention to these matters. For example, in September 1998, the Chinese government showed great concern for attacks against Chinese in Indonesia. At the same time, large-scale investments in China by some wealthy groups of Indonesian Chinese influence

Indonesia's economy to some degree and inspire doubts on the part of the Indonesian government concerning the loyalty of these Chinese groups to Indonesia.

Problems concerning ethnic Chinese are common throughout Southeast Asia because of the rather large share that they and their descendants have in the Southeast Asian economies. In Malaysia, they account for 61 percent of economic activity, in Thailand 95 percent, in Indonesia 73 percent, and in the Philippines 60 percent.[14]

The third problem relates to territorial water boundaries between China and Indonesia. Some Indonesians are very suspicious of China, and some in the Indonesian military even regard it as the potentially largest direct threat to Indonesian sovereignty. China's rapid growth over a period of many years has focused the attention of the Indonesian military on the parallel growth of Chinese military forces. The Indonesian military believes that continued development will enable China to become the strongest economic and military power in the region, raising the possibility of military clashes over territorial demands between China and Southeast Asian countries. According to the U.N. Law of the Sea, which took effect in November 1994, Indonesia enjoys the rights of an archipelagic state and can lay sovereign claim to 3 million square miles of land and sea as well as possessing an exclusive economic zone. Indonesia's rights conflict with China's sovereignty and territorial claims in the South China Sea as well as its claim to an exclusive economic zone. In 1996, diplomatic disputes flared between the two countries as Indonesia asserted China's actions in the islands of the South China Sea violated international law. China supports the proposal made by Indonesia and other countries to make Southeast Asia a free, peaceful, and neutral area. ASEAN foreign ministers formally introduced this proposal in November 1971.

Indonesia adopted a contradictory standpoint in its dialogue on cooperation with China. On the one hand, Indonesia welcomed and supported China's joining ASEAN's dialogue system and hoped that the system could establish and maintain peace and stability in the region. Peace and stability are essential to economic development in both China and Indonesia. On the other hand, Indonesia worried that China's increasing involvement in Southeast Asia would weaken its own traditional position as the leading country in ASEAN. Indonesia hoped to further its cooperation with China via China's participation in the ASEAN dialogue, but, at the same time, anxious about China's growing influence in the region, it hoped to check China's influence via ASEAN.

To achieve these two purposes, Indonesia sought to draw U.S. and Australian power into the region as a counterbalance to China. Indonesia provided the U.S. Navy a port of call for ship repair. In addition, in 1995 Indonesia signed a security agreement with Australia declaring that the two countries would cooperate to protect their common security interests and even could take necessary joint action, including military action.

Indonesia even agreed to Singapore's proposal to make India a member of the ASEAN Forum, a proposal that was likewise intended to balance China. In fact, the main threat to Indonesia comes not from China but from inside Indonesia itself.

Ambivalence: Malaysia, the Philippines, Vietnam, and Brunei. These countries see China's path toward becoming a world power as an important opportunity for their own economic development, but one that may also pose a potential threat to their security and stability. They have in common disputes with China regarding sovereignty over the Nansha Islands and are concerned about China's action to protect its sovereignty in the South China Sea, especially the increase of China's military power.

At present, however, their discomfort with China's development is not the main trend. For example, the Philippines sees any threat from China as lying in the distant future. In fact, the internal problems of the Philippines are far more serious than the so-called China threat. These countries are also well aware of the great benefits that cooperation with China may deliver. China's stand during the 1997–1998 financial crisis served to promote such cooperation. Therefore, these countries publicly choose to cooperate with China, avoid opposing China openly, and generally welcome China's cooperation with ASEAN.

Among these countries, Malaysia has been most in step with China's policies. Under the leadership of former premier Mahathir, it was particularly active in promoting cooperation in Southeast Asia. Mahathir was critical of Western culture and values and actively upheld the histories and cultures of Southeast and East Asia. Malaysia played a leading role and, to a certain degree, acted as spokesman in strengthening and consolidating cooperation among Third World and developing countries. Shared values served as the foundation for cooperation between China and Malaysia. Therefore, Malaysia opposed attempts to contain China and favored engagement.

Malaysia opposes using China's growth as an excuse to view China as a threat. Mahathir said publicly that viewing China as a threat could be a self-fulfilling prophecy. He thought that basing U.S. troops in East Asia to keep an eye on China was a waste of effort. Many high-ranking Malaysian officials expressed the same opinion arguing that engagement, not containment, was the right policy.

By engaging China, Malaysia aims to establish a normal framework and a multilateral connection so that China can play a role in maintaining peace and stability. Engagement serves a dual purpose. A multilateral system helps Malaysia hedge against the possibility of a Chinese threat to its security while, at the same time, providing opportunities for Malaysia to benefit economically from China's ascent to the status of a major world power. Malaysia hopes to establish increasingly close economic links with China on the basis of mutual respect. Both countries can benefit from this interdependent relationship. For that purpose, Malaysia welcomes China's entry into the international community and supports bringing it into the multilateral system of Southeast Asia. Some Americans even think that Malaysia has formed an alliance with China to oppose Western economic aggression and international financial speculators.

China's firm stance of nonintervention in the internal affairs of other countries and the attitude that Malaysian leaders display toward ethnic Chinese in Malaysia facilitate the solution of sensitive problems in relations between the two countries. Malaysian leaders have refuted the notion that investments in China by Malaysian Chinese indicates that they are disloyal to their own country. China's firm commitment to helping ASEAN countries weather the East Asian financial crisis also won favor in Kuala Lumpur, and Malaysian leaders publicly expressed their appreciation of China's position.

Nevertheless, Malaysia and some other countries do not trust China completely. In private, they are suspicious of China to one degree or another and on guard against potential conflicts of interest with it. Malaysia's military and security institutions are wary of the instability caused by China's development, especially its competition with the United States and Japan. Of course, Malaysia is concerned not only about China but also about other countries, because it is the only Southeast Asia country that has territorial sea disputes with all its neighbors. Yet it views the most important of these disputes as that concerning sovereignty over the islands in the South China Sea. Although China and Malaysia both support a peaceful solution or joint exploration as the way to resolve this issue, no concrete measures to implement this approach have yet been taken. Therefore, Malaysian military authorities remain on the alert vis-à-vis China.

Apart from the military threat, Malaysia has another concern with respect to China. Because ethnic Chinese account for 29 percent of the population of Malaysia, the Malaysian government worries that, if China's economic reform falters, large numbers of Chinese will pour into Malaysia and constitute a serious threat to the country's stability.

In addition, Malaysia is concerned about economic competition from China. China has absorbed a great deal of foreign investment, and its exports compete with those of ASEAN for foreign markets. However, some ASEAN leaders believe that China's market economy, together with the development of the economies of Japan and the United States, provides an impetus to ASEAN economic growth.

Although Malaysia is ambivalent toward China, in actuality there is a lot of space for the development of relations between the two countries. Malaysia's suspicion of China does not affect the development of its relations with China. From the 1990s, political relations between the two countries have been strengthened and solidified. The frequent exchange of visits of the two countries' leaders improved mutual trust. Improvements were even made in military cooperation, the most sensitive field. Visits to China by large Malaysian business delegations in the 1990s jump-started the development of trade relations between these two countries. In just a decade, the trade volume between them increased fivefold. Despite the impact of the East Asian financial crisis of 1997 and 1998, the volume of two-way trade continued to increase at a rapid pace.

Approbation: Thailand, Burma, and Singapore. These countries believe that China's ascent to the status of a world power provides them more opportunities than threats. Consequently, they are more actively engaged with China and hope that it can establish closes relations with Southeast Asia. Although they have lingering doubts about the implications of China's growth, this is by no means the main current in their thinking. These countries are the primary force promoting the establishment of political and economic relation between China and Southeast Asia.

Burma, Thailand, and Singapore all are committed to engaging China and reject the opposite policy of containment, which, they believe, would produce negative outcomes. They see the further development of mutually beneficial economic relations as the main form of engagement with China and a way to integrate China into the regional and the global economies, each of which possesses its own rules and regulations. A second form of engagement is political. Viewing China as a legitimate competitor rather than an adversary, Singapore has long advocated and supported China's participation in regional forums, including granting China observer status in ASEAN. Singapore advised it to take part in the APEC forum and the Asia-Europe conference, and it actively supported its application to join the WTO. The purpose of Singapore's political communication with China is to make China respect international rules and solve disputes with diplomatic methods and negotiation. Singapore's leaders, beginning with Lee Kuan Yew, enjoy frank and sincere communications with their Chinese counterparts. At the same time, Singapore strongly rejects the notion that it is a "third China" and emphasizes that its cooperation with China is based on mutual economic benefit, not the politics of ethnic affinity. It is always wary about being viewed as an agent of China in Southeast Asia. The third aspect of Singapore's cooperation with China involves the modernization of its armed forces as a defensive measure in light of the strategic instability in the Asian-Pacific region.

Like South Korea, Singapore changed its policies toward China after deriving benefits from contact with China. In the 1960s, Singapore tended to regard China as its enemy and harbored strong suspicions of China. The year 1978, when Deng Xiaoping paid a visit to Singapore, was the turning point in the relationship between the two countries. China viewed Singapore as a model of a state open to the world and invited Singaporeans to offer advice on its reform and opening-up policy. Dr. Wu Qingrui, the architect of Singapore's economic strategy, accepted the position of special adviser for China's economic special zones. Lee Kuan Yew himself was a senior adviser to the Chinese government as well. China learned the concept of economic reform and opening up from Singapore's experience. Singapore showed it the way to reform and openness and encouraged it to develop trade, investment, technology transfer, and technical cooperation as means to improve its economy and its people's standard of living. As Lee Kuan Yew said, China's decision on opening up was the most notable factor resulting in Asian peace, stability, and growth. China viewed Singapore as a source of capital, enterprises, and technical management. Therefore, Singapore's assistance was a factor in China's growth.

Singapore also helped the world secure a better understanding of China's bedrock national interest. In 1995, when the Sino-U.S. relationship was strained owing to the Taiwan issue, Lee Kuan Yew warned Chinese leaders that, if Sino-U.S. relations remained unstable and the situation in the Taiwan Strait tense, then Singapore's industrial park in Suzhou could not be started on schedule. Three days later, Chinese leaders informed him that Taiwan would not be allowed to take the path of independence and that, if it did, China could not exclude using force to prevent this from happening. Therefore, Lee clearly understood that Chinese leaders valued the Suzhou industrial park project less than China's unification and territorial integrity. Afterward, Lee repeatedly advised U.S. and other leaders that they must accept that Taiwan and Tibet are parts of China and stop challenging China on this issue.

China's path toward becoming a great power via the policy of reform and opening up conveyed benefits to Singapore inasmuch as China became a huge potential market and a business partner of Singapore's. Singapore concluded that China's top priority was to modernize its economy and become an industrialized country by 2020, tantamount to becoming a world power. If it failed to achieve this goal, its relationship with the international community would suffer. Therefore, it is in the interest of the international community to facilitate its transition to becoming a world power since an economically modernized China will contribute to world peace and stability as a responsible member of the international community.

What China Must Do to Secure ASEAN's Support

First, China must respect Indonesia's role and position as the biggest member country in ASEAN and abjure any intention to compete with it regarding leadership in ASEAN. In 1997, when the Southeast Asia financial crisis erupted, China offered Indonesia an extraordinary export credit of US$200 million and an additional loan of US$400 million arranged by the International Monetary Fund. Altogether, it provided US$600 million to help Indonesia. In July 1997, it issued a special invitation to Indonesia's foreign minister and secretary of state to attend the ceremony marking Hong Kong's return to the motherland. China has taken a low-key approach to several instances of Indonesia's official contact with Taiwan. It consistently supports the statement proposed by Indonesia and other

ASEAN countries that the Southeast Asian region should be free, peaceful, neutral, and nonnuclear. Meanwhile, it actively pushes and develops its trade relationship with Indonesia.

Second, China should actively participate in multilateral dialogues with ASEAN countries, including Indonesia. In July 1993, it began to take part with ASEAN countries at the ASEAN security forum attended by seventeen countries, including Russia, South Korea, Japan, and the United States. In April 1995, ASEAN held its first security dialogue with China in Hangzhou. In July 1995, Vietnam was accepted into ASEAN. Then, in July 1997, Laos and Burma became the eighth and ninth members of ASEAN, respectively. With Cambodia's entry, the organization embraced all ten countries in the region.

It should be pointed out that the ASEAN members favor multilateral cooperation with China, not only to advance economic development, but also to troubleshoot and resolve any disputes between ASEAN and China since they view a collective approach as useful in balancing China's greater power vis-à-vis any individual ASEAN member state.

Furthermore, there are conflicts among member countries of ASEAN. Thus, it is reasonable that some member countries make use of the regional organization framework to restrain other member countries whose state interests are in tension with their own. Thus, it makes sense for the countries of ASEAN to reinforce the multilateral regional organization because, by so doing, not only can they prevent any powerful country from outside the region from controlling the area by itself, but they can also prevent any large power inside the area from achieving unilateral domination.

It also should be mentioned that the establishment of the ASEAN regional multilateral mechanism also supports the trend toward East Asian regionalism. Malaysia has consistently promoted an East Asian economic nucleus forum as a response to the formation of the NAFTA and European Union trade zones. One outstanding question is whether a multilateral East Asian economic organization without U.S. participation would be capable of managing its own regional economy and trade. Japan harbors doubts on this score but has not expressed its own attitude clearly. The concept, however, is congruent with the ideas advocated by Mao Zedong and Zhou Enlai in the 1950s and 1960s, namely, that Asia belongs to the Asians. China should support Malaysia's idea and should also skillfully manage the relation between East Asian economic cooperation and APEC, which includes countries such as the United States and Australia. In 1997, China's positive response to Malaysia's ten plus three proposal (ten countries from ASEAN plus China, Japan, and South Korea) was a significant measure.

China's active cooperation with ASEAN is also of great significance in facilitating its contribution to developing a peaceful and stable regional environment in Southeast Asia. Such cooperation can indirectly soften the element of containment in the U.S. dual strategy of engaging and containing China. In order to sustain the further development of its relationship with China, ASEAN is also inclined to persuade the United States not to carry out its containment strategy because it inhibits the development of multilateral cooperative mechanisms with China. Thus, ASEAN plays a conciliatory role in potential conflicts between the United States and China.

In addition, China's proposal in late 2001 to establish a free trade zone between ASEAN and China was of great significance. At their meeting on May 16, 2002, China and the ASEAN countries resolved to establish a free trade zone in ten years. Such a zone, embracing a population of 1.7 billion, will be the largest in the world, with a collective GDP of more than US$2 trillion.

Such actions on the part of China serve to neutralize the impact of the China threat theory among ASEAN countries. Close economic integration between China and ASEAN indicates that China is willing to develop its economy in tandem with those of ASEAN countries and willing to let them share the economic benefits of its own rapid growth. Knowledgeable officials point out that, after the establishment of a China-ASEAN free trade zone, trade inside it will increase by 50 percent; the economic growth rate of ASEAN countries will rise by 1 percent, and China's economic growth will advance by 0.3 pecent. In sum, China's active cooperation and dialogue with ASEAN plays an important role in its participation in the political and economic order of peace and stability in Southeast Asia.

Third, China respects ASEAN's strategy of inducing the great powers to act with restraint and does not regard this strategy as one aimed at China. To be sure, there can be no doubt that ASEAN's attempt to get the United States, Japan, Russia, the European Union, and India to cooperate within an ASEAN framework implies its desire to have these countries balance the impact of China on Southeast Asia. Nevertheless, China should not be hypersensitive and should not view such action simply as a strategy aimed at China. This is only one of a number of different objectives that ASEAN is pursuing. If conflicts of interest should occur in the future between members of ASEAN and Japan or the United States, then the practice of self-restraint on the part of the major powers will be useful in managing any such conflicts. More important is that China should try to convince the members of ASEAN that its becoming a world power is a development that does not clash with their own national interests. This is because China will not resort to force to solve the problems and conflicts between itself and the ASEAN countries. It should also be pointed out that the ASEAN countries do not necessarily fully trust the United States, as former Malaysian prime minister Mahathir pointed out some time ago. The United States is just one factor in the Southeast Asian balance of power. ASEAN is inclined to assume that security and stability in Southeast Asia mainly depend on the establishment of its own multilateral security dialogue and trust-building mechanisms, including the cooperative mechanism between ASEAN and China. Malaysia and other countries do not desire either Chinese or U.S. domination or control of Southeast Asia.

From the perspective of international relations theory, the countries of Southeast Asia, which are medium and small states compared to China, facing the rise of a large neighboring state such as China, find it difficult to choose between the strategies of jumping on the bandwagon or going along, but it is also difficult for them to fully choose the strategy of aligning themselves against China and with the United States, the status quo world power. The reason is that such a strategy may benefit the United States, but it would be of no practical benefit to the Southeast Asian states. Even worse, they may run a great risk of conflict with their large neighboring country of China and achieve results that are directly contrary to their interests. This would not accord with the interests of Southeast Asian countries and with their desire to establish a zone of peace and neutrality.

Fourth, China should be especially cautious in managing conflicts over territory and sovereignty in the South China Sea with Southeast Asian countries. It should persist in avoiding armed conflicts and in resolving disputes peacefully on the basis of mutual respect and benefit.

To sum up, regarding how the countries of Southeast Asia deal with China's emergence as a world power, what China must do is to respect the interests of the ASEAN states, actively promote its cooperation with them in developing trade, let them share its growing benefits, and act as the driving force behind their economic development. It should strive for a relationship that, even though it contains an element of competition, is not a zero-sum game or does not involve intense competition. The ASEAN states should not think of China's growth as an obstacle to their own development.

In recent years, a number of ASEAN states have developed a more mature understanding of China's growth. Where before they emphasized the elements of competition and threat associated with its development, they now advocate adapting to this new reality and promoting a higher degree of economic relations with China. This shows that they have successfully adjusted their attitudes toward the reality of China's emergence as a world power.

The former prime minister of Singapore, Goh Chok Tong, put it well: "We should see China as an opportunity, not a threat. If we look at China as a threat, we will be scared to death. On the contrary, if we think of China as an opportunity, then we will be more creative and develop rapidly. We have established a good relationship with China. In the past, we shared our own developmental experience with China, but now we expect that we can benefit from China's rapidly growing economy." His conclusion: "China's development is not the end of us. Actually it can offer us endless opportunity."[15]

China's economic development also stimulates that of East Asia. In the early years of the twenty-first century, the growth rate of East Asia was around 6 percent, and East Asia was the region with the fastest growth rate in the world, a phenomenon that was inextricably linked to the China's growth and the growth of its market. With the help of the Chinese economy, trade within East Asia has increased quickly to the point where it finally exceeds exports to the United States. Intraregional exports accounted for more than one-third of all exports by 2003. China's economic power does not negatively affect the interests of Southeast Asian countries whose industry is labor intensive. On the contrary, with respect to clothing, footwear, and home products, China, along with Southeast Asia, is striving for higher levels of industrialization, which indicates that its development is healthy and mutual. For example, Malaysia has increased its exports of low-technology palm oil to China by a factor of three, and Thailand greatly benefits from large numbers of Chinese tourists. Those enterprises and countries that are connected with China on the supply chain will obtain new benefits from its development. In short, for Asia and even the whole world, China's revitalization will by no means be a zero-sum game.[16]

South Korea: From Skeptical Neighbor to Development Partner

The Korean Peninsula has special significance for China. North and South Korea are not only neighbors of China; they also have special historical and cultural relations with it. The Korean Peninsula was once a trap in which China fell, paying a huge price as a result. In the history of its feudal dynasties and Korea, China not only invaded and ruled Korea at one time but also fought wars with Japan over it and paid a great price to defend its interests. In the Sui dynasty, it fought three wars with Korea but met with resistance and was held in check. The failure of these wars resulted in domestic peasant uprisings, which was one of the important factors contributing to the rapid disappearance of the Sui dynasty. Tang Taizong, too, conducted several unsuccessful campaigns against Korea. Later on, the Tang dynasty became involved in Korea's civil wars. The Yuan dynasty once ruled the Korean Peninsula, established administrative divisions, and directly ruled Korea. During the Ming dynasty, China maintained close relations with Korea. In the late sixteenth century, the Ming dynasty dispatched forces to Korea on three occasions. These armies fought against Japan alongside with Korean forces and, ultimately, expelled the Japanese military forces from Korea. The Qing dynasty continued to maintain a special relationship with Korea, which led to the 1894–95 War against Japan, a war that cost China heavily in both treasure and territory. China was forced not only to concede suzerainty over Korea to Japan but also to cede Taiwan and pay large sums of money to Japan. In 1950, the military conflict between South and North Korea drew China into war again. Though the United States was ultimately compelled to sign a cease-fire in the first war it did not win, the war escalated the confrontation between China and the United States and made Taiwan an object of strategic competition between the two countries. During the Cold War, China and the Korean Peninsula occupied a special status. China supported North Korea, while the United States supported South Korea.

Obviously, the question of how to manage affairs on the Korean Peninsula has always been of great importance to China as a regional power. As China rises to the status of a world power, how well will it be able to handle its relations with the two states that occupy the Korean Peninsula? By continuously drawing lessons from history, it will not follow the same old road as before.

The development of relations between China and South Korea demonstrates that, in the process of becoming a world power, China can assure neighboring countries that its own development is not a threat but an opportunity for mutual development. South Korea is a model in this respect, inasmuch as the relations between South Korea and China have progressed from mutual hostility, mutual containment, and lack of dialogue, through mutual acceptance and normalization, to improved cooperation in many political and economic spheres of activity. During this process, both sides gained the opportunity to develop, and it may be predicted with confidence that their mutual relations will further progress because there are no significant impediments toward this end. This sea change in relations occurred at the same time as China's rise to the status of a world power.

The relations between China and South Korea present two different pictures before and after 1990. South Korean attitudes toward China underwent a qualitative change in the second of these two periods.

Prior to 1980, South Korea regarded China as a threat. South Koreans viewed China as a revolutionary country dissatisfied with the existing international order and determined to overturn it. China's Communist ideology and support for the North Korean government sufficed to convince South Korea that it faced a unified threat from North Korea and China. Thus, South Korea had no choice but to follow the United States and Japan in dealing with China and considering it a Cold War threat that needed to be contained. At the same time, China viewed South Korea as a camp follower supporting aggressive U.S. policies in Asia. South Korea appeared to be a hostile country in league with U.S. imperialism and Japanese militarism and one of the few Asian countries to support the Taiwan regime. Therefore, China had no choice but to support North Korea in order to deal with the threat from the south. It often publicly criticized South Korea as a fascist regime. This was the first stage of the two countries' relations.

The second stage began with the reform and opening up of China from 1979. Although both parties still clung to a hostile attitude toward each other, there were some hints of improvement. South Koreans came to view China not as a country that sought to overturn the existing international order but rather as one that sought to revise the world order in a reasonable way that could be accepted by the international community. Moreover, South Korea calculated that it could surely benefit from China's economic reform and opening up. Therefore, the two countries circumvented the political obstacles and began trading with each other, initially through third parties. In 1985, China's trade with South Korea amounted to US$1.161 billion, compared to US$480 million with North Korea. China and South Korea were able to separate economic and political affairs on the basis of their changing attitudes toward each other.

The latest stage began in 1990. In that year, the South Korean Trade Agency was established in Beijing, thus initiating direct trade between the two countries. In 1991, both parties granted most-favored-nation trading status to each other, and, in 1992, formal diplomatic relations were established after South Korea severed relations with Taiwan. Ever since then, the South Korean people have no longer viewed China as an enemy because it will not encourage North Korea to pursue reunification by force and it treasures stability and development on the Korean Peninsula. In 1989, when Western countries applied severe sanctions against China, South Korea opposed those sanctions. Instead, it initiated positive cooperation with China.

In the late 1990s, the relations between China and South Korea developed smoothly. China pursued evenhanded policies toward both North and South Korea and opposed outside pressure on North Korea. On the other hand, it insisted that the Korean Peninsula be a nonnuclear zone and supported peaceful unification through equal negotiations. It hopes to develop not only trade and economic relations with South Korea but also political relations. For South Korea, the rapidly developing Chinese economy not only provided commercial opportunities and markets but also contributed to the stability and prosperity of the entire region. The best example was the 1997 Asian financial crisis.

The further development of bilateral relations fostered increased trade, investment, and personnel exchanges. Trade turnover in 1992 was US$6.4 billion. By 2001, it had grown to US$35.9 billion, by which time both countries were each other's third largest trading partners. South

Korea is the second biggest investor in China, and China became the top destination country for South Korean tourists.

In sum, the relations between China and South Korea have undergone several phases, from enemies, to neither friend nor foe, to equal partners and neighbors; from China as a threat to it promoting stability on the Korean Peninsula. South Korea has changed from viewing China as a revolutionary state that supported North Korea's strategy of unifying Korea by armed force to seeing China as a country that supports peace and the status quo on the Korean Peninsula. South Korea's government has altered its course toward China from one of automatically following the United States and Japan to one of recognizing and communicating with China and viewing it not only as a reliable partner but also as one with which it even shares the same perspective on issues such as criticizing Japan on historical issues left over from the era of Japanese aggression.

In sum, the transformation of China's relations with South Korea demonstrates that China's rise to a world power presents no threat to its neighbors. On the contrary, it provides further opportunities for cooperation and development. China's growth has benefited from Korean experience, capital, technology, and talents. South Korea enjoys new economic motivations and markets. The South Korean people themselves consider their relations with China to be quite successful.

Among China's neighbors, the China threat theory has the least influence in South Korea. This is because, in its exchanges with China, South Korea has gained not only experience but confidence as well. The Koreans believe that they are generally more advanced than the Chinese, and they advanced the notion that China was the world's factory while South Korea was the world's research and development center. The South Koreans thought that, if they could maintain this technological edge, China would remain a golden market for a long time to come.

On the foundation of this historic change, China should further advance its policy toward the Korean Peninsula via the following measures: (1) Maintain peace and stability on the peninsula, oppose any attempt to change the status quo through force, and demonstrate that China is a defender and supporter of the status quo. (2) Continue an evenhanded policy toward both parties on the Peninsula, support the political and economic stability of North Korea, and develop political and economic cooperation with South Korea. (3) Support the nonnuclearization of the peninsula; nonnuclearization is in the interests of China, the

Korean Peninsula, and the whole world. (4) Advocate peaceful and independent efforts to achieve the unification of the peninsula and oppose any outside interference into the process of reunification, especially the threats of certain great powers to engage in war or apply sanctions against North Korea.

On the basis of such policies, China and the two countries on the Korean Peninsula can enjoy a bright future sustained by the stability and prosperity resulting from China's rise to the status of a world power.

6

China and Unification

Strategic Choices on the Taiwan Issue

THE RELATIONSHIP BETWEEN UNIFICATION
AND WORLD POWER STATUS

In Antiquity World Powers Achieved Their Status by Unifying the Core and Integrating Neighboring Territories

Unification is closely tied to the growth of great powers. Without unification, great powers cannot emerge. The development of world civilizations illustrates this point, which is one that China should bear in mind: "From the perspective of the Chinese people, China can become a great power in the true sense of that term only after it completes the process of unification. In the present world no country that has not completed its unification can be said to be a great power. In this sense, U.S. actions with regard to the Taiwan problem not only challenge China's history but also challenge its future insofar as they constitute an impediment to its rise."[1]
As historians like Bai Shouyi have pointed out:

The emergence and development of civilization are linked to varying degrees of unification. At the beginning of a civilization, tribes evolve into states. Only then do city-states, states, and unions of states develop. The civilization of ancient Egypt was built on the base of its integration as a state. There followed the states of the Middle Kingdom and the New Kingdom. In the two rivers area of Western Asia, unified kingdoms likewise emerged. Babylonian civilization reached its peak of prosperity after integration. Assyrian civilization was based on the unification of Egypt, Syria, Palestine, and the land of the two rivers. The Persian Empire was based on the unification of Iran, the land of the two great rivers, Palestine, and Asia Minor. The Macedonian Empire unified Persia and Greece successively. The Roman Empire, whose glory endured for several centuries, was based initially on the unification of Italy.[2]

In the history of world civilizations, China is viewed as a special country. In addition to the continuity of its language, scholarship, and culture stretching far back in time, its major distinguishing feature is its deeply rooted culture of unification. In other cultures, unification was only a temporary phenomenon. Empires were built on the conquest of numerous small states and territories. But, as soon as the empires disintegrated (for whatever reason), they lacked the capacity to recover. These empires quickly dissolved into a multitude of small states and territories, and the process began all over again. Only Chinese history is entirely based on unification. Although China has experienced numerous periods of disunity, it differs from foreign countries because these periods of disunity were merely interludes in the vast narrative of unification. Unity is the main theme of Chinese history.

Unification and the Growth of Great Powers: Germany, the United States, the Soviet Union

In the process of becoming great powers, Germany, the United States, and the Soviet Union all faced the problem of unification, especially Germany, which went through it three times. However, unification had very different effects on the three countries. In the nineteenth century, the process of unification had largely positive effects and greatly accelerated the growth of these countries. Unification enhanced their overall strength and quickly made them world powers. Moreover, international society did not significantly influence or interfere with their unification. The process of unification basically involved competition among various domestic forces, the most powerful among these being the one that achieved unification.

In the twentieth century, however, it seems that negative elements increasingly entered into the unification process. To a certain extent, uni-

fication increased the strength of a country, but, compared with the nineteenth century, the effect was limited. No country could achieve its full
growth solely via unification. Furthermore, international society became
more and more of a factor in unification via pressure and interference.

Looking at the experience of Germany and the United States in the
nineteenth century, we can see that unification significantly accelerated
their rise as world powers. A lack of integration had greatly hindered the
growth of these two countries. When Germany was divided into dozens of
small states, it was impossible to form a large economic unit. This became
a great impediment in the competition with Great Britain, France, Russia,
and the Hapsburg Empire. In January 1871, after Germany announced the
completion of its unification, its political, economic, and military power
increased significantly. By the 1880s and 1890s, it had already become a
new center of Europe, advancing from a second-rate power to the main
power in Europe. Without unification, Germany could not have developed, let alone become a world power.

If the United States had not solved the division between North and
South, it would not have achieved its present status in the world. The two
sides were both very strong even though they were not equal in strength.
Without unification, the United States would not have developed very
much. The population of the Confederacy was 8 million; the North had
20 million people. The North had an army of 1 million, and the South
had more than 460,000. Although the South was nowhere near as strong
as the North, still it embraced the area of nine states with a quarter of the
total population of the United States. After the unification of the United
States in 1865, the fast pace of development demonstrated the great effect
of unification on growth.

Another important element with respect to the unification of Germany and the United States in the nineteenth century was that international society did not intervene in these processes. Yet there was
a significant difference in the case of Germany and Russia (the Soviet
Union) when they experienced a renewal of their power in the twentieth
century. Unification did not just fail to produce positive effects on their
growth; on the contrary, it had negative effects.

After the collapse of czarist Russia, Poland, Finland, and the three
Baltic countries successively declared their independence. Ukraine and
the countries of the Caucasus also established independent regimes. Yet,
in the early 1920s, Soviet Russia reunited Ukraine, Belarus, and the coun-

tries of the Caucasus and founded the Soviet Union in 1924. In 1939, after reabsorbing the three Baltic states, the Soviet Union in essence reestablished the boundaries of the former Russian Empire. The reabsorption of the Baltic states, however, had little impact on the growth of the Soviet Union. By 1939, Russia was already a world power. Apart from adding defense in depth to Leningrad in a military sense, the reintegration of the Baltic states was of no direct or positive help in the economic growth and political influence of the Soviet Union. Moreover, later on, the three Baltic states became the Achilles heel of the Soviet Union and spearheaded the dissolution of the Soviet Union. Taking advantage of glasnost and democratization, the three states promoted movements for complete national independence, first establishing so-called sovereign republics, and then formally declaring their independence. These actions created an irresistible trend toward the dissolution of the Soviet Union, destroying its structural foundation.

The two reunifications of Germany that occurred in the twentieth century had a different impact on its growth than the original unification in the nineteenth century. In the 1930s, Germany resumed the process of integration. It regained the Rhine area, which had been ceded to France, by dispatching troops in March 1936 to occupy the demilitarized zone. In March 1938, it sent troops to Austria and carried out the *Anschluss,* in effect swallowing up that country. This unification swelled the wild ambitions of the Nazis and encouraged their further aggression. Germany sought by means of war to regain its historical territory that had been ceded to Poland after World War I. This evoked opposition from the international community and culminated in Germany's defeat in World War II. In order to prevent Germany from again becoming a launching pad for war, the Soviet Union, the United States, France, and Britain initially divided it into four zones of military occupation. Thereafter, it was divided into two states. Austria regained its independence. Part of Germany's former territory was ceded to the Soviet Union (what is now Kaliningrad in Russia) and another part to Poland. Thus, Germany's second attempt at unification and expansion failed.

The second unification that Germany attempted in the twentieth century occurred in the 1990s. Owing to the collapse of the Soviet Union, the reunification of the two Germanies was carried out without a single shot being fired. (Of course, Germany expended a lot of money to accomplish the objective.) In reality, Germany was the biggest winner at the end of the

Cold War. After reunification, its strength was greatly enhanced with the addition of land and population. Even before reunification, it was the most powerful country in Europe. Afterward, its position was further reinforced.

At the same time, Germany chose a path of development in concert with the rest of Europe rather than going it alone. German reunification became an important step in the process of European unification. Therefore, reunification did not cause Germany to become a world power. Only when Europe achieves integration can Germany play a more important role in the world as a component of a unified Europe. Yet the road to unification is not smooth, and the result may turn out not to be what people expected. On the surface, the process of integration is conducive to building a powerful Europe because a unified European Union will have a population of some 400 million people, 100 million more than the United States, with a territory one-third the size of the United States and a GDP 80 percent that of the United States. In December 2002, the European Union launched a new round of expansion in which the number of its member countries reached twenty-five, its population increased to 450 million, and its GDP increased to US$8 trillion. However, this expansion did not bring a new dynamic to the European Union. While in 1979 the GDP of the then nine-member European Community was US$2.38 trillion, surpassing that of the United States, which was US$2.368 trillion, and in 1990 it had reached US$6.231 trillion, still surpassing that of the United States, which was US$5.465 trillion, by 2000 the U.S. GDP of US$9.834 trillion had shot ahead of that of the fifteen-member European Union, which was US$7.766 trillion.

Unification in Chinese History and China's Status as a World Power

The significance and function of unification in the history of China's various dynasties were similar to those of Germany and the United States in the nineteenth century. Unification and the process of becoming a world power went hand in hand. The completion of unification guaranteed the attainment of world power status. Moreover, the process of unification was barely affected by outside forces.

For example, during the Warring States period (475–221 B.C.), the state of Qin, which was already a major power, was able to impress the other six states with its might. But only after it unified the whole nation did Qin become the most powerful state in the Chinese and East Asian systems. From then on, unification was the key to becoming a world power.

The Han, Tang, Yuan, Ming, and Qing dynasties all became world powers by virtue of first unifying China. Unification depended on whether these dynasties were able to bring order out of chaos and ensure the social stability that was the precondition for prosperity.

Although the Song dynasty had once flourished, it did not complete the unification of China. Initially, it coexisted with the Liao and Xia kingdoms. Moreover, it often suffered defeats at the hands of the northern Liao and was compelled to cede territory and pay indemnities. Therefore, the Song could not be considered a world power, not to mention the Southern Song dynasty, which had fewer qualifications in this regard.

Taiwan: The Core of China's Unification Problem

While developing into a world power, China has upheld and strengthened national unity and safeguarded its sovereignty and territorial integrity. The return of Hong Kong in 1997 and of Macao in 1999 represented two important achievements in the process of Chinese unification. With respect to unification and territorial integrity, however, China still faces five challenges. These are the problems of the Diaoyu Islands, the South China islands, countering Xinjiang separatism, Tibetan independence, and Taiwanese independence. As some scholars have pointed out, whether one focuses on expanding the army and improving its combat effectiveness, adjusting ethnic relationships, increasing investments in western China, or strengthening ground forces and developing the navy, no single one of these measures by itself can resolve the five problems simultaneously. To safeguard China's territorial integrity, what is required is an integrated set of strategies and, in particular, some innovative ideas regarding how to proceed. The reunification of Taiwan with the mainland is still the key to restoring China's greatness. If this key issue is managed well, it will positively influence the resolution of the other issues.

U.S. INTERVENTION IS THE KEY OBSTACLE TO CROSS-STRAIT UNIFICATION

Brief Review of the Cross-Strait Relationship

Taiwan, a territory of thirty-six thousand square kilometers with a population in 2000 of some 23 million, had a GDP in that year of US$311 billion, which equates to a per capita income of US$13,838.

Since ancient times, Taiwan has been an inseparable part of China. In the distant geologic past, Taiwan and the mainland were physically joined. Then, because of the shifting of the earth's crust, the Taiwan Strait was formed, and Taiwan was divided from the mainland. In the period of the Three Kingdoms, Sun Quan sent Wei Wen at the head of a ten-thousand-man army to Yi Zhou (Taiwan). During the Yuan dynasty, the Penghu Patrol and Inspection Bureau was established to govern Taiwanese affairs. From early times, the Chinese considered Taiwan as a base for expeditions and commerce. From there, one could set out for the Liuqiu Islands, southern Korea, Kyushu in southern Japan, the Philippines, Indonesia, Thailand, etc. In 1604, the Dutch invaded Penghu. From 1624 to 1639, the Netherlands built castles in southern Taiwan. Around 1626, the Spanish occupied Keelung in northern Taiwan, but they were defeated by the Dutch in 1642. In 1661, the national hero Zheng Chenggong led troops to take back Taiwan and the following year expelled the Dutch. In 1683, Emperor Kangxi dispatched troops led by Shi Lang that defeated Zheng Chenggong's army and realized the unification of Taiwan with the mainland. Prior to 1895, when Japan defeated China in the Sino-Japanese War and China was forced to cede Taiwan to Japan, there was no doubt whatsoever that Taiwan was a part of China. In the fifty years from 1895 to 1945, Japan controlled Taiwan as a colony. At the Cairo Conference in November 1943, Chinese leader Chiang Kai-shek reached an agreement with U.S. president Franklin Delano Roosevelt and British prime minister Winston S. Churchill that Taiwan would be returned to China. This decision was reaffirmed at the July 1945 Potsdam Conference, which dealt with postwar arrangements of various sorts. After its surrender in August 1945, Japan returned Taiwan to the Guomindang government, and the Guomindang government exercised limited sovereignty rights over Taiwan during the following years. In 1949, the defeated Guomindang government escaped to Taiwan with 2 million mainlanders following it.

Owing to the outbreak of the Korean War, the United States, which had intended to give up Taiwan, now included it in the strategic defensive zone designed to contain the expansion of communism and, in July 1950, stationed the Seventh Fleet in the Taiwan Strait. In 1954, the United States signed a so-called mutual defense treaty with Chiang Kai-shek's government. That marked the separation of Taiwan from the mainland. However, not only did the government of the People's Republic of China consistently assert that Taiwan was an inseparable part of China, but the

Republic of China on Taiwan also declared that the mainland and Taiwan were inseparable. There was no difference between the two on this fundamental issue.

This common stance was later reflected in U.S. policy toward China. The framework of U.S. policy was defined by the three joint communiqués of 1972, 1978, and 1982. (The Taiwan Relations Act, passed in 1979 in the face of opposition from China, was also often invoked by the United States.) This framework consisted of four core elements: (1) The United States acknowledges that the Chinese people on both sides of the Taiwan Strait assert there is only one China, that Taiwan is a part of China, and that the People's Republic of China is the only legal government of China. (2) The United States maintains a nongovernment relationship with Taiwan. (3) The United States will reduce the quantity and quality of its weapons sale to Taiwan step by step. (4) The United States is concerned that the differences between the two sides of the strait be resolved peacefully. Thereafter, China and the United States have consistently dealt with the Taiwan issue within this framework.

In the late 1980s and early and mid-1990s, the cross-strait relationship underwent a great change. First, from 1979 on, the mainland more and more clearly declared that one country, two systems and peaceful unification were the basic policies to solve the Taiwan problem. Taiwan's leader, Chiang Ching-kuo, responded by announcing in 1987 that residents of Taiwan could return to the mainland to visit their relatives. For a number of years afterward, there was an upsurge of nongovernment communication and contact across the Taiwan Strait. In 1991, Taiwan issued a set of guiding principles for unification restating the position that both sides of the Taiwan Strait belong to one China and laid out a policy of three stages—short-term, medium-term, and long-term—for achieving unification. Through meetings between officials of the Straits Exchange Foundation (SEF) and the Association for Relations across the Taiwan Strait (ARATS), the two sides reached agreement on the one China principle. In 1995, President Jiang Zemin's Eight Point proposal regarding Taiwan advanced the conciliatory trend to a new stage. Had this trend continued, the prospects for cross-strait relations would have been bright.

Around this same time, however, in the late 1980s and early 1990s, three significant events occurred that influenced the cross-strait relationship and the framework of Sino-U.S. policy. First was the Tiananmen

Incident of 1989. Second was the dramatic change and dissolution of the Soviet Union and the East European Communist states. Third was political change in Taiwan. Lee Teng-hui succeeded Chiang Ching-kuo as Taiwan's top leader, and, starting in 1995, he promoted his policy of so-called Taiwanization, the Republic of China on Taiwan, and "special state-to-state relationship." He shredded the one China consensus achieved in 1992. Ultimately, he revealed his proindependence views to the world. The situation became even more complicated when the openly proindependence party that followed in his footsteps, namely, the Democratic Progressive Party (DPP), took power in 2000. In 1989, the United States applied sanctions against China, and, in 1992, it sold a large quantity of advanced fighter planes to Taiwan, an action that violated the U.S. commitment in the joint communiqué of 1982. In 1995, the United States, despite China's stern warnings, permitted Lee Teng-hui to visit the United States notwithstanding Washington's long-standing promise not to have official relations with Taiwan. Under these circumstances, the mainland was forced to respond to the changes carried out by Taiwan and the United States. In 1996, in response to Lee's visit to the United States and his enunciation in 1999 of the two states theory, the mainland carried out several rounds of military exercises.

Although President Jiang Zemin's visit to the United States in 1997 and President Clinton's visit to China in 1998, especially Clinton's public declaration of "three nonsupports," helped ease tension on the Taiwan problem, U.S. policy toward Taiwan still had changed a lot. This was mostly reflected in sympathy in the United States for Taiwan's democratization and its economic achievements. This phenomenon influenced official U.S. policy toward China. Nevertheless, the cross-strait relationship retrogressed in the process, and Taiwan refused to accept the one China principle. It took a series of covert proindependence measures as its policies deviated further and further away from the one China policy and posed an increasing obstacle to unification.

How to manage the issue of Taiwan posed a real conundrum during the process of China's rise to great power status. Which should be given priority: unification or development? Could China become a great power without first uniting the two sides of the Taiwan Strait? How could Taiwan be returned to the path of unification? If, in the end, China was compelled to use military force to bring about unification, how would this affect its rise to great power status?

Taiwan's Three Challenges to China's Unification and Growth

How to solve the Taiwan problem, or, put differently, how to attain and preserve unity, is a major problem facing a rising China. There are three dimensions to this problem.

New Challenges from within Taiwan

On May 20, 2000, the DPP, which advocates Taiwanese independence, came to power. This initiated a new stage in both Taiwanese politics and the cross-strait relationship. In his inaugural speech on May 20, 2000, Chen Shui-bian proclaimed the "Four Never and One No" policy: (1) The constitution will never contain a clause promising a referendum on Taiwanese independence. (2) The name *Republic of China* will never be changed, and the policy of unification will never be abrogated. (3) If the mainland does not use force against it, Taiwan will never declare independence. (4) In light of the tension aroused by Lee Teng-hui's two states theory, the government will avoid making any more trouble. Abrogation of the Guidelines for National Unification (adopted by the government in 1991) is out of the question. Subsequently, Chen talked about the possibility of holding discussions with the mainland regarding the topic of one China, but he rejected the one China principle. He said that the cross-strait talks should occur without preconditions and that the one China principle was just one of many topics. In his 2001 New Year's speech, he reiterated his views: "The people on both sides of the Taiwan Strait are one family and share the same goals of coexistence and mutual prosperity. They are living under the same roof and, therefore, should be considerate of each other. They should start with the integration of trade and culture, progressively build up mutual trust, and then seek a new structure of permanent peace and politic integration."

Two years after coming to office, Chen felt secure in power and was ready to initiate more extreme policies. He felt that he could depart from the aforementioned "Four Never and One No" policy to which he committed earlier. He began to put into effect his clandestine proindependence policy. He openly repudiated the 1992 one China policy agreement. He continued the Guomindang's so-called practical diplomacy, invoking Taiwan's so-called democracy to expand its international influence and seek access to various international organizations. He further strength-ened Taiwan's relationship with the United States and awarded impor-tant positions to proindependence overseas Taiwanese who returned to Taiwan from the United States, including even those who retained their nationality as Americans. He became complicit in proindependence, anti-China plots and emphasized the so-called Taiwanese-U.S. relation-ship, dispatching his defense minister to visit the United States with the aim of placing Taiwan under the protective umbrella of the United States and using the United States to confront the mainland. He rarely, if ever, referred to the Republic of China, deliberately sought to deemphasize Taiwan's Chinese roots, and peddled Lee Teng-hui's line, "China is China, and Taiwan is Taiwan." He changed the inscription in Taiwanese pass-ports from "Printed in the Republic of China" to "Printed in Taiwan." At the same time, he underscored Taiwanese localism and distorted the his-torical relationship between the mainland and Taiwan in order to boost so-called Taiwanese nationalism.

When the Guomindang and the People First Party, which support unification, were divided and defeated in the elections against the back-ground of economic decline, Chen's influence became even stronger. He served simultaneously as chairman of the DPP and president of the Republic of China, consolidating both party and government power in his own hands.[3]

In recent years, Taiwan has increased its purchases of U.S. weapons. Since the 1990s, it has spent an average of US$2 billion per year on U.S. weapons and, on numerous occasions, surpassed Saudi Arabia as the larg-est arms buyer. After the DPP took office, it went even further. Accord-ing to Taiwan's military plans, in the decade from 2001 to 2010, Taiwan intended to spend NT$4 trillion on military expenditures, or US$116.6 billion, more than US$11 billion per year, most of it to buy U.S. arms. From 1994 to 2000, each person in Taiwan was burdened with US$1,400 of military expenditure. From 2001 to 2010, this number was scheduled to increase to US$4,700.[4]

These developments posed an enormous challenge to the process of unification. In the past, although there were charlatans pretending to favor unification but actually supporting independence, such as Lee Teng-hui, who disrupted the unification process, at least the two sides had reached agreements on a one China policy and the concept of future unification. Within this framework, SEF and ARATS had initiated a process of negotiation. If the key problem in the past in the cross-strait relationship was *how* to achieve unification, now it became the problem of choosing between independence or unification. The question of *how* to achieve unification became a second-order priority. This is a new challenge to China's rise to world power status.

The New Challenge from the United States

The U.S. attitude toward Taiwan also became more changeable. Indeed, in the future, U.S. policy may constitute a huge barrier to peaceful unification of the two sides of the Taiwan Strait. Although after taking office President George W. Bush asserted that there would be no fundamental change in U.S. policy on the Taiwan problem and that the United States would adhere to the one China policy, oppose China using force to unify Taiwan, and oppose any Taiwanese declaration of independence, in reality he retreated from the Clinton administration's policy on this issue. During his 1998 visit to China, President Clinton had openly proclaimed the "Three Nos" policy, that is, no support for Taiwan joining world organizations open only to sovereign states, no support for a one China and one Taiwan or a two Chinas policy, and no support for Taiwanese independence. After Bush came to power, he not only violated the Three Nos policy but also openly announced that, if the mainland attacked Taiwan, the United States would go all out to protect it, although he later backed away from such statements. He also intended to upgrade the quality and quantity of U.S. weapons sales to Taiwan, although this did not actually occur, for a variety of reasons.

In sum, the Bush administration's policy toward Taiwan was a retreat from that of Clinton. There are always anti-China forces in the United States that are inclined to use Taiwan as a chess piece to contain China's rise, a strategic base to deal with the so-called China threat. Therefore, it is likely that U.S. Taiwan policy will experience further fluctuations and serve as a factor that impedes China's unification and rise to a world power.

New Challenges from Changing Attitudes of Mainland Chinese

In general, with respect to how to resolve the Taiwan issue, people on the mainland were inclined to support and uphold Deng Xiaoping's policy of "one country, two systems, and peaceful unification." This began to change in the late 1990s. Lee Teng-hui's 1995 visit to the United States, the mainland's 1996 maneuver against Taiwan, the 1999 U.S. bombing of the Chinese embassy in Belgrade, Lee's two states theory, the DPP's assumption of power, President Bush's 2001 speech on Taiwan policy that contravened the three communiqués, and Chen Shui-bian's covert independence policy all induced mainlanders to feel pessimistic about the prospects of peaceful unification and fed extremism. Some scholars and members of the news media believe that war between the two sides is inevitable and that there is no longer any room for a peaceful unification policy. They think that it is better to fight sooner rather than later. At the midpoint of the first decade of the twenty-first century, it was hard to be optimistic about trends in the cross-strait relationship. Various elements stood in the way of a smooth development of cross-strait relations over the longer term.

First, there was no clear answer to the question of unification versus independence. Taiwan's attitude toward unification versus independence was ambiguous, and, during the administration of Chen Shui-bian, the Taiwanese leadership was drifting away from unification. There was no political force in Taiwan able to unify the fragmented will of the Taiwanese people. Second, even if at some point a majority supports unification, there still remains the problem of how to achieve it. In Taiwan, even those supporting unification have deep differences with the mainland's policy of one country, two systems. This is the result, inter alia, of Taiwan's long-time "hate communism, dread communism, and defame communism" education as well as desiring unification on the basis of two equal political entities, the effects of localism, and consideration of personal interest. Third, there are long-existing conflicts between the two sides on the timing of unification. Contrary to mainland views that unification should occur as soon as possible, Taiwanese supporters of unification believe that the question of unification should be left for the future to solve, with no timetable. In any case, throughout most of the first decade of the twenty-first century, supporters of independence held power in Taiwan. U.S. support for Taiwanese independence (whether open or covert), motivated by the desire to contain China, will dim the prospects of unification for a long time to come.

If, in the past, mainlanders basically supported the, one country, two systems formula, reflecting the optimism engendered by the return of

Hong Kong in 1997, now that support is fragmenting as the optimism that sustained it has dissipated.

THE FUTURE OF TAIWAN: AN ANALYSIS OF SEVERAL OPTIONS

Two Improbable Scenarios

Considering the political, economic, military, and cultural aspects of the two sides, there are two extreme options with virtually no possibility of their ever occurring. The first is for China to take the initiative and announce that it is giving up Taiwan or allowing it to conduct a referendum in which the choices are unification or independence. If the majority in Taiwan vote for independence, China announces its acceptance of this result, and Taiwan becomes an independent country. The other equally unlikely scenario is for Taiwan to announce that it will become a province or special region of the People's Republic of China.

Eight Possible Scenarios

Any one of the following scenarios could actually be played out in the future.

First, after China has experienced a long period of economic and military development and its comprehensive national strength has gradually increased, the issue of national reunification will move to the top of the mainland's action agenda. Assuming that Taiwan continues its clandestine independence policy, mainland China insists that it will not tolerate Taiwan's open-ended stalling with respect to reunification. Beijing announces a deadline for peaceful reunification; Taiwan ignores this and persists in its de facto independence policy. Judging that the possibility of peaceful reunification has been exhausted, mainland China opts to use military force. Before the expiration of the deadline comes, mainland China takes successfully military action to achieve reunification, after which Taiwan becomes the third special administrative region in the People's Republic, along with Hong Kong and Macao.

Second, as China increases its economic and military strength over a long period, there is a big change in the power correlation between China and the United States, and their relationship also changes in qualitative terms. With China adhering to the guidelines of peace and development and opening to the outside world, mutual distrust between the two countries dissipates. The United States comes to realize that China's reunification is not a strategic threat, or that it faces more imminent threats than the hypothetical China threat, or, finally, that owing to domestic changes U.S. power is no longer what it used to be. In these circumstances, the Taiwan issue will further diminish in importance, and the two countries will enter an era of all-around cooperation the continuation of which becomes of paramount importance to the United States. The benefits deriving from such cooperation exceed those deriving from a policy of seeking to contain China. With respect to a number of important national interests, the United States needs closer cooperation with China. Therefore, it declares that it will never interfere in the Taiwan issue, which exerts much more pressure on Taiwan to accept peaceful reunification and leads to important changes in public opinion on the island. Proponents of peaceful reunification become the mainstream, and reunification is achieved under the principle that "the Taiwanese people are masters of their own destiny."

Third, after constant and consistent development over a period of many years, China achieves economic prosperity and political stability. Democracy and the development of a legal system have progressed greatly, which attracts Taiwan. The development of mainland China has created good opportunities for Taiwan. The two sides of the strait are developing at the same time. Most people in Taiwan realize that the status quo of neither unification nor independence cannot meet the developmental needs of either side. Or, when the proindependence forces develop further, they reach their limit, and a backlash occurs as people realize that all kinds of internal problems will lead to a serious economic and political crisis. They also come to understand that the clandestine proindependence policy pursued by the Taiwanese authorities is the main factor responsible for the island's erratic economic development. So support for a change in policy grows, as does approval of or support for mainland China. This gradually increases sentiment in favor of peaceful reunification. The two sides reach short-, medium-, and long-term agreements to reunify China through peaceful negotiation.

Fourth, the political environment changes in Taiwan as a result of domestic evolution. Possible causes for such a change include significant factional splits in the DPP as a result of an intraparty power struggle, a poor job of managing domestic affairs causing supporters to rethink their allegiance to the DPP, and, the reemergence after several years' in the political wilderness of the Guomindang and the People First Party and their cooperation in seeking long-term advantage over the DPP in the electoral process, resulting in a stable pan-Blue alliance[5] undergirding a joint administration supported by middle forces. Meanwhile, the mainland is developing its economy and politics on a foundation of stability. In this situation, the cross-strait relationship is reestablished along the the lines set forth in the Guidelines for National Unification, and the prospects for unification are bright once again. Although there may still be conflicts over how to effect unification, the two sides finally reach a definite agreement on peaceful unification. The trend toward unification becomes irreversible.

Fifth, a long-term split between the Guomindang and the People First Party encourages the DPP to pursue its wild ambition for independence regardless of warnings from the mainland and international community. It misjudges the support of the United States or, spurred on by anti-China forces in the United States, openly holds a referendum on independence and proclaims the founding of a so-called Republic of Taiwan. The mainland, bolstered by long-term economic and military development, possesses ample power to counter Taiwanese independence forces. It launches a war of unification that swiftly achieves its goal.

Sixth, if the mainland's politics and economy falter, Taiwan seizes the opportunity to declare independence, and the mainland then establishes a military blockade and imposes economic sanctions against Taiwan, a state of war will exist between the two sides. Initially, Taiwan will make some progress toward independence, but most of the world will not recognize its split from China. The two sides will remain hostile to each other. Subsequently, because of the effects of the mainland's blockade and sanction, anti-independence forces inside Taiwan will bounce back and get the upper hand; the two sides will initiate talks, and unification will be back on track.

Seventh, the only possibility of a break between the two sides of the Taiwan Strait is if the mainland fails to solve its political and economic problems. Not only are the original problems unsolved, but additional problems have accumulated. During a prolonged economic crisis, large-scale political upheavals occur such as those in Russia during the reform era. The proindependence forces in Taiwan wield political power, take advantage of the opportunity to promote Taiwanese independence, and manage to secure support from the United States and other countries.

Eighth, the mainland, whether it has developed successfully or not, misgauges the domestic, cross-strait, and international situations and hastily launches a war of unification that results in a significant military defeat and evokes internal political upheavals. The United States, Japan, and other Western countries seize the opportunity to carry out the conspiracy of splitting China and supporting Taiwanese independence.

Summing up, the probability of unification is far greater than that of a split as world leaders, including former U.S. president Bill Clinton, acknowledged.

DEVELOPMENT AND UNIFICATION ARE TWO SIDES OF THE SAME COIN

The View That Unification Precedes Development

In the cross-strait relationship, unification is more likely than a split. Regardless of whether one is speaking of unification or split, peaceful unification or coercive unification, the key question/prerequisite in all cases depends on the mainland's developmental prospects. As long as the mainland maintains a relatively stable political environment and keeps up the pace of economic development, Taiwan will be unable to proclaim independence, and the forces in favor of unification will grow. But, if economic and political problems arise, or if the mainland commits significant strategic errors even while things are going smoothly, Taiwanese independence forces may engage in reckless behavior. Even if the mainland's development does not proceed smoothly, Taiwanese independence is just one possibility among others. Moreover, the proindependence forces might first appear to be succeeding but wind up failing in the end. Therefore, overall, the prospects for unification far exceed those for independence. If one wishes to put this in numerical terms, unification has an 80 percent chance of occurring, independence only a 20 percent chance.

Therefore, the mainland should develop its own long-term unification strategy on the premise that the final resolution of the Taiwan problem and cross-strait unification depends on the its own development. To do this, the first key problem to solve is the relationship between cross-strait unification and the process of China's becoming a world power. There are four possible views on this issue.

Unification is a necessary condition if China is to become a world power. As long as the two sides of the Taiwan Strait remain separated, China must waste its limited resources to maintain a high degree of military pressure on Taiwan lest Taiwan go ever further down the path of independence. Therefore, if unification does not occur, China cannot become a leading world power, for no country can become a world power if it is not united. In other words, the Taiwan issue has been a major obstacle to China's growth, and, if that obstacle is not overcome, China will be unable to advance toward its goal of becoming a world power.

An inevitable war over unification will destroy the fruits of China's development. If the mainland first focuses on development with the aim of becoming a world power and sets aside the Taiwan problem, all the fruits of development may be destroyed by the war over unification that is sure to come sooner or later. Therefore, it is premature for China to talk about becoming a world power. Only after the resolution of the Taiwan problem can China move toward this objective.

The DPP's campaign to suppress Chinese culture and emphasize Taiwanese localism has rendered unification impossible. The campaign to suppress Chinese culture and emphasize Taiwanese localism intensified starting in Lee Teng-hui's second term and further accelerated after the DPP came to power in 2000. If this situation, which is cause for concern, lasts for a long time, young Taiwanese will accept the proindependence viewpoint that Taiwan has no connections with China, that Taiwan is Taiwan and China is China. Although their parents, to one degree or another, may have contacts with the mainland, under the influence of an education system that suppresses Chinese culture and emphasizes Taiwanese localism, young Taiwanese may think that China has played no role in Taiwan's history except to betray it. After twenty or thirty years, if these young people who know only Taiwan and not China become the mainstream of Taiwanese society, then raising the issue of unification with them will be like searching for fish in a desert.

Maintaining China's rapid development requires the resolution of the Taiwan problem. This view holds that, if in the 1970s and 1980s in its discussions with the United States and other countries it could postpone dealing with the Taiwan and South China Sea problems, China must now assert its claims in these areas, having entered the fast track of the global market economy. Although this is a difficult choice for the Chinese, who have a tradition of taking the middle road, the fact of the matter is that, since China established the goal of a market economy, it must at least exercise maritime rights in its own sovereign territory. Without such maritime rights, it can never be a leading world power.

Though these four perspectives differ, they all converge in the assertion that unification trumps development, that unification takes precedence over and is more urgent than development.

Development Promotes Unification, and They Are Two Sides of the Same Coin

I think that the processes of China's unification and development as a world power are one and the same. As China becomes a world power, this in itself will accelerate progress toward achieving the goal of unification.

Cross-strait unification should take into account two important factors. First, what effect will unification have on China's development as a rising world power? Will it be positive or negative? Is unification the prerequisite and precondition of growth or the largest obstacle to China's becoming a leading power? Second, we must consider the international conditions for unification.

I contend that there is no direct connection between the unification of Taiwan and the mainland, on the one hand, and China's historic rise as a great power, on the other. A case in point is the Ming dynasty. Although it put Taiwan under the administration of the Pescadores, in reality the Dutch controlled Taiwan at that time. When Zheng Chenggong recovered Taiwan, the Ming dynasty had already been replaced by the Qing dynasty. The Qing dynasty was a great power even before it reoccupied Taiwan in 1681 during the reign of the Kangxi Emperor. The return of Taiwan reinforced the Qing's strength, but it was not the determinative factor. Taiwan was less important to both the Ming and the Qing than Prussia was to the integration of the German states, the surrender of the South in the U.S. Civil War to the North, or the control of central China to the Han, Tang, Yuan, Ming, and Qing dynasties. There are many points of difference between the history of China and the history of other countries. In this context, China's rise may also present a new phenomenon, just like the concept of one country, two systems introduced a new theory of government to the international community. China may succeed in becoming a great power within the context of the current status quo in cross-strait relations.

Both development and unification are core interests of China. If the separation between Taiwan and the mainland persists for a long time, this will degrade the mainland's strength and cause serious damage to its development. The Taiwan problem is a difficult and central issue of Chinese sovereignty, but we cannot say that, without unification, there will be no development and that unification is the top priority. I think that development should be promoted along with unification, but development is the key factor. Modernization should continue to be given strategic priority. As long as the Taiwan problem has not worsened to the point that it must be solved by military action, development should be the prime goal. At the same time, there is no contradiction between development and unification. Development will lead to unification, creating a momentum toward it. The more developed mainland China is, the better the chances for peaceful unification, the less space for Taiwanese independence, and the greater the pressure on Taiwan.

There is no need to determine whether China's growth or the question of unification takes priority. They are two aspects of the same process. Progress in growth enhances the prospects for peaceful unification. The final stage of China's rise as a world power is the time to solve the cross-strait problem. Because unification is a long-term project, as is China's rise as a world power, the two processes are bound to overlap in time, space, and even in content.

First, past experience demonstrates that resolving the question of unification or independence is not a prerequisite for growth on either side of the Taiwan Strait. In reality, without having resolved this question, both sides have achieved a great deal. Since China's opening up and reform and pursuit of a policy of peaceful unification and Taiwan's opening to the mainland, both sides have unquestionably benefited.

Second, there is still room within the current status quo for both sides to continue developing. After the DPP came to power, there was continuing tension in cross-strait relations; the economic and political policies adopted by the DDP were unsuitable and led to a decline in Taiwan's economy and virtual chaos. The advocates of independence, however, rather than reflecting on the DPP's administrative incompetence, concluded that cross-strait relations were too intimate and were responsible for the flight of Taiwanese capital to the mainland and Taiwan's economic decline. Therefore, they asserted that the only way to improve Taiwan's economy would be to cut off economic relations with the mainland and for Taiwan to be completely independent. Others on Taiwan with a better grasp of the situation argued that only via closer cooperation between Taiwan and the mainland could the two sides better meet the various challenges presented by entry into the WTO. Without cross-strait cooperation, Taiwan would have no future. Even some advocates of independence recognized that the mainland was the biggest market for the further development of Taiwanese enterprises and that, without this avenue of growth, these companies would fail. As for the mainland, Taiwan's investment, human resources, and experience have become important factors in the mainland's economic growth. Now even more Taiwanese come to Shanghai, Beijing, and other cities to invest their capital. It is evident that, even under the continuation of the current status quo, there is still room for development, contrary to the thesis that the question of unification or independence must be settled for development to occur.

A demonstration of this is that the number of people traveling back and forth across the strait is unaffected by the problem of unification or independence, rising in a straight line. According to Taiwanese government statistics, from 1987 to 1999, Taiwanese made 14.7 million trips to the mainland, while mainland Chinese made 420,000 trips to Taiwan. Such events as the mainland's military exercises in 1996 and Lee Teng-hui's enunciation of the two states theory in 1999 had no influence on these unofficial exchanges. In 1997, Taiwanese made only 500,000 trips to the mainland, yet, in 2000, this figure reached 3 million, while the volume of trade reached US$30.5 billion. Taiwan enjoyed a more than US$20 billion surplus. From 1987 to 2000, it obtained a US$204.9 billion trade surplus vis-à-vis the mainland. These unofficial exchanges increased support on Taiwan for the one country, two systems policy, according to a Gallup poll. Taiwanese investment in the mainland already surpassed US$80 billion by 2001.

In sum, there are still grounds for optimism with regard to the prospects for peaceful unification. China scholars in the United States even think that the increase of Taiwanese investment in the mainland has brought about some political changes. This trend suggests the possibility that some form of unification is possible, if not immediately, then at least in the distant future. As for the United States, if Taiwan pursues unification, there is not much Washington can do to prevent it. If Taiwan desires unification and believes that talks with the mainland will be mutually beneficial, it will have no further need to accumulate weapons, and the United States will have no further means to exert its influence. If the will of the Taiwanese people turns to support of unification and elected officials likewise declare that the time for unification has arrived, the United States will have no grounds for opposing it. No one can obstruct the progress of economic unity or the removal of geographic and man-made obstacles on the road to establishing a Greater China open economic zone.

Considering China's opportunities, growth should be prioritized over unification. We must recognize that China faces enormous, historic opportunities in the age of the digital economy. Just as Meiji Japan grasped opportunities in the Steam Age to become the only non-Western great power by developing its industry, the coming Digital Age may help China and other ethnic Chinese states and regions take their place among the small number of leading non-Western powers by developing the Internet and the information industry. The Chinese people are intelligent, hardworking, creative, and innovative. The Information Age affords a great opportunity for them to unleash their economic potential. Chinese characters are quite suitable for the Internet era, and Chinese may become the second largest Internet language after English. Before long, there may be more Chinese than any other people using the Internet. This presents a great opportunity for the Chinese Internet economy and a great impetus for Chinese commerce. The Internet era is a heaven-sent opportunity that people on both sides of the Taiwan Strait should grasp. It would be the greatest tragedy if such a rare opportunity is lost owing to the use of force to resolve the unification issue.

As some scholars have argued, in order to solve the Taiwan problem, the mainland should show magnanimity. As Wang Yizhou puts it: "Considering the huge disparity in territory, population, natural resources, and international status between the two sides, we should have the confidence that, provided the mainland adheres to the policy of reform and opening up and maintains the development trend of the past twenty years, time is on our side. The hopes of the Chinese people for unification will finally be achieved."[6]

Reflections on the Pluses and Minuses of the Former Taiwan Strategy

If we hold that China's rise to great power status and the unification of the two sides of the Taiwan Strait are parts of the same process, we should confidently map out a long-term strategy to achieve unification over the next twenty to fifty years and not press to solve the Taiwan problem in the next three to five years. Before elaborating such a strategy, we must first review and reflect on the recent phase of our Taiwan strategies.

The high point of cross-strait relations occurred around 1991. On January 1, 1979, when China and the United States established diplomatic relations, the Standing Committee of China's National People's Congress issued a proposal regarding the "Three Openings and Four Exchanges" (the opening of post, information, and shipping and exchanges in academic, cultural, sports, and economic fields). On September 30, 1981, Chairman Ye Jianying put forward the famous "Nine Principles," the first comprehensive presentation of the mainland's framework for unification. These principles were the following: (1) Hold negotiations between the Guomindang and the CCP to achieve cooperation for the third time. (2) Follow the "Three Openings and Four Exchanges." (3) After unification, Taiwan will be a special district, enjoying a high level of autonomy. (4) No changes will be made in the framework of Taiwan's society, economy, and way of life. (5) Taiwanese leaders may take posts in the mainland. (6) If Taiwan is in trouble, the mainland will help. (7) Taiwanese can settle in mainland China and move freely back and forth. (8) Taiwanese investment in the mainland is welcome. (9) The Taiwanese are welcome to make suggestions on state affairs.

Influenced by this policy, the Guomindang authorities responded to the mainland's Three Openings with their own "Three Nos" policy, that is, "no compromise, no negotiation, no contact." Finally, on November 2, 1987, they opened the door for Taiwanese compatriots to visit the mainland, responding positively rather than negatively. At the same time, they began to prepare a comprehensive response to the mainland's policy. In February 1991, they established the Mainland Affairs Council and the SEF to deal with mainland affairs, and, in March 1991, they passed the Guidelines for National Unification, which was drafted in the third meeting of the National Unification Council. The guidelines stipulated the so-called 1234 formula, namely, (1) there is only one China; both the mainland and Taiwan are Chinese territory; (2) at present, the two sides of the Taiwan Strait are governed by two equal political entities; (3) national unification will occur through three stages, namely, short-, middle-, and long-term; and (4) the Four Principles, that is, the rationality of national unification, peace, equality, and mutual benefit, should be followed. The preface of the

Guidelines indicated: "China's unification should be built on rationality, peace, equality, and mutual benefit. Through communication, cooperation, and negotiation, [the two sides may] reach a common understanding of democracy and freedom and on that basis reconstruct a unified China."[7]

Apart from the contentious reference to the so-called two equal political entities, most of the Guidelines for National Unification was acceptable to the mainland because they made it clear that the cross-strait relationship would be dealt with under the principle of one China. Under this premise, the two sides held two meetings between Taiwan's SEF and the mainland's ARATS, culminating in a meeting in Singapore between the ARATS chairman, Wang Daohan, and the SEF chairman, Koo Chen-fu.

Thereafter, the Taiwanese authorities restated the Guidelines in a number of documents. For example, on July 4, 1994, they held a mainland affairs conference and issued a white paper on cross-strait relations indicating that China should be unified under Sun Yet-sen's Three People's Principles and that there was no difference between the two sides over the one China principle. The issue between the two sides was, not whether there should be unification, but rather how it should be effected. In essence, it was a conflict between the two political systems. The white paper claimed: "The Chinese Communist Party is the critical obstacle to China's unification." It admitted: "One China means a China with the same history, geography, culture, and kinship. . . . The existence of separate governments is just a temporary, transitional phenomenon. . . . The two sides must inevitably unite." It reiterated that the Taiwanese side recognized there was only one China and opposed the concept of two Chinas and one China, one Taiwan.[8]

On January 30, 1995, President Jiang Zemin published a speech about cross-strait relations that was subsequently called Jiang's Eight Points. The main contents of this document were as follows: (1) Cross-strait relations should be based on the principle of one China and peaceful unification; China's territory and sovereignty cannot be divided. (2) The mainland does not oppose Taiwan developing nongovernment relations with foreign countries but opposes it expanding its international status under the rubric of two Chinas or one China, one Taiwan. (3) The two sides should hold peace talks in which all parties and personages should take part. Jiang reiterated the position he put forward at the Fourteenth Party Congress in 1992—that, as long as the one China principle is respected, any-thing can be put on the table. (4) Strive to achieve peaceful unification; Chinese do not fight against Chinese, but the mainland cannot forswear the use of force as an ultimate deterrent against Taiwanese indepen-dence. (5) Develop cross-strait exchange and cooperation, and speed up the Three Links (i.e., direct postal, transportation, and trade links). (6) Chinese culture is the foundation of cross-strait exchange. (7) Taiwanese compatriots are Chinese; the mainland will respect the principle of the self-governance of the Taiwanese people. (8) Taiwanese leaders are wel-come to visit the mainland under appropriate conditions. Mainland lead-ers may also visit Taiwan. Chinese matters should be handled by Chinese. They should not become an occasion for international intervention.

On April 8, 1995, Lee Teng-hui gave a speech responding to Jiang's Eight Points in which he reiterated Taiwan's Guidelines for National Unification and acknowledged that national unification is the common responsibility of the Chinese people. If this trend had continued, there might have been a breakthrough in cross-strait relations.

But, starting in mid-1995, Lee abruptly changed his position. Around 1991, in his capacity as chairman of the National Unification Council, he appeared to support the Guidelines for National Unification, but, since his position in Taiwan was insecure, he devoted most of his efforts to strengthening his own power and paid little attention to cross-strait rela-tions. Therefore, he was unwilling at that time to oppose the Guidelines. But, by 1995, he felt himself securely in power and believed that he pos-sessed the political capital to obstruct the process of peaceful reunifica-tion. He began to use his power to advance his Taiwanese independence plot. Although he intentionally dissembled, his close associates quickly discerned that he was prounification on the surface but proindependence in his bones.

Lee's actions led to a decisive response from the mainland that achieved some results. The most important of these was the military exer-cises in 1996 in response to Lee's abandonment of the one China prin-ciple; these exercises clearly demonstrated to the world, to the United States, and to the Taiwanese public the mainland's unshakable determi-nation to uphold national unity. At the same time, during these years, the mainland conducted a critical reexamination of its Taiwan strategy. For example, it lacked a clear understanding of and correct judgment about Taiwan's elections in 1996 and 2000. Attacking the Taiwanese proinde-

pendence forces did not prevent their candidates from being elected. To
the contrary, there were some negative consequences. Many people in
Taiwan switched from supporting one China to supporting the status quo
of separation between the mainland and Taiwan.

In the process of reexamining its policy, in February 2002 the mainland changed its position on the DPP. It decided to differentiate between
a small handful of hardcore proindependence DPP members and the
majority. It concluded that rank-and-file DPP supporters were different
from the proindependence activists. The Sixteenth Party Congress proposed that, provided the one China principle was accepted, the two sides
of the Taiwan Strait could discuss such issues as a formal end to mutual
hostility, Taiwan's international status, an appropriate space for its economic, cultural, and social life, and the political position of the Taiwanese
authorities. Such thinking greatly expanded the options for the mainland's Taiwan strategy.

Winning Popular Support: Key to the Mainland's New Taiwan Strategy

The Core Content of the Mainland's New Strategy toward Taiwan

The mainland's strategy toward Taiwan should be decided on the basis of
previous experience and lessons learned. In accordance with the distinctive features of China's development, we should devise a loftier, broader,
and more proactive strategy whose core content is the following:

1. As long as the mainland adheres to the principle of peaceful unification, maintains political and economic stability, sustains economic
development, and solves various problems that emerge in the process of
development, peaceful unification will, ultimately, occur. Taiwanese independence is basically impossible.

2. While maintaining a degree of military pressure against Taiwanese independence forces, the Mainland should make winning over and
attracting the support of its Taiwanese compatriots its priority. Only
through sustainable development and social progress can it attract more
and more Taiwanese. If domestic problems in the mainland increase, this
will serve only to alienate the Taiwanese.

3. While continuing political and economic development, the mainland should be more tolerant, more confident, more concerned, more

respectful, and more understanding toward the people in Taiwan. Time is on the side of the mainland. Unification is the future of the cross-strait relationship.

4. If Taiwan declares its independence, the mainland will take effective measures to respond. However, as long as the possibility of peaceful unification remains, it will never use military force to realize unification. China is a big country; the national defense should be viewed from the perspective of protecting the security of the entire nation, not just in terms of the Taiwan issue. Even apart from the Taiwan issue, China must develop its national defense and enhance its military strength.

5. The mainland should adopt a more strategic attitude that takes into account the overall situation and long-term national interest with respect to solving the Taiwan issue. It is unnecessary to respond to each proindependence action or engage in excessive criticism of every proindependence statement or action.

6. The practical application of one country, two systems should be more flexible and diverse. Anything that can promote progress toward the goal of one China should be given due consideration. Indeed, the final outcome may be what is in reality, if not in name, a kind of federal system. This could be based on four points: (1) Taiwan clearly declares that it will never become independent, and the mainland forswears the use of military force. (2) Both sides reach an agreement about the one country issue, and, as a part of China, Taiwan will be accorded a higher political position than Hong Kong and Macau, something less than a sovereign state, but higher than a special administrative region or a province. Taiwan will be wholly responsible for managing its own internal affairs. At the same time, in its capacity as a part of one China, it will be able to take part in mainland affairs. (3) Under the rubric of Chinese Taiwan and other conditions such as China's acquiescence to its exercising voting rights, Taiwan can take part in international organizations. (4) There can be international guarantees for such arrangements.

At the same time, the mainland should adopt a more practical attitude to various parties on Taiwan, including the DPP. It should establish contacts, not only with rank-and-file DPP members, but also with the party leadership. This new strategy must manage three key issues effectively, namely, how to win the support of the majority of Taiwan's citizens, how to deal with the DPP should it return to power in Taiwan, and how to deal with the U.S. factor in the process of unification.

How To Win over Majority Opinion in Taiwan

Peaceful unification will be possible only if the majority of the Taiwanese people agree to it. Therefore, winning the support of a majority of Taiwanese citizens is the critical issue. Even if the mainland's economy continues to develop smoothly, the question of winning over ordinary Taiwanese citizens remains.

If a majority of the people of Taiwan accepts the one China principle, then peaceful unification will be guaranteed. The question, however, is whether we can win them over. This question must be considered from three angles, namely, the international community in which China is becoming a major power, the mainland's development, and changes within Taiwan itself.

First, with respect to the international community, can China become a true world power within the next thirty to fifty years? We must be cognizant of the reality that there are forces within the international community trying their utmost to prevent China from becoming a world power. Yet, if China has faith in its own capacity to develop, consistently adheres to peace and the policy of opening, abjures pursuing hegemony and expansionism, and manages international affairs cautiously and prudently, then no force can prevent it from becoming a world power. Once it becomes a world power, unification will be even more of a certainty.

Second, the mainland also faces various problems and difficulties in the course of development. Presently, the greatest of these are the struggle against corruption, the effort to establish the rule of law in Chinese society, and problems related to state-owned enterprises. Yet these are all problems associated with the process of development that can gradually be solved and overcome through concerted efforts. If China can maintain its current pace of development and social progress, it will be easier to solve the problem of unification. Taiwan has already in recent years been attracted by the mainland's economic development, and this attraction will increase if its own economy suffers a decline.

Finally, the mainland should have confidence in the judgment and choices of the majority in Taiwan. Most people in Taiwan are well educated, rational, and practical. They can understand the overall situation. Therefore, presently only a minority has made up their minds about unification versus independence. The majority is still undecided. Most Taiwanese are still very flexible and, thus, amenable to persuasion. The majority knows that, if Taiwan declares independence, the mainland will adamantly oppose such an action and that war will be inevitable. Even if Taiwan achieves independence as a result of such a war, the outcome would be disastrous. If the mainland allows the Taiwanese people to choose unification, they might think that, although it is developing very quickly, it still has too many domestic problems, not to mention the significant differences in political systems, standard of living, and ways of thinking. Even if unification occurs under the principle of one country, two systems and the mainland guarantees that the political and economic systems and lifestyle of Taiwan will remain unchanged, the people of Taiwan will still feel uneasy because of political corruption on the mainland and the shaky foundations of the rule of law.

Therefore, if the mainland can effectively deal with corruption, improve the legal system, and continue the rapid economic growth that raises living standards to the level of Taiwan, the attitudes of our Taiwanese compatriots toward it may change, and the prospect that they will finally accept peaceful unification under the principle of one country, two systems or one country, multiple systems will be greatly enhanced.

If the problem of unification versus independence is not one that needs to be solved in the short term, then we should view the issue in the long-term perspective of twenty to thirty or even forty to fifty years. Our task then becomes one of gaining the understanding and winning the support of young people on Taiwan who are now in their twenties because it is they who twenty, thirty, forty, even fifty years from now will be in power. They will make a rational choice between unification and independence. Now, most young people in Taiwan look at things from the perspective, What is most in our interests? What will be in our best interests in the future? What practical benefits can unification deliver? What influence will independence have on our futures?

With political stability and economic growth prevailing in mainland China, there can be no doubt that peaceful reunification will bring more scope for activity, greater freedom, and a brighter future for people on both sides of the Taiwan Strait. If we consider that many young people from the DPP in Taiwan want to pursue their studies on the mainland, we can grasp that, even though they may have supported the DPP when it was in power, by no means did they entrust their future to so-called Taiwanese independence. Even some core members of the DPP, who publicly proclaimed their belief in independence, were not loathe to investing in and doing business with the mainland and even to declaring when they came to the mainland, "In fact, we, too, are Chinese." They also use connections to secure a Taiwan compatriot permit or pursue the opportunity to get an academic degree on the mainland. Their behavior is justified by the following consideration. They benefit from supporting the DPP in Taiwan, and they also benefit from acknowledging their Chinese identity to cozy up to the mainland. As the publisher of the Taiwan magazine *Business Weekly*, Jin Weichun, has said, the inherent defect of most people in Taiwan is their great attachment to pursuing personal interests. Therefore, the crux of unification versus independence is the problem of interest. If we can solve this problem, then the relationship between the two sides will advance by leaps and bounds.[9] If, in the course of a few years, a decade, or even several decades, the mainland can show that unification can, not only preserve the Taiwanese people's political freedom, but also ensure a much brighter future, there is no doubt that they will support unification. Deemphasizing Chinese culture and promoting a Taiwanese identity have not yet played a significant role in promoting independence.

To win the support of the Taiwanese people, the mainland should understand four points related to the history of the Taiwanese people's resistance to the mainland.

The first is the historical tragedy experienced by the Taiwanese people. This derived from the fact that they were not masters of their own destiny. They suffered numerous times from foreign invasions. First the Spanish and then the Dutch exercised colonial rule over Taiwan. After Zheng Chenggong recovered Taiwan, the Qing dynasty sent troops in 1681 and achieved reunification. However, in 1895, the Qing dynasty ceded Taiwan to Japan, an act that greatly damaged the relationship between the Taiwanese people and the mainland. This is one of the main roots of Taiwanese independence. Then fifty years of Japanese colonial rule, accompanied by an attempt to impose Japanese culture, contributed to the hostility of some Taiwanese people toward the mainland.

The second is the 2/28 Incident during Guomindang rule in 1947. This is what Taiwanese proindependence forces have used to promote a sense of separate Taiwanese identity and hostility toward the mainland. Taiwanese separatists categorize the Guomindang as an outside colonial power no different than the Dutch or the Japanese. This hostile attitude has persisted until the present and is the foundation for the ill-will of a portion of the Taiwanese people toward the mainland.

The third is that, after the Guomindang lost the civil war and fled to Taiwan, it inculcated the people with anti-Communist ideology so that, even today, a certain portion of the Taiwanese people fail to understand the reality of contemporary China. This is true notwithstanding the large numbers of Taiwanese people and even some officials who have visited the mainland in recent years.

The fourth is that Taiwanese politics has greatly changed. In the past, just a handful of leaders on Taiwan could exert a large influence regarding the question of independence and unification. For the most part this is no longer so. It is increasingly important to win over the majority of people, and it takes time to persuade them to favor unification with the mainland.

How to Think about the Proindependence DPP

Proindependence forces on Taiwan gained strength in the first years of the new century. They were in power from 2000 to 2008. Although this tide has recently receded, it is imperative that we still consider this problem.

First, given that parties alternate in power on Taiwan, the Guomindang or some other party may hold power in the future. The DPP held power for eight years before being voted out of office in 2008. Different parties will implement different policies on the Taiwan issue. The proindependence DPP was able to come to power because the path of independence that Lee Teng-hui advocated caused a split in the Guomindang, giving rise first to the New Party, then to the People First Party. The Guomindang itself greatly declined in strength. At a critical point in the 2000 electoral campaign, Lee Teng-hui threw his support to the DPP, resulting in the defeat of the Guomindang and the People First Party.

The victory of the DPP in 2000 and again in 2004, however, represented only one swing of the electoral pendulum and was no indication that that party would retain power indefinitely. The return to power of the Guomindang in 2008 enhanced the possibility for cooperation across the Taiwan Strait and raised hopes that the two sides can reach agreement on the one China principle and get back on track toward reunification.

Second, one must understand the relationship between voters and parties. Voters tend to judge a party on the basis of reality rather than ideology. If the party fails to deliver on its promises, then it will be voted out in the next election. This is what happened to the DPP in 2008.

After the DPP came to power in 2000, it encountered many problems owing to its lack of able and experienced leaders. Many problems remained unsolved throughout its tenure in office. Changes in political leadership occurred, along with a slump in Taiwan's economy. Survey data showed declining support for Chen Shui-bian. By 2002, more than two-thirds of DPP supporters deemed the domestic situation very serious. Chen barely squeaked to victory—and under dubious circumstances—in 2004, but support for the DPP continued to erode in the following years.

Third, the DPP itself was far from being a unified party; its inner circle was split, and its policy toward independence and cross-strait relations was a subject of intraparty dispute and liable to change. Like the Guomindang, the DPP was ridden with factions divided between extremists and moderates on the issue of independence. Therefore, the mainland had to distinguish between the DPP, which supported independence, and the Guomindang, which generally supported unification. Second, it had to distinguish between the hardcore proindependence faction of the DPP and those within the DPP who might be persuaded to change their views. Third, it had to distinguish between voters who supported the DPP because they were proindependence and voters who supported it because they opposed the previous Guomindang administration.

Fourth, the mainland had to distinguish among proindependence Taiwanese fundamentalists or hard-liners, moderate factions, middle-of-the-road factions, and opportunistic factions.

Therefore, although it is not easy to promote cross-strait unification on Taiwan, neither is it easy to promote independence. Since 1996, the military pressure that the mainland applied put the Taiwanese people on notice that there is no future for independence and that independence means war. Objectively speaking, there is not much room for the independence forces to grow, and, after peaking in the early years of this century, the tide of independence may already be receding.

The majority of the Taiwanese people favor the maintenance of the status quo, but the number of those who support the one country, two systems policy has increased. So long as the mainland maintains its development momentum and treats the Taiwanese people with sincerity, openness, tolerance, generosity, care, and a willingness to help, the future of peaceful unification is bright. In addition, U.S. China policy will hold independence forces in check. One of the basic features of that policy is to maintain a situation of neither unification nor independence with regard to cross-strait relations. Therefore, if the DPP disregards the mainland's firm opposition and insists on pursuing independence, this would increase tension in the Taiwan Strait and create a dilemma for the United States. Washington does not want this to happen. The Rand Corporation's report on Taiwan suggested that the U.S. government "should tell Taiwan that any effort to pursue unilateral independence will be prevented. . . . The U.S. supports the development of Taiwan's democracy but does not support independence."[10] Therefore, even should the DPP intend to push for independence, it will find it difficult to achieve this objective.

How to Deal with the U.S. Factor vis-à-vis the Taiwan Problem?

Cross-strait relations are greatly influenced by the United States. Its policies and standpoint regarding the Taiwan problem are the following: First, the United States uses Taiwan to contain and tie down China. Second, its weapons sales to Taiwan benefit the U.S. arms industry. Third, it maintains its influence on China and safeguards its interests with its policy of neither unification nor independence. Fourth, it invokes Taiwan's experience with democracy to promote peaceful evolution in China. Fifth, it maintains stability in East Asia by keeping the peace in the Taiwan Strait. The influence of the United States can be discerned by examining the recent situation on both sides of the Taiwan Strait.

Considering how the DPP dealt with cross-strait relations after it took power, it is evident that its policy was basically dependent on the United States. A number of U.S. scholars clearly pointed out that President George W. Bush's assertion that the United States would take action to protect Taiwan in case it was attacked by the mainland did not really change Washington's ambiguous position on the Taiwan issue but further muddied the waters.[11] On April 18, 2002, the U.S. Pacific commander, Admiral Dennis Blair, stressed that the Bush administration's Taiwan policy had not fundamentally changed.[12] There was no reason to suppose that Washington supported Taiwan's independence. Nor should U.S. arms sales to Taiwan be regarded as an action in support of an independent Taiwan. A stable cross-strait military balance is merely one of the prerequisites for China's peaceful unification. The United States still adheres to a one China policy.

During Hu Jintao's visit to the United States in May 2002, President Bush and Vice President Dick Cheney not only indicated that the United

States would abide by the three communiqués with China agreed on in the past and restated the one China policy, but also added that it would not encourage the growth of proindependence forces on Taiwan. This came as a blow to proindependence forces, which had taken heart from some earlier statements by President Bush that seemed to indicate his support for an independent Taiwan. When Hu visited the United States, Washington clarified its one China stance. Nevertheless, the U.S. Taiwan policy of neither unification nor independence, no war and no peace, and upgrading the quality and scale of arms sales to Taiwan has the effect of supporting the expansion of Taiwan's role and influence in the world and represents a huge obstacle to unification. Yet cross-strait relations may still develop in a healthy manner independent of Sino-U.S. relations.

The history of cross-strait relations suggests that it is not outside the bounds of possibility for the two sides to shake free of U.S. influence and develop healthy interactions. For example, after the June 4 incident in 1989, the United States applied sanctions against the mainland, and the Sino-U.S. relationship hit rock bottom, but cross-strait relations did not retrogress, and Taiwanese investment in the mainland actually peaked. Not only did economic and trade connections develop greatly, but political relations also advanced, as manifested by the Wang-Koo meeting in 1993. So, even though cross-strait relations cannot escape U.S. influence, neither are they controlled by it. If China develops smoothly and grows in strength, the common interests between it and the United States will increase, while U.S. interests in Taiwan will diminish. The unification of Taiwan and the mainland is a core interest of China, but protecting Taiwan is not a core or even an important interest of the United States. Taiwan will be gradually marginalized in U.S. foreign policy interests. The more developed and stronger China is, the less likely the United States will engage in a full-scale confrontation with it over Taiwan.

Therefore, the mainland should possess the self-confidence to realize that China is a great power in the world and has enough strength and determination to prevent Taiwanese independence. As long as the mainland does not abandon unification, there is no power in the world that can hold back this process. Taiwan cannot be independent of China. Time is on the mainland's side, and Taiwan's future is in association with the mainland.

Postscript

In May and June 2002, while I was lecturing at East China University in Taiwan, I finished writing *Inside China's Grand Strategy*, a book that was published by the Chinese Academy of Social Sciences in November 2003. More than seven years have passed since then, and there have been many changes regarding various subjects that the book discusses. Some things I wrote have been confirmed, and others have become a reality. Nevertheless, the Chinese people must still continue their efforts to achieve what I posited as the ultimate objective of China's grand strategy, namely, the renascence of the Chinese people (*zhonghua minzu*). At the same time, after further reflection, I have developed some new ideas concerning a number of topics addressed in the book. In what follows, I would like to present them as a modest supplement to the English translation.

An examination of China's national renascence requires that we look at its pursuit of its goal from a historical perspective, namely, that of recovering the great power position and influence that China once enjoyed in the East Asian region. The objective is to attain a position and wield influence in international society commensurate with its historic culture, population, size, economy, and comprehensive national strength. This, however, is not enough. The real question is what sort of great power should China become now that it has become a modernized and powerful state in a globalized world? What follow are my thoughts regarding this subject.

First, China should strive to the utmost to undertake certain obligations and responsibilities with regard to the contemporary world. I do not like the expression *to act as a responsible great power* because it insinuates that, in the past, China has not behaved responsibly. One of the great changes with respect to contemporary China is that it has demonstrated a strong economic capability in the current financial crisis. Its US$2 trillion foreign currency reserve provides it a capacity to solve the crisis that other countries lack. Moreover, this capacity is not only very useful in helping solve China's crisis but also very important with respect to solving the world financial crisis. Therefore, China's great economic power should be used not only to solve the current economic crisis but also with an eye toward advancing international economic development in the direction of greater stability. Regarding this point, however, China lacks strategic thinking. It is especially unfamiliar and inexperienced regarding the proper use of financial power. On the one hand, its foreign currency reserves have been influenced and restrained by U.S. financial markets; on the other hand, it has been unsuccessful in its initial attempts at investing its foreign currency in international markets. Therefore, it faces the enormous challenge of how to transform its wealth into the kind of strategic financial power that can exert a larger and healthier influence on international financial development. The financial crisis has shown how invisible and omnipresent financial powers can instantaneously destroy a country's wealth and plunge it into political and economic crisis. If China wishes to become an influential world power, it must also become a financial power with global influence and not simply attract Western financial resources for its own development. At the same time, its so-called international obligations and responsibilities should not be understood as meaning simply that, once a financial crisis occurs, it should use even more money to purchase foreign goods and debt or to make more investments in Western markets to stabilize them. But, if it lacks influence in and is excluded from the international economic and financial system that gave rise to the financial crisis, how can it discharge its so-called international obligations and responsibilities?

In addition, what are considered China's international obligations and responsibilities is subject to Western influence and constraints. There are certain responsibilities, such as China's dispatch of its navy to the waters off the Somali coast in Africa to protect ships against piracy, that both protect its own interest and uphold the interests of international society. But, if this should take place somewhere else, would Western countries be similarly accepting? For example, if the its navy were to protect shipping in the Pacific Ocean, would others see this as an example of China acting responsibly or an example of it acting irresponsibly and provocatively? Further thought must be given to the question of what constitutes China's international obligations and responsibilities.

The second question relates to the development of strategic thinking regarding China's continental and maritime power. China is a great continental power with a very long coastline. It is located in the eastern part of the Eurasian landmass and is the crossroads where East, Central, South, and Southeast Asia converge, yet part of its territory is in the hinterland of Eurasia. However, it also possesses extensive maritime territory. How to manage the relations between the development of its land-based power, on the one hand, and its maritime development, on the other, is, likewise, a question of its grand strategy to which thought must be given. Not much attention was paid to this issue in *Inside China's Grand Strategy* Subsequently, as this question emerged, I began to follow it more closely. In 2007, I published *The Development of Land Power and the Rise and Fall of Great Powers* (*Lu quan fazhan yu daguo xingshuai*). This book examined the various roles that the development of land-based power played in the rise and fall of different great powers throughout history. It showed that, even for maritime powers, the development of a certain measure of land-based power was a prerequisite. The development of land-based power was of decisive significance for continental powers. I pointed out that land-based power cannot be understood simply in terms of control but should be thought of primarily in terms of survival, development, and influence. The Eurasian landmass is still the central stage of world geopolitics. China is essentially a land power. Most of its great accomplishments historically were on land. The geopolitical proposition I would offer regarding contemporary China's course of peaceful development is the following: China, the first country in world history to become a great continental power and one that achieved dominant influence in East Asia via land-based power, should develop its maritime power in a suitable manner, particularly since its maritime power is insufficiently developed, but it should emphasize maritime power as an auxiliary form of power. Fundamentally, however, it cannot position itself as a global maritime power, nor should it accord maritime power equal weight with land-based power. For China, continental power is the key from start to finish.

Another topic that was inadequately addressed in *Inside China's Grand Strategy* was how, in the course of reestablishing its status as a great power, China should manage its relations with the international system. Let me now say a few words about this in light of my latest reflections. China's view of the international system has gone through a process of change. At first, it sought the revolutionary overthrow of the Western system and followed the lead of the Soviet Union. Then it put forward the Five Principles of Peaceful Coexistence and simultaneously laid down a challenge to the Soviet system while continuing to seek the overthrow of the Western system and proposing to establish a new international political and economic order. Finally, on the foundation of the Five Principles of Peaceful Coexistence, it upheld the primacy of the current Western international system while seeking to carry out partial reforms and revisions. In sum, China's views on the international order have undergone great ups and downs like a ride on a roller coaster. At present, its fundamental notion is to uphold the current international system with international law at its core and, on this foundation, carry out transformation and improvements. China does not seek the fundamental transformation of the international system, and it has all but abandoned its past, loudly proclaimed intention to establish a new international political and economic system.

My views on this are as follows:

First, China's relationship with the current international order is neither one of integrating with the world nor one of transforming it, neither one of complying with the current order nor one of overthrowing it, but rather one of partially changing, transforming, and improving the world system while becoming integrated into it. It is one of building a new international system on the foundation of the existing one.

Second, even though China has been a victim of the current system, it has also been a beneficiary. That it has been a victim of the international system is shown by the aggression, exploitation, and oppression it suffered in recent times at the hands of the great powers. The Western great powers forced it to sign a series of unequal and unjust treaties that seriously harmed it interests and whose consequences are still felt today. To a certain extent, the issue of Taiwan is the outgrowth of this old system of inequality and injustice. That China has been a beneficiary of the international system is shown by the fact that, as one of the five permanent members of the UN Security Council, it enjoys the right of veto. During its process of reform, it has also benefited from the international economic system by drawing on international capital, technology, and the free movement of goods. It has derived significant benefits from the current system of international trade.

Third, one must apply a rational analysis to the current system; one cannot treat it in an undifferentiated manner. The current system contains both reasonable and unreasonable elements, both overt and covert regulations. On the one hand, international law and generally acknowledged international norms constitute the foundation of the current system. They are a reasonable part of it and should not be discarded. Although they were established by the West, they reflect the progress and development of human civilization. China's Five Principles of Peaceful Coexistence are, likewise, a reflection of this civilization. Therefore, they should continue to be upheld and observed. On the other hand, great power prerogatives, hegemonism, unilateralism, preemptive war, power politics, privileging Western civilization, the practice of forcing Western values onto developing countries in the name of universal standards, the privileged position developed countries enjoy in the international system and international organizations, these are all the unreasonable and hidden rules of the current system.

Fourth, even with respect to the unreasonable elements of the current system, one must distinguish between those that are unreasonable but accord and those that are unreasonable and do not accord with the current situation. The former include great power prerogatives that are unreasonable and should be completely abolished but will be necessary for a long time. Not only does this formulation safeguard China's current interests; it is essential for reform of the United Nations, upholding world peace, and solving major problems in the world. The present is a transitional period, one in which we are moving toward achieving a more just and more rational world order. Under these circumstances, the major powers will continue to enjoy certain special privileges as these are necessary for upholding the authority of the United Nations and maintaining its practical work. Other prerogatives, such as only the major powers possessing nuclear weapons and the pursuit by them of nuclear nonproliferation, have become constituent elements of the present international order. They are inherently reasonable but do not accord with current reality. If the major powers can possess nuclear weapons, why not India? And, if all states must observe the Nuclear Test Ban Treaty, why cannot North Korea and Iran possess nuclear technology? Finally, the United States abused its power to bypass the United Nations and unleash the Iraq War in clear violation of international law. This illegal action was neither restrained nor punished.

Fifth, the establishment of a new order is a very lengthy process. Therefore, at the present stage, China should lay stress on respecting and upholding international law and generally accepted norms in its relations with the international system. This is not only because the present international order facilitates the achievement of its national interests but also because most states are unlikely to accept much of what it desires to incorporate in a new international system. More work must be done toward this end.[1]

In *An Analysis of the International Environment for China's Peaceful Development,* I pointed out that, in order to achieve the goal of national renascence that I posited in *Inside China's Grand Strategy,* China must correctly manage its international relations.[2] There are two key points. China must correctly manage its relations with the United States, and it must correctly manage its relations with the international order. The history of international relations shows that the majority of rising powers in the West have tried to establish their hegemony and that, in the process, strategic conflicts have arisen with the existing hegemonic states that eventuate in wars. The other important reason is that rising powers try to establish a new international order that serves their own interests. This is the root of the major wars in the world. But part of China's grand strategy to achieve its goal is to avoid challenging the United States—that is, not to confront it in East Asia and not to contend with it in its North American sphere of influence, let alone replace it as a global hegemon. China and the United States not only can, but in fact are, molding a new kind of great power relationship. A large-scale war between the two countries can and certainly will be avoided. China is not seeking to overthrow the current international system with the United States at its center; rather it is actively trying to integrate itself into that system. Far from challenging the U.S.-led international system, it is actively respecting and upholding the existing system based on international law and generally recognized international norms. In many instances, China is more willing than the United States to uphold the mechanisms of the United Nations and the WTO. These two points demonstrate that its quest for national renascence does not necessitate a zero-sum conflict with the hegemonic power or the existing international system. Instead, there is a positive-sum game.

The implementation of China's grand strategy must be guided by Chinese-style thinking, namely, the mode of thinking contained in the *Book of Changes.* After the publication of *Inside China's Grand Strategy,* a number of related books appeared in China, among which several were quite impressive. But on the main questions they were heavily influenced by Western, and particularly U.S., modes of strategic thought. I believe that there is a great difference between the nature of China and that of the United States. There are significant limits to the utility of transferring U.S. scholarly thought and grand strategy to China. I believe that there are merits in Western methods for studying the humanities and social sciences, but they are also problematic in many ways. While continuing to study and draw lessons from these methods, we should give priority to the ways of thought in China's own *Book of Changes* and combine them with Chinese studies of the humanities and social sciences. The *Book of Changes* is the first of the Six Classics and the source of all the classics. Grand strategy requires grand thought. The outstanding feature of the *Book of Changes* is its systematic thought. Compared to holistic thought, the Yin-Yang school, and dialectics, it is particularly well suited to grand strategic thinking.[3] For example, domestic issues, relations with neighboring states, and the question of maritime rights are not pressing issues for the United States; therefore, it can focus its energy on the international arena. Consequently, the so-called strategy or grand strategy of the United States generally focuses on the study of international strategy. But China is a different case. Any kind of international grand strategy for China must be linked to a solution of and studied in tandem with its domestic problems. The *Book of Changes* views heaven, earth, and humankind as a whole, as a single system. Under this premise, one can engage in more profound and concrete study. What is not a strategic question in the United States may be a question of grand strategy in China, even an extremely important question. Therefore, *Inside China's Grand Strategy* consistently stresses the solution of China's domestic problems as an important element in its grand strategy. More than that, I now contend that the solution of domestic rather than foreign problems is the most important key to achieving the renascence of the Chinese nation. If China can successfully manage its domestic problems, this will have a huge international impact. Indeed, it is not by focusing its energies on solving international issues but by tackling its domestic problems that China can influence the outside world.

In sum, I recognize that the content of *Inside China's Grand Strategy* needs to be supplemented and that further study of the questions it addresses is in order.

Notes

Introduction

1. For contending views on the rise of China, see Avery Goldstein, *Rising to the Challenge: China's Grand Strategy and International Security* (Stanford, CA: Stanford University Press, 2005); C. Fred Bergsten, Bates Gill, Nicholas R. Lardy, and Derek Mitchell, *China: The Balance Sheet: What the World Needs to Know Now about the Emerging Superpower* (New York: Public Affairs, 2006); Robert G. Sutter, *China's Rise in Asia: Promises and Perils* (Lanham, MA: Rowman & Littlefield, 2005); Michael Brown et al., eds., *The Rise of China* (Cambridge, MA: MIT Press, 2000); Michael D. Swaine and Ashley J. Tellis, *Interpreting China's Grand Strategy: Past, Present, and Future* (Santa Monica, CA: Rand, 2000); and Quansheng Zhao and Guoli Liu, eds., *Managing the China Challenge: Global Perspectives* (London: Routledge, 2009). For comparative perspectives on international studies of China's economy, politics, and foreign policy, see Robert Ash, David Shambaugh, and Seiichiro Takagi, *China Watching: Perspectives from Europe, Japan and the United States* (New York: Routledge, 2007).

2. Wang Hui's *China's New Order: Society, Politics, and Economy in Transition* (ed. Theodore Huters [Cambridge, MA: Harvard University Press, 2003]) is more about China's internal transition than its foreign policy. Zheng Bijian has given some important speeches on China's peaceful rise (see, e.g., Zheng Bijian, "China's Peaceful Rise and Opportunity for the Asian-Pacific Region" [speech, Roundtable Meeting between the Bo'ao Forum for Asia and the China Reform Forum, April 18, 2004], in *China's Peaceful Rise: Speeches of Zheng Bijian, 1997–2004* [Washington, DC: Brookings Institution, 2005], available at http://www .brook.edu/fp/events/20050616bijianlunch.pdf [accessed May 31, 2010], and "China's Development and Her New Path to a Peaceful Rise" [speech, Villa d'Este Forum, September 2004], in ibid. [accessed May 31, 2010]). But he is a political adviser and policy analyst, not an academic scholar.

3. The reference here is to Mark Leonard's *What Does China Think?* (New York: Public Affairs, 2008). For an in-depth analysis of recent intellectual debates in China, see Joseph Fewsmith, *China since Tiananmen: From Deng Xiaoping to Hu Jintao*, 2nd ed. (New York: Cambridge University Press, 2008).

4. Ye Zicheng, *Opening to the Outside World and China's Modernization* (Beijing: Peking University Press, 1997), *Geopolitics and Chinese Diplomacy*

(Beijing: Beijing Chubanshe, 1998), *New China's Diplomatic Thought: From Mao Zedong to Deng Xiaoping* (Beijing: Peking University Press, 2001), *China's Diplomatic Thought during the Spring, Autumn, and Warring States Periods* (Hong Kong: Hong Kong Social Sciences Press, 2003), and *The Development of Land Rights and the Rise and Fall of Great Powers: Geopolitical Development and Geostrategic Choice of China's Peaceful Development* (Beijing: New Star Press, 2007).

5. See Ye Zicheng, "Zhongguo shixing daguo waijiao zhanlue shizai bixing" (The imperative for China to implement a great power diplomatic strategy), *Shijie jingji yu zhengzhi* (World economics and politics), 2000, no. 1:5–10.

6. The other two were the Chinese People's University and Fudan University. According to the initial division of area specialization in the 1960s, Peking University would emphasize Asia, Africa, and Latin America, Fudan University North America and Western Europe, and the Chinese People's University the Soviet Union and Eastern Europe. Since the early 1980s, each of the three universities has tried to develop comprehensive international studies programs.

7. See James Kynge, *China Shakes the World: A Titan's Rise and Troubled Future—and the Challenge for America* (Boston: Houghton Mifflin, 2006); and Ted C. Fishman, *China Inc.: How the Rise of the Next Superpower Challenges America and the World* (New York: Scribner, 2005).

8. For an analysis of Sino-U.S. relations with an emphasis on the changing power relationship, see Quansheng Zhao, "Managing the Challenge: Power Shift in US-China Relations," in Zhao and Liu eds., *Managing the China Challenge,* 230–54.

9. For contending perspectives and in-depth analysis of the Taiwan issue, see Richard C. Bush, *Untying the Knot: Making Peace in the Taiwan Strait* (Washington, DC: Brookings Institution, 2005); and John F. Cooper, *Playing with Fire: The Looming War with China over Taiwan* (Westport, CT: Praeger Security International, 2006).

10. See Sujian Guo and Baogang Guo, eds., *China in Search of a Harmonious Society* (Lanham, MA: Lexington, 2008).

11. See Cheng Li, *China's Changing Political Landscape: Prospects for Democracy* (Washington, DC: Brookings Institution, 2008).

12. Elizabeth J. Perry and Merle Goldman, *Grassroots Political Reform in Contemporary China* (Cambridge, MA: Harvard University Press, 2007).

13. See Lowell Dittmer and Guoli Liu, eds., *China's Deep Reform: Domestic Politics in Transition* (Lanham: Rowman & Littlefield, 2006).

14. Samuel P. Huntington, *The Clash of Civilizations and the Remaking of World Order* (New York: Simon & Schuster, 1996); and John Mearsheimer, *The Tragedy of Great Power Politics* (New York: Norton, 2001).

15. See, e.g., Gordon G. Chang, *The Coming Collapse of China* (New York: Random House, 2001).

16. For a comparative analysis of China in East Asia, see Joseph E. Stiglitz and Shahid Yusuf, eds., *Rethinking the East Asian Miracle* (New York: Oxford University Press, 2001).

17. For China's changing role in the world economy, see Barry Naughton, *The Chinese Economy: Transition and Growth* (Cambridge, MA: MIT Press, 2007); and Thomas G. Moore, "China as an Economic Power in the Contemporary Era of Globalization," *Journal of Asian and African Studies* 43 (2008): 497–521.

1. China's Development as a World Power

1. Peng Ming, *The Fourth Monument* (Taipei: Shangzhi Cultural Publishing House, 1999), 155.

2. Sheng Lijun, "China and the United States: Asymmetrical Strategic Partners," *Washington Quarterly* 22, no. 3 (1999): 145–64.

3. Joe Studwell, *The China Dream: The Quest for the Last Great Untapped Market on Earth* (New York: Atlantic Monthly Press, 2002), 268.

4. Yu Xilai, "The Growth of New Rising Power: Glory and Dream," *Strategy and Management*, 1999, no. 6:6.

5. *World Development Report* (Washington, DC: August 1998); *World Development Report* (Washington, DC: April 2002).

6. Wilhelm Fucks, *Formeln zur Macht: Prognosen über Völker, Wirtschaft, Potentiale* (Stuttgart: Deutsche Verlags/Anstalt, 1965).

7. Ray S. Cline, *World Power Assessment: A Calculus of Strategic Drift* (Washington, DC: Center for Strategic and International Studies, Georgetown University, 1975), and *World Power Trends and U.S. Foreign Policy for the 1980s* (Boulder, CO: Westview, 1980).

8. Nicholas John Spykman, *The Geography of the Peace* (New York: Harcourt, Brace, 1944); Hans J. Morgenthau, *Politics among Nations: The Struggle for Power and Peace* (New York: Knopf, 1978). On Cox and Jackson, see Huang Shuofeng, *New Theory of Overall National Strength* (Beijing: China Social Sciences Press, 1999), 8.

9. Joseph Nye, *Soft Power: The Means to Success in World Politics* (New York: PublicAffairs, 2004).

10. Wu Chunqiu, "Comprehensive National Strength and Its Implications for China's Development Strategy," *Journal of International Technical Economics Institute*, no. 3 (1990): 4; Li Tianran, "Studies of Comprehensive National Power," *International Studies*, 1990, no. 2:54; Sheng Lijun, "China Lacks Three Critical Elements for Becoming a World Power," *Hong Kong Fax*, no. 46 (1999); Wang Yizhou, "Chinese Foreign Policy in the 21st Century: Seeking and Balancing Three Demands," *Strategy and Management*, 1999, no. 6:54.

11. Mu Tao et al., *Yutah Kingdom* (Shanghai: East Normal University Press, 2002), 2; Mu Tao et al., *Egypt* (Shanghai: East Normal University Press, 2002), 10; Chen Xiaohong, *Babylon* (Shanghai: East Normal University Press, 2002), 43; Chen Huan, *Ancient Greece* (Shanghai: East Normal University Press, 2002), 137–56.

12. Peng Shuzhi, "On the History, Civilization, Interchange of Hegemony,"

preface to *The Rise and Decline of World Hegemony,* vol. 1 of *The Russian Empire* (Xi'an: Sanqin Publishing House, 2000).

13. Samuel P. Huntington, *The Clash of Civilizations and the Remaking of World Order* (1996; reprint, New York, Simon & Schuster, 2003), 210.

14. Bai Shouyi, *General History of China,* 12 vols. (Shanghai: Shanghai People's Publishing House, 1989–99), 1:349, 352, 359.

15. Guo Changgang, *Ancient Rome* (Shanghai: East China Normal University Press, 2002), 1–2, 146.

16. Bai, *General History of China,* 5:453–56.

17. Denis Twitchett and Michael Loewe, eds., *The Ch'in and Han Empires, 221 B.C.–A.D. 220,* vol. 1 of *The Cambridge History of China* (Cambridge: Cambridge University Press, 1992), 78.

18. Bai, *General History of China,* 9:498–514, 625.

19. Jacob d'Ancona, *The City of Light: The Hidden Journal of the Man Who Entered China Four Years Before Marco Polo,* trans. David Selbourne (New York: Citadel, 2000).

20. See Paul M. Kennedy, *The Rise and Fall of the Great Powers: Economic Change and Military Conflict from 1500 to 2000* (New York: Random House, 1987).

21. Ibid., 176, 228.

22. Huntington, *The Clash of Civilizations,* 86.

23. Angus Maddison, *Monitoring the World Economy, 1820–1992* (Paris: OECD Publishing, 1998).

24. *Selected Works of Deng Xiaoping,* 3 vols. (Beijing: People's Publishing House, 1983–93), 3:213.

25. These Western scholars' views are discussed in Peng, *The Fourth Monument,* 97–99.

26. Ezra F. Vogel, *Japan as Number One: Lessons for America* (Cambridge, MA: Harvard University Press, 1979).

27. Tang Shiping, "On the Grand Strategy of China Again," *Strategy and Management,* 2004, no. 4:31.

28. Editorial, *South China Morning Post,* April 3, 2003.

29. Kennedy, *The Rise and Fall of the Great Powers,* 455.

30. Chu Shulong, *The Trend of the Sino-American Relationship after the Cold War* (Beijing: China Social Sciences Press, May 2001), 605.

31. Dwight H. Perkins, "How China's Economic Transition Shapes Its Future," in *Living with China: U.S.-China Relations in the Twenty-first Century,* ed. Ezra F. Vogel (New York: Norton, 1997), 141–43.

32. On the Rand study, see Hu Angang, "The Challenge of Economic Development and Social Employment," and Chen Xikang, "The Challenge from the Security of Economics, Finance, and Information," both in *12 Challenges Facing China in the 21st Century,* ed. Lu Yongxiang (Beijing: World Affairs Press, 2001).

33. World Bank, *China 2020: Development Challenges in the New Century* (Beijing: China Financial and Economic Publishing House, 1997), 69–72.

34. Asia Development Bank, *Emerging Asia: Changes and Challenges* (Beijing: China Financial Publishing House, 1997), 83–86.

35. Angus Maddison, *Chinese Economic Performance in the Long Run* (Paris: OECD Publishing, 1998), 98–101.

36. Julia Chang Bloch, "Commercial Diplomacy," in Vogel, ed., *Living with China*, 185–87.

37. National Conditions Analysis and Research Group of the Chinese Academy of Sciences, ed., *Opportunities and Challenges: On China's Strategic Goals of Economic Development and Basic Development Strategies on Its Way to 21st Century* (Beijing: Science Press, 1995).

38. Sustainable Development Study Group of the Chinese Academy of Sciences, ed., *A Strategic Report on China's Sustainable Development* (Beijing: Science Press, 1999), 121–22.

39. Lu Zhongwei, *Estimation of the International Strategy and Security Situation* (Beijing: Current Affairs Press, 2002), 4.

40. Communiqué from the Bureau of Statistics, February 28, 2003.

41. See *Global Times* (Beijing), November 11, 2002.

42. Hu Angang, *The Construction of Strategy of China* (Hangzhou: Zhejiang People's Publisher), 2.

43. "The Chinese Economic Achievement Is Real," *South China Morning Post*, February 26, 2002.

44. Paul Wolfowitz, "The Policy of One China Is Not Changed," *China Times* (Taiwan), June 4, 2002.

45. Xie Guozhong, "Why China Can Dominate the World Economy in the Next 10 Years," *South China Morning Post*, February 12, 2003.

46. *Beijing Morning News*, February 28, 2003.

47. Zhao Yanyun, "Where Is China's Competitiveness?" *Global Times* (Beijing), June 17, 2002.

48. Hu Angang, "How to Build an Overall Relatively Comfortable Life in Different Areas," *Qinghua Communication of Development Research*, February 18, 2002, 2.

49. See *People's Daily* (Beijing), November 25, 2002.

50. "Money, New Car Style," *Nanhua zaobao*, March 18, 2003.

51. "The Future of Developing China," *Voice* (Tokyo), February 2003.

52. *Editor's note*: China's foreign trade exceeded US$2.17 trillion in 2007.

53. See *People's Daily* (Beijing), November 14, 2002.

54. Yu, "The Growth of New Rising Power," 9–11.

55. Ibid., 3.

56. Zhang Wenmu, "Kosovo War and the New Century Security Strategy," *Strategy and Management*, 1999, no. 3:8; Zhang Wenmu, "The Chinese National Interest in the Globalization," *Strategy and Management*, 2002, no. 1:54; Wang Sirui, "The Times' Characteristics and the Opportunity for China," *Strategy and Management*, 1999, no. 6:50–60.

57. Zhang Ruizhuang, "Reassessment of International Environment for Chinese Diplomacy," *Strategy and Management,* 2001, no. 2:27.

58. "National Security Strategy of the United States" (September 2002), at http://www.globalsecurity.org/military/library/policy/national/nss-020920.pdf.

59. Ibid.

60. Yang Duogui, "The Challenge of the International Environment," in Lu, ed., *12 Challenges Facing China in the 21st Century,* 415.

61. Zhang, "Reassessment of International Environment."

62. Li Changjiu, "Some Issues about Contemporary Capitalism," *Pacific Journal,* 2002, no. 2:9–15; Lin Shuiyuan, "On Economic Globalization," *Pacific Journal,* 2002, no. 2:19–29.

63. Communiqué from the Bureau of Statistics of China, at http://www.stats.gov.cn/tjgb/ndtjgb/qgndtjgb/t20030228_69102.htm.

64. See *People's Daily* (Beijing), September 29, 2002.

65. Peng, *The Fourth Monument,* 42.

66. Cheng Jianming, *The Contemporary Middle East* (Beijing: Peking University Press, 2002), 225.

67. Zhao Zhihui, "Franklin Roosevelt's Perspective on China," *America Studies,* February 2002, no. 2:93–108.

68. Shi Yinhong and Song Dexing, "Reflection on the Chinese International Attitude, Philosophy of Diplomacy, and Basic Strategy," *Strategy and Management,* 2001, no. 1:12.

69. Wang, "Chinese Foreign Policy in the 21st Century," 26.

70. See Jawaharlal Nehru, *The Discovery of India* (Oxford: Oxford University Press, 1982), 38.

71. Sun Shihai, *The Development of India and Its Outward Strategy* (Beijing: World Knowledge Publisher, 1958), 57.

72. *Selected Works of Deng Xiaoping,* 2:54, 358, 383.

2. China's Rise

1. Yan Xuetong, "The National Security Interest Is More Important Than That of the Economy," *Global Times* (Beijing), February 14, 2002.

2. Kennedy, *The Rise and Fall of the Great Powers,* 605.

3. Qian Qichen, "Address to the Faculty and Students of the School of International Studies," *Studies of International Politics,* January 2002, 6.

4. Si Xing, "Economic Development Is Fundamental to National Security," *Global Times* (Beijing), March 7, 2003.

5. Shi and Song, "Reflection on the Chinese International Attitude."

6. Wang, "Chinese Foreign Policy in the 21st Century."

7. Yu, "The Growth of New Rising Power."

8. Wang, "The Times' Characteristics," 61.

9. Yu, "The Growth of New Rising Power," 14.

10. Chen Lemin, "The Western Cultural Tradition and World History," *Pacific Journal*, 2002, no. 2:8.

11. Zheng Yongnian, "Strategic Reflections on the World System: Relationship between China and the U.S.," *Strategy and Management*, 2001, no. 5:77.

12. Z. Brzezinski, "Order or Anarchy," *Handelsblatt* (Dusseldorf), January 28, 2003.

13. Wang Yushan, "The Strategy of Hiding Capacities Is Not a Temporary Measure," *Global Times* (Beijing), August 17, 2001.

14. *Selected Works of Deng Xiaoping*, 3:354.

15. Yang, "The Challenge of the International Environment," 418.

16. Arnold Toynbee, *A Study of History*, 12 vols. (New York: Oxford University Press, 1961), 12:195.

17. Hou Ruosi, "How to Revive the East Asian Economy," *Global Times* (Beijing), May 16, 2002.

18. Central Compilation and Translation Bureau, ed., *Complete Works of Marx and Engels*, 50 vols. (Beijing: People's Publishing House, 1956–85), 19:431, 451.

19. Central Compilation and Translation Bureau, ed., *Selected Works of Lenin*, 4 vols. (Beijing: People's Publishing House, 1972), 4:501.

20. Central Compilation and Translation Bureau, ed., *The Complete Works of Lenin*, 60 vols. (Beijing: People's Publishing House, 1990), 40:64.

21. Zheng, "Strategic Reflections on the World System."

22. Shi and Song, "Reflection on the Chinese International Attitude."

23. Tang, "On the Grand Strategy of China Again."

24. *Editor's note:* This part came from chapter 6 of the Chinese edition. Following the author's advice, we moved this section here.

25. Xiao Gongqin, "Post-Totalitarian Neo-Authoritarian Regime of China," *Strategy and Management*, 2002, no. 6:87.

3. Relations with the United States

1. Lu, *Estimation of the International Strategy and Security Situation*, 96.

2. Richard Holbrooke, "A Defining Moment with China," *Washington Post*, January 2, 2002.

3. Wang, "The Times' Characteristics."

4. Zheng Yongnian, "World System, Sino-US Relationship, and the Strategic Examination of China," *Strategy and Management*, 2001, no. 5:68.

5. Huntington, *The Clash of Civilizations*, 218, 232–33.

6. Zhang, "Kosovo War."

7. Quoted in Zhang Ruizhuang, "Which Diplomatic Philosophy Should China Choose?" *Strategy and Management*, 1999, no. 1:57.

8. Mearsheimer, *The Tragedy of Great Power Politics*, 402. See also Wang Yigui and Tang Xiaosong, "International Politics Is Power Politics," *Global Times* (Beijing), March 14, 2003.

9. Qian, "Address to the Faculty and Students of the School of International Studies," 7.

10. Colin Powell, "Talk at the Annual Meeting of Asian Society," June 10, 2002, provided by the News and Culture Department of the U.S. Embassy to China.

11. Zhang, "Reassessment of International Environment," 29.

12. Zhang Wenmu, "China's National Interests in the Process of Globalization," *Strategy and Management*, 2002, no. 1:54.

13. Mearsheimer, *The Tragedy of Great Power Politics*, 402–3. See also Wang and Tang, "International Politics Is Power Politics."

14. Transcript of CNN interview with President Jiang Zemin, Xinhua Agency, Beijing, May 9, 1997.

15. Qian Qichen, "Establishing Sino-U.S. Relationship Facing toward the 21st Century," Xinhua Agency, Washington, April 29, 1997.

16. Peng, *The Fourth Monument*, 42.

17. Zhang Yijun, "Sino-U.S. Relationship Will Not Follow Soviet-U.S. Cold War," *Global Times* (Beijing), June 20, 2002.

18. George W. Bush, "It Is in Accordance with U.S. Interests to Keep Close Communication with China," *People's Daily* (Beijing), February 22, 2002.

19. Powell, "Talk."

20. "Liberal Imperialism," *Le monde*, February 28, 2003.

21. Y. Wolkeph, "International Totalitarianism," *Russia* (Moscow), January 3, 2003.

22. Paul Kennedy, "Dangerous Ambition," *Wirtschafts Woche*, (Stuttgart), January 30, 2003.

23. Spencer Johnson, *Who Moved My Cheese? An A-Mazing Way to Deal with Change in Your Work and in Your Life* (New York: Putnam, 1998).

24. Immanuel Wallerstein, "The Eagle Has Crash Landed," *Foreign Policy,* July–August 2002, 63.

25. John Hughes, "American Eagle Is Not Down," *Christian Science Monitor,* July 10, 2002.

26. Oswald Spengler, *The Decline of the West,* trans. Chen Xiaolin (Harbin: Heilongjiang Education Press, 1988), 423–29.

27. *Editor's note:* See Ye Zicheng's further thoughts on this subject following his preface to this English edition.

28. On Toynbee, see David Horowitz, *From Yalta to Vietnam: American Foreign Policy in the Cold War* (Ringwood: Penguin, 1967), 5.

29. Andrew Hacker, *The End of the American Era* (New York: Athenaeum, 1970).

30. Louis M. Hacker, *The Triumph of American Capitalism: The Development of Forces in American History to the End of the Nineteenth Century* (New York: Simon & Schuster, 1940).

31. Richard N. Rosecrance, *America as an Ordinary Country: U.S. Foreign Policy and the Future* (Ithaca, NY: Cornell University Press, 1976).

32. On Kennedy, see Donald W. White, *The American Century: The Rise and*

Decline of the United States as a World Power (New Haven, CT: Yale University Press, 1996), 512.

33. Toynbee, *A Study of History,* 4:124.

34. *Editor's note:* See Samuel P. Huntington, *Who Are We? The Challenges to America's National Identity* (New York: Simon & Schuster, 2005); and Peter J. Katzenstein, ed., *Civilizations in World Politics: Plural and Pluralist Perspectives* (New York: Routledge, 2010).

35. See *China Statistical Yearbook* (Beijing: China Statistics Press/National Bureau of Statistics), various years.

36. L. Yiwasov, "Setting 'Boa Harness' around Russia," *Duma News* (Moscow), April 8, 2002.

37. See Jim Lobe, "Unilateralism Path Scored as Self-Defeating," *Foreign Policy in Focus,* July 2, 2002.

38. Tan Zhong, "The 10 Contradictions Influencing Bush Policies," *Singapore United Morning Post,* April 26, 2002.

39. Thomas E. Ricks, "Empire or Not? A Quiet Debate over U.S. Role," *Washington Post,* August 21, 2001.

40. Niu Jun, "Chinese Views and Considerations on the USA in the Post–Cold War Era," *International Economic Comment,* 2001, nos. 7–8:1–8.

41. Zhang, "China's National Interests."

42. Andrew J. Nathan and Robert S. Ross, *The Great Wall and the Empty Fortress: China's Search for Security* (New York: Norton, 1997), 260.

43. *Selected Works of Deng Xiaoping,* 3:233, 104–5.

44. Meng Xiangqin, "China's Security: Dilemma and Outlet," *Global Times* (Beijing), June 13, 2003.

45. Michel Oksenberg, "Taiwan, Tibet and Hong Kong in Sino-American Relations," in Vogel, ed., *Living with China,* 55.

46. See, e.g., Zhang Linhong, "Sino-U.S. Relationship in the 21st Century: Confrontation or Cooperation?" *Strategy and Management,* 1997, no. 3:21–28.

4. China's Relations and Strategic Choices with Other Developing World Powers

1. *People's Daily* (Beijing), May 28 1994, September 4, 1994.

2. Anderei Kozyrev, *Transition* (Moscow: International Relations Press, 1994), 241.

3. *Overview of China's Diplomacy* (Beijing: World Affairs Press, 1994), 252; *Overview of China's Diplomacy* (Beijing: World Affairs Press, 1995), 270; Li Jinyu, "Thoughts on Sino-Russian Economic and Trade Cooperation Trend toward the 21st Century," *International Observation,* 1999, no. 2:48–50; *Today's Russia* (Russian Embassy to China, June 24, 1996); *International Trade* (Beijing), December 2001.

4. Alexander Lukin, "Oracle Bone of Partnership," *Red Star* (Moscow), January 21, 2002.

5. *Today* (Moscow), January 17, 1995.

6. Alexander Lukin, "Three Intentions inside Russia toward Its China Policy," *International Forum* (Beijing), 1999, no. 5:78–80.

7. G. Ilichev, "We Like the USA, but China Is More Important," *Information* (Moscow), June 7, 2002.

8. *Translator's note:* In March 2009, France announced that it was rejoining NATO's defense apparatus as a full member, more than forty years after President de Gaulle downgraded its defense cooperation with NATO.

9. Charles A. Kupchan, *The End of the American Era: U.S. Foreign Policy and the Geopolitics of the Twenty-first Century* (New York: Knopf, 2002).

10. Mearsheimer, *The Tragedy of Great Power Politics*, 4.

11. "Is China a Threat?" *Japan Industrial News* (Tokyo), December 11, 2002.

12. "Another Side of the China Threat," *Japan Business News* (Tokyo), October 6, 2002.

13. Japanese Ambassador to China Tanino, "Review and Forecast of Japan-Sino Relationship" (speech delivered at the School of International Studies, Peking University, May 1999).

14. Data edited by Beijing Agency of Japan Bank for International Cooperation, October 1999.

15. Tabata Nagamicu, "Tasks Facing Japan and China in the Twenty-first Century," in *The Trans-Century Sino-Japanese Relationship*, ed. Gao Kuanhai (Beijing: World Affairs Press, 1998), 262–64.

16. Zalmay Khalilzad et al., *The United States and Asia: Toward a New U.S. Strategy and Force Posture* (Santa Monica, CA: Rand, 2001), 5.

17. Nalaeyo Suke, "Some Thoughts on the Japan-Sino Relationship," in Gao, ed., *The Trans-Century Sino-Japanese Relationship*, 184–85; Tabata, "Tasks Facing Japan and China in the Twenty-first Century," He Li, "Criticism of the Militarist Historical Viewpoint—Comments on Some Japanese's Attitude toward Historical Issues," *Research on the Anti-Japanese War*, 1998, no. 12:10–11.

18. Kakegawa Emiko, "How the Japanese View Sino-Japanese Emotion," *Global Times* (Beijing), April 11, 2002.

19. Michael Green, "Coping with China—Ideas from Japan," in Vogel, ed., *Living with China*, 198–99.

20. Alastair Iain Johnston and Robert Ross, eds., *Engaging China: The Management of an Emerging Power* (Beijing: Xinhua Publishing House, 2001), 209, 218, 220.

21. Ge Lide et al., "Japanese Right Wing Forgets Who It Is," *Global Times* (Beijing), April 11, 2002.

22. Ishihara Shintaro, "Defeating China and Rebuilding Japan's Road," *Art Age* (Tokyo), March 2002.

23. Wunosi Geaki, "East Asian Situation and Japan-China Relations in the 21st Century," in *China and Japan in the Twenty-first Century*, ed. Li Yu (Beijing: Peking University Press, 1996), 311.

24. "China and Japan Issued the Communiqué on Establishing Friendly Cooperative Partnership for Peace and Development," *People's Daily* (Beijing), November 27, 1998.

25. *Global Times* (Beijing), October 8, 1999, 14.

26. Nakasone Yasuhiro, "China and Japan Should Cooperate for the Future," *Global Times* (Beijing), July 4, 2002.

27. Takeshi Igarashi, "Seeking the Establishment of Asia's International Pattern" (paper presented at the symposium "China's Development and the International Pattern in the Twenty-first Century," Peking University, May 5–7, 1998).

28. Watanabe Osamu, "Koizumi Regime Gave Itself Away—Wild Ambition to Become a Military Power," *Friday Weekly* (Hong Kong), March 1, 2002.

29. Xue Yong, "Viewing Future Asian Economic Configuration from Japanese Yen's Depreciation," *Singapore United Morning Post,* January 4, 2002.

30. Kimuraka Zumi, "Japan and China Should Encourage New Kingly Way," *Industrial and Economic News* (Tokyo), February 8, 2000.

31. Michael Sheridan, "Economically Stagnant Japan Ties Itself to Rapidly Developing China," *Sunday Times,* June 16, 2002.

32. Sun Shihai, ed., *India's Development and Foreign Strategy* (Beijing: China Social Sciences Press, May 2000), 1–15, 315.

33. Nehru quoted in Song Guotao et al., *Report on China's International Environment* (Beijing: China Social Sciences Press, 2002), 155.

34. Ibid., 149.

35. Cheng Ruishen, "On the Sino-Indian Relationship in the New Century," *International Studies,* 2002, no. 1:44.

36. *India Today* (New Delhi), no. 40 (March 2002).

37. Qian Feng, "Indian High-Level Officials Show Good Intention to China," *Global Times* (Beijing), February 7, 2003.

5. China and Its Neighbors

1. *Global Times* (Beijing), June 10, 2002.

2. *Selected Works of Mao Zedong on Diplomacy* (Beijing: Central Party Literature Press, 1994), 137.

3. *Selected Works of Zhou Enlai on Diplomacy* (Beijing: Central Party Literature Press, 1990), 8–10, 70, 207–9.

4. Jiang Zemin, "Hold High the Great Banner of Deng Xiaoping Theory and Push forward the Great Cause of Building Socialism with Chinese Characteristics into the 21st Century," *People's Daily* (Beijing), September 18, 1997.

5. *Selected Works of Mao Zedong on Diplomacy,* 3, 4, 5, 15, 17, 51, 78, 223, 96, 245.

6. *Selected Works of Deng Xiaoping,* 3:82, 128, 319–22, 311–12.

7. Vladimir Putin, "Russia at the Turn of the Millennium," *The Independent* (Moscow), December 30, 1999.

8. Gan Ailan and Lin Limin, "On the Change of the World Geopolitical Situation and Analysis of the Chinese Geopolitical Environment," *Modern International Relations*, 1999, no. 7:8; Tang Yongsheng, "The Strategic and Geopolitical Relations among America, Russia and Europe," *Contemporary World*, 1999, no. 9:15.

9. H. J. Mackinder, *Democratic Ideals and Reality: A Study in the Politics of Reconstruction* (New York: Holt, 1919), 186.

10. Zbigniew Brzezinski, *The Grand Chessboard: American Primacy and Its Geostrategic Imperatives* (New York: Basic, (1997), 47.

11. Ibid., 49, 261–62, 251, 149.

12. Lin Limin, "On China's Geo-Strategic Environment in the Twenty-first Century," *World Economy and Politics*, 1999, no. 12:9.

13. Lee Kuan Yew, Speech at Tokyo Conference on the Future, May 22, 2002.

14. David S. G. Goodman, "The Ethnic Chinese in East and Southeast Asia: Local Insecurities and Regional Concerns," in Johnston and Ross, eds., *Engaging China*, 195.

15. *Singapore United Morning Post*, August 19, 2002.

16. *Global Times* (Beijing), January 29, 2003.

6. China and Unification

1. Niu, "Chinese Views and Considerations," 7.

2. Bai, Bai, *General History of China*, 1:360–62.

3. *Editor's note:* Chen Shui-bian was narrowly reelected in March 2004 and served until March 2008, when the Guomindang candidate, Ma Ying-jeou, was elected president by a large majority.

4. *Global Times* (Beijing), May 20, 2002.

5. *Editor's note:* The "pan-Blue alliance" is the alliance of the Guomindang and the People First Party.

6. Wang, "Chinese Foreign Policy in the 21st Century," 21.

7. Su Qi, *Answering Questions on Mainland Policy and Cross-Strait Relations* (Taipei: Mainland Affairs Council, February 2000), 1–9.

8. *Editor's note:* The white paper and related analysis of cross-strait relations can be found in *Asian Affairs: An American Review* 26, no. 2 (Summer 1999): 93–100.

9. Jin Weichun, "'Interest' Is the Critical Issue Regarding Unification or Independence," *Business Weekly* (Taipei), May 27, 2002.

10. Michael D. Swaine and James C. Mulvenon, *Taiwan's Foreign and Defense Policies: Features and Determinants* (Santa Monica, CA: Rand, 2001), xvii.

11. For example, Kurt M. Campbell and Derek J. Mitchell, "Crisis in the Taiwan Strait?" *Foreign Affairs*, July/August 2001, 14–25.

12. *South China Morning Post* (Hong Kong), April 19, 2002.

Postscript

1. Readers interested in this topic should consult Ye Zicheng, ed., *Major Aspects of China's Diplomacy: Sixty Years of Diplomatic Activity* (Beijing: Contemporary World Publishers, 2009).

2. Ye Zicheng, *An Analysis of the International Environment for China's Peaceful Development* (Beijing: Economic Science Press, 2009).

3. I have written elsewhere about these ideas. See my "Several Questions regarding the Relationship between the Thought of the *Book of Changes* and International Relations," *Study and Explorations,* May 2009, 130–36.

Index

Assyria, 26
Australia, *20,* 209
Austria, 226
automobile production, 52
"axis of evil," 178
Azerbaijan, 193, 195

Babylonian Empire, 26
Baghdad, 33, 34
Bai Shouyi, 223–24
Balkans, 195
Baltic countries, 193, 225, 226
Bandung Conference, 168
Bank of America, xi
Bank of China, 134
Beijing Declaration, 132, 133, 134
Beijing Olympics, 59
Belarus, 193, 225
bilateral relations
    China and, 180, 181
    Franco-German, 156
biological weapons, 61
Blair, Dennis, 255
Bloch, Julia Chang, 46
"Blue Sky" missiles, 167
Bohai Sea, 203
Book of Changes, The, 262, 263
Brazil, *20*
bridges, 33
British Empire, 29, 30
Brunei, 209
Brzezinski, Zbigniew, 82–83, 195, 196
Buddhism, 169
Burma, 168, 207, 211–12, 214
Bush, George W.
    foreign policy aims under, 108–9
    identifies the "axis of evil," 178
    North Korea and, 66, 178
    relations with India and Pakistan,
        120–21
    Sino-U.S. relations under, 94, 99, 107
    Taiwan unification issue and, 234,
        255–56
    U.S. national security strategy and, 56
Business Weekly, 252
Byzantine Empire, 27, 28
Byzantium, 34. *See also* Constantinople

Cairo Conference, 229
Cambodia, 214
Canada, *20*
capital, global circulation of, 63–64
capitalism
    as incompatible with socialism, 94–95
    opening socialism to, 86–87
    relations with Chinese socialism,
        99–100
Caspian Sea region, 195
Caucasus, 193, 225
cell phones, 52
center-periphery relations, 53
Central Asia
    in China's geostrategic thinking, 205
    pipeline for oil producers, 195
    Sino-Russian cooperation in, 133, 135
    the Soviet collapse and, 193
Central Intelligence Agency (CIA),
    42–43
centralization of state power, 39
Chang, Gordon, 14
Changan, 33, 34
Chechnya, 138
chemical weapons, 61
Chemical Weapons Convention, 120
Cheney, Dick, 255–56
Chen Shui-bian, 8, 232–33, 235, 254,
    276n3
Chiang Ching-kuo, 230, 231
Chiang Kai-shek, 229
China
    APEC and, 160
    ASEAN and (*see* Association of
        Southeast Asian Nations)
    attitude toward militarism, 118–19
    continuity of its historical civilization,
        31
    Cultural Revolution and, 72
    developing the international role of, 84
    development as a world power: the
        advancement of international
        economic development and,
        257–58; Chinese military capacity
        and, 23; Chinese shortcomings, 26;
        Chinese-style strategic thinking
        and, 262, 263; comprehensive

challenges of the new economic era,
63
China's relations with, 192
competition among, 128
negative impact of economic
globalization on, 60–62
development
as China's main goal, 69–72
Deng Xiaoping's theory of, 118
is preceded by unification, 239–41
promotes unification, 241–44
See also China, development as a
world power
developmental capacity, 22
*Development of Land Power and the Rise
and Fall of Great Powers* (Ye), 259
Diaoyu Islands, 6, 149, 154, 155, 162
Digital Age, 244
diplomatic strategy, 179
domestic problems, 5, 14, 88–90, 125
double-headed eagle strategy, 197–98
DPP. *See* Democratic Progressive Party

"Earth" missiles, 167
East Asia
arms sales to, 178
in China's geostrategic thinking, 205
China's interests and participation in,
84, 180, 182–83
economic circle, 160
economic cooperation system, 175
impact of Chinese economic growth
on, 217–18
model of development in, 80–81
multilateral cooperation in, 160–61,
163–66
post–Cold War geopolitical changes,
193–95
security system, 164
Sino-Japanese cooperation and,
148–49
unchanging geopolitical elements in,
195–99
East Asian economic nucleus proposal,
214–15
East Asian financial crisis (1997–1998),
71, 72, 152, 161, 181, 182–83

East Asian model, 80–81
East Asian regionalism
ASEAN and, 214–15
role of China in, 182–83
East China Sea, 203
Eastern Han dynasty, 31
Eastern Roman Empire, 33
East European bloc, 30
East Turkistan, 202
economic crises
of 2008, xi, 10
as a cause of war, 53
East Asian financial crisis, 71, 72, 152,
161, 181, 182–83
implications for China's development,
10–11
military expansion and, 78
economic development
as a cause of war, 54
China's rise and the international
advancement of, 257–58
relationship to military development,
77–79
See also Chinese economic growth
economic disparity, 89
economic globalization
benefits and opportunities for
developing countries, 62, 64
impact on Chinese economic growth,
63, 65
the Information Revolution and, 63
major trends in, 63–64
negative impact on developing
countries, 60–62
polarization and, 62
Westernization and, 61
See also globalization
Economist, 43
Egypt, ancient, 26
elephant mentality, 13
Eleventh Central Committee, 190
Emerging Asia (report), 45
empires, 26, 27–28
End of the American Era, The (A.
Hacker), 112
End of the American Era, The
(Kupchan), 142

CPSIA information can be obtained
at www.ICGtesting.com
Printed in the USA
BVOW03*0215190117
473920BV00002B/11/P